Also by Damian Cox

INTEGRITY AND THE FRAGILE SELF (*with Marguerite La Caze and Michael Levine*)

Also by Michael Levine

THE PHILOSOPHICAL FOUNDATIONS OF ARCHITECTURAL DISCOURSE (*forthcoming with Bill Taylor*)

PANTHEISM: A Non-Theistic Concept of Deity

HUME AND THE PROBLEM OF MIRACLES: A Solution

RACISM IN MIND (*co-editor with Tamas Pataki*)

THE ANALYTIC FREUD: Philosophy and Psychoanalysis (*editor*)

Also by Saul Newman

FROM BAKUNIN TO LACAN: Anti-Authoritarianism and the Dislocation of Power

POWER AND POLITICS IN POSTSTRUCTURALIST THOUGHT: New Theories of the Political

UNSTABLE UNIVERSALITIES: Poststructuralism and Radical Politics

THE POLITICS OF POSTANARCHISM (*forthcoming*)

Politics Most Unusual

Politics Most Unusual
Violence, Sovereignty and Democracy in the 'War on Terror'

Damian Cox
Bond University

Michael Levine
University of Western Australia

Saul Newman
Goldsmiths – University of London

© Damian Cox, Michael Levine and Saul Newman 2009

All rights reserved. No reproduction, copy or transmission of this publication may be made without written permission.

No portion of this publication may be reproduced, copied or transmitted save with written permission or in accordance with the provisions of the Copyright, Designs and Patents Act 1988, or under the terms of any licence permitting limited copying issued by the Copyright Licensing Agency, Saffron House, 6-10 Kirby Street, London EC1N 8TS.

Any person who does any unauthorized act in relation to this publication may be liable to criminal prosecution and civil claims for damages.

The authors have asserted their rights to be identified as the authors of this work in accordance with the Copyright, Designs and Patents Act 1988.

First published 2009 by
PALGRAVE MACMILLAN

Palgrave Macmillan in the UK is an imprint of Macmillan Publishers Limited, registered in England, company number 785998, of Houndmills, Basingstoke, Hampshire RG21 6XS.

Palgrave Macmillan in the US is a division of St Martin's Press LLC, 175 Fifth Avenue, New York, NY 10010.

Palgrave Macmillan is the global academic imprint of the above companies and has companies and representatives throughout the world.

Palgrave® and Macmillan® are registered trademarks in the United States, the United Kingdom, Europe and other countries.

ISBN-13: 978-0-230-53539-8   hardback
ISBN-10: 0-230-53539-9   hardback

This book is printed on paper suitable for recycling and made from fully managed and sustained forest sources. Logging, pulping and manufacturing processes are expected to conform to the environmental regulations of the country of origin.

A catalogue record for this book is available from the British Library.

Library of Congress Cataloging-in-Publication Data

Cox, Damian.
   Politics most unusual : violence, sovereignty, and democracy in the
  "war on terror" / Damian Cox, Michael Levine, Saul Newman.
     p. cm.
  Includes bibliographical references (p.) and index.
  ISBN 978-0-230-53539-8
  1. War on Terrorism, 2001– 2. Political violence. 3. Sovereignty.
4. Democracy. 5. World politics—1995–2005. 6. World politics—
2005–2015. I. Levine, Michael P., 1950–II. Newman, Saul, 1972–
III. Title.

HV6432.C7 2009
363.325—dc22   2008034633

10 9 8 7 6 5 4 3 2 1
18 17 16 15 14 13 12 11 10 09

Printed and bound in Great Britain by
CPI Antony Rowe, Chippenham and Eastbourne

To Jean Charles de Menezes, and the countless other victims of the 'war on terror'

Contents

Acknowledgements		viii
Preface		ix
1	The Politics of Security	1
2	Religion, Prejudice, Violence and Politics	24
3	Lying in the War on Terrorism	43
4	Sovereignty, Violence and the State of Exception	68
5	American Empire and its Discontents	90
6	The Lesser of Two Terrors: Ethical Questions	116
7	On Ways Forward	143
Bibliography		181
Index		188

Acknowledgements

We wish to acknowledge the generous support of the British Academy in supporting this book project. Thanks also to Marguerite La Caze for her insightful comments on Chapter 6.

Preface

The changes in political landscape wrought by the events on and after 9/11 – the move to what we call in this book 'politics most unusual' – have brought about a significant revitalization of political theory and close scrutiny of the relation between political theory and moral philosophy. It seems that there is hardly a political theorist or moral philosopher around that has not in some way turned their attention to these events. After all, the conglomeration of political actions traced back to 9/11 (sometimes accurately, sometimes not) has resulted in massive loss of life and has changed the lives of a great many.

Some of the academic work that has been produced post 9/11 rehashes old issues in old ways. Moral philosophers working in 'just war' or 'human rights' traditions, as well as philosophers working more broadly within the 'analytic' tradition of moral philosophy, continue to be embroiled with the problem of defining terrorism and the question of whether terrorism can ever be morally justified. Many are obsessed with, and tend to overstate, the practical significance of non-combatant immunity and criteria for distinguishing combatants from non-combatants. (In a sense, they are conceptualizing the issue as if armies still lined up to face each other in a field of battle.) Many continue to finesse the doctrine of double-effect in an effort to make it seem practical; as if it could be enlisted to do the analytical and explanatory work needed to get clear about the moral challenge of terrorism. The conclusions of some other moral philosophers are trite. Is something of real significance uncovered when a philosopher discovers that at least one reason why terrorism is immoral is that terrorists instill fear, thereby undermining the tranquility and comfort of ordinary life? And what value is there in the re-emergence of those old Machiavellians, only recently 'out of the closet', who argue for the moral permissibility of torture and assassination? Part of the motivation for writing this book is a sense of the inadequacy of so much of the philosophical response to politics after 9/11.

However, where mainstream academic philosophy has come up with very little that is new or worthwhile, new perspectives have emerged from other sources, with analyses that draw from many disciplines. Responses to 9/11 are being scrutinized, theorized and problematized in relation to democratic theory, notions of sovereignty and the so-called state of exception. What is to be made of the fact that some Western nations, notably the US and its allies such as Israel, have endorsed and practised torture and have sought either a legal justification for it or a redefinition of it? Just how much of a threat to democracy is the creeping normalization of a 'state of exception' given that exceptions allow torture, invasions of privacy and curtailment of many other human rights and freedoms? What has become and what is to become of the very idea of a democracy given the lawlessness and barbarity of democratic nations like the US? Democracy is not an all or nothing thing. But even those who see democracy as largely procedural, constitutional and institutional are beginning to claim that contemporary institutions of democracy fall too far short of standards of equity and fairness to be called fully democratic. And for those who believe that democracy must be substantive as well as procedural – that it must guarantee the kinds of rights and conditions that make democratic life possible; that it must adhere to the principle of equal consideration of interests[1] – the self-claimed democracies of the West fall a very long way short of a fully democratic condition; they are partial democracies at best.

This book argues that the current political climate has been a long time coming. It seeks to describe deeper issues and underlying dynamics that are causally related to the violence, lies, prejudices, curtailments of freedoms, religious fervour, neoliberal and neoconservative ways of thinking and other threats to democracy constitutive of what we term 'politics most unusual'. It is a book that eschews easy answers and solutions along with unwarranted optimism. It does not counsel despair but is meant to engender serious concern – perhaps even useful worry.

The argument of the book is developed through seven chapters. Chapter 1 examines the authoritarian nature of responses to terrorism characteristic of Western democracies after 9/11, particularly, but by no means only, those of the US and the UK. The underlying logic of this response – in which demands for security are established on the basis of the manipulative creation of *insecurity* – leads to a highly anti-democratic political environment. We set out to describe the logic of the security paradigm: its power as well as its paradoxical and anti-democratic nature. Underlying the vulnerability of a population to manipulation in a politics of security – at the hands of the security industry and its political masters – is a pervasive psychological vulnerability. We explore a number of aspects of this vulnerability in the next two chapters.

The politics of security relies on an extreme sensitivity to threats of violence: sensitivity out of all proportion to actual levels of risk. The general vulnerability of people to this kind of fallacy is well known and not at all mysterious. Of deeper concern is the vulnerability of people to violent responses *per se*. One feature of the politics of security is a kind of violence directed against those who threaten and those who *might* threaten or indeed those who somehow *resemble* or *represent* people who might threaten. The violent response to threat (real, perceived or invented) characterizes much of post-9/11 politics. The US response to the assault of 9/11 was a murderous one: a rampage of violence, a violent reassertion of power, shock and awe as television therapy. Our aim in Chapter 2, therefore, is to try to explain something of the psychological basis of this violent reflex. We find the most explanatorily useful term in which to understand this phenomenon is that of prejudice, and the most powerful explanation of the operations of prejudice and its translation into violence to be a psychoanalytic one in which prejudicial mental states function primarily as modes of ego-defence. The crucial feature of a threat of violence is not the risk of harm *per se*, but the affront to one's sense of self and to the narcissistic comforts of one's self-image (an image which, in the prejudicial mind, is constructed out of a denigration of others). We concentrate on two kinds of prejudice, both central features of post-9/11 politics: racism and religion. Racist attitudes and religious belief are both kinds of prejudicial mental states, and are both ubiquitous sources of violence.

Another psychological vulnerability – another crucial piece of the puzzle – is the vulnerability of people to lies and distortion, and to political mendacity in particular. In Chapter 3, we take up the task of explaining this vulnerability. What primarily needs explaining is not the fact that politicians lie or that their lies often go unexposed. What needs explaining is the fact that politicians get away with lies when they are transparently caught out by them. A politician lies. We accept that they have lied. And yet we are disposed to believe their very next claim. What accounts for this gullibility and this unwillingness to hold politicians to account for their lies? Why did it not matter that George W. Bush lied so transparently and manipulatively about Iraqi weapons programmes in the lead-up to the 2003 US invasion and subjugation of Iraq? This has even been confirmed by his former press secretary Scott McClellan, whose recently published book exposing the Administration's deceit and propagandistic manipulation of the American public has created quite a stir.[2] We look for the explanation of our vulnerability to political lies and to the other mendacious characteristics of political discourse – to spin, distortion, rhetorical manipulation and so on – in aspects of group psychology.

In Chapter 4, we turn to the question of the political character of violence and, in particular, the violence at the heart of the idea of sovereignty. The idea of sovereignty presupposes the possibility of operating under a state of exception: a state in which ordinary, constitutional and legal protections are suspended. The decision to operate under a state of exception is a prerogative of sovereignty. The state of exception is therefore a crystallization of the power of the state, a strange no-man's-land beyond the law in which the sovereign can act with violent impunity. We argue that this situation applies increasingly to political life in contemporary Western societies, societies which define themselves as formally liberal democratic but which implement 'security' measures that are more akin to those of authoritarian police states.

Chapter 5 examines the internationalization of the violence of post-9/11 politics in the guise of what we call the project of American Empire. We argue that while imperialism has long been a feature of US foreign policy, under the Bush Administration the project of empire became fully explicit. This is something that could be seen in that administration's overt militarism, its doctrine of pre-emptive strikes and regime change, and in the ideological and political discourse of neoconservatism. We also develop a critique of imperialist politics on both ethical and pragmatic grounds, taking issue with those who attempt to justify US empire in terms of either liberal humanitarianism or the promotion of a stable world order.

The project of American Empire is morally bankrupt, and the paradigm of security leads to authoritarian excess, the violent assertion of sovereignty and the permanency of a state of exception. If we are right about all this, then what are the prospects for a more just, morally legitimate and democratic politics in the future? We turn to this question in the next two chapters. First we consider the question as a purely ethical one. What prospects are there for pursuing a security agenda within the basic ethical framework of liberal democracy? In Chapter 6, we examine Michael Ignatieff's attempt to do just this through an ethics of the lesser evil. Ignatieff tries to show how liberal democracies, as they currently stand, are capable of responding to the threat of international terrorism – are capable of fighting a 'war on terror' – without compromising fundamental ethical commitments of a liberal democracy. He does this by trying to articulate a compromise ethics: an ethics in which a greater evil (the destruction of democracy) may be averted by allowing lesser evils (preventative imprisonment, extra-judicial killings, war). His attempt unravels very easily, as we show. Although we have not the space to explore every possibility, we suggest that there is no ethically legitimate compromise to be had between pursuit of the security paradigm and the maintenance of the ethical conditions of liberal democracy. This paves the way for our discussion of the politics of anti-security in the final chapter.

In Chapter 7, we move at last to the task of advancing positive suggestions for ways forward. How do we respond to contemporary political situation in full knowledge of the depth and complexity of the problems we face? How do we respond in ways that are neither politically naive nor assume that the psychological vulnerabilities which underlie so much of the condition of contemporary politics can be wished away? We argue for a range of concrete measures that would ameliorate many of the worst aspects of this politics, including the promotion of a politics of anti-security, but we also recognize that there is no honest hope for them without a profound re-invigoration of democratic culture. The challenge of a politics most unusual is first and foremost a challenge to this culture. We examine a major ideological obstacle to democracy today – neoliberalism – and suggest ways of getting around it. We highlight some of the principal conditions for bringing democracy back to life.

As we write this Preface, Bush's reign is in its twilight hour, and we are witnessing the unseemly and interminable nomination contest between the two Democrat presidential contenders. The future political situation in the US is unclear. Some perceive a new politics of hope, and believe a Democratic administration (assuming McCain doesn't get in!) will mean an end to the disastrous 'war on terror' in the form we have endured it for six long years, and a radically new direction in US foreign and domestic policy. We are not quite so sanguine. Indeed, the Clinton–Obama spectacle over the past few months – with its overtones over race and religion and with the same talk of God, 'national security' and support for Israel – seems to suggest little grounds for optimism. The 'controversy of the two pastors' sums it all up: Jeremiah Wright, Obama's pastor, was vociferously condemned from every quarter (including from Obama himself) for his 'inflammatory rhetoric' over (in our view perfectly reasonable) comments about racism, the oppression of the Palestinians and the US bearing some of the blame for 9/11. And, on the other side, a certain evangelical Reverend Hagee, who has endorsed McCain, caused quite a stir himself when he said that God sent Hitler to chase the Jews out of Europe so they could go to Israel. Somehow, this speaks for all the things we talk about in this book: the deeply troubling mix of religious extremism, political spin and image control, blind support for Israel (driven in reality by anti-Semitism), racism, economic inequality, imperialism, double standards and the denial of moral culpability that characterizes much of what passes as politics in the US at the moment. As we have argued, it is only through a democratic transformation of politics – not only in the US but everywhere – that there can be any hope for a different kind of future.

This work is collaboration by a political theorist and two philosophers. It is a very different work than one of us could have produced and in virtually all ways it is better. Three heads are sometimes better than one and we can each heartily recommend collaborative work. Of course, broad agreement on the important issues, along with a shared concern about the moral condition of contemporary politics, does not guarantee agreement on all particular points. Each of the chapters is the result of considerable collaboration that often altered an initial draft considerably.

In his *Essay on Liberty* Mill discussed the importance of dissent and various liberties, not least of which was freedom of speech. He believed that something good, or at least better, could often come of disagreement (even profound disagreement), whereas idle agreement and blind or cockeyed adherence to tradition merely enshrined 'dead dogma' and impeded all kinds of progress – political, social and personal. Like most great philosophers, Mill was mistaken about a great many things, indeed most things. Let's hope he got this one right.

Notes

1. See T. Christiano (2002) 'Democracy and Equality', in D. Estlund (ed.) In *Democracy* (Oxford: Blackwell), p. 46, pp. 315–50.
2. S. McClellan (2008) *What Happened: Inside the Bush White House and Washington's Culture of Deception* (Public Affairs).

1
The Politics of Security

On the 22 July 2005, a day after the attempted bombings on the London transport system, a young, semi-employed Brazilian electrician was shot dead at point blank range by plain clothes police officers as he boarded a train at a subway station in South London. At the inquest into the killing of this innocent commuter, the police defended their 'shoot to kill' policy, claiming this was justified given the present fears about further terrorist attacks; and claiming, moreover, that the victim had been behaving 'suspiciously', vaulting over the turnstiles, running from the police, and wearing a padded jacket – the apparently unmistakable signs of a suicide bomber. It later transpired that the police had lied about these details – that he did not in fact jump over the ticket barriers but passed through as any commuter would, and that rather than wearing a bomb-concealing jacket, he was wearing a light summer shirt. But no matter – his death was put down to collateral damage in the 'war against terrorism', and he was after all, as the newspapers dutifully reported, in the country 'illegally'. Despite protests and legal campaigns by the victim's family, the police were exonerated – indeed, the police commander in charge of this operation was later promoted.[1]

The slaying of Jean Charles de Menezes, the lies and dissimulations in the official version of events, the lack of police accountability, the government spin and media complicity – all symbolize, in a profound and powerful way, what can be seen as a new political paradigm that is starting to emerge before our very eyes. Of course, police brutality and incompetence are nothing new, and nor are government cover-ups. However, what gives this case a particular and brilliant resonance is the broader discursive and ideological context in which it appeared – that which goes by the name of the 'war on terror'.[2] Ever since that global event, September 11, there has been – under the dubious banner of 'security' – an unprecedented accumulation of state powers of control, detention and surveillance and a severe curtailment of what were formally regarded as vital civil liberties, legal protections and democratic rights. Everything from the expansion of electronic and biometric surveillance,[3] to the indefinite detention without charge of terrorist suspects, to restrictions on protests, to the formalization of 'shoot to kill' powers for police forces, and, perhaps most disturbingly of all, the use of torture in interrogation – all suggest that a fundamental transformation is taking place in modern liberal democracies. That these regimes are uncannily coming to resemble the very authoritarian police states and fundamentalist societies (a fundamentalism of security) that Western governments like to distinguish themselves from – witness the desperate insistence from leaders like Bush and Blair about the 'free and open' nature of their societies, something which the terrorists and extremists apparently despise us for – points to a kind of mutation in modern political life.

The restriction of freedoms and rights, the undermining of due process and the constant intrusions into private affairs, is accompanied, in this new 'security' paradigm, by the increasing unaccountability of government power.[4] Once again, democratic governments lying to their citizens is nothing new. But when the lies and prevarications are so blatant, when governments so clearly mislead their citizens about their reasons for going to war and manipulate public opinion in such a shameless way; when they ignore the protests of millions of people, as they did in 2003 – it would seem that even the mere semblance of democratic accountability and the consent of the governed has begun to disintegrate. What it reveals, increasingly, is naked power and illegitimate violence – the state of exception at the heart of state sovereignty. As we witness the passing of liberal-democratic politics and the emergence of the security state, it is time to reflect more seriously on the dangers posed by the so-called war on terror. These include what the war obfuscates and underwrites; how it subverts meaningful oppositional discourse, as well as crucial elements of morality like truthfulness; and how, in related ways, it repudiates fundamental human rights, respect for persons and democracy (both procedurally and substantively understood) itself.

In this chapter, we propose to explore the contours of this 'security' paradigm – by which we mean an *episteme*[5] of discourses, speech acts, power relations, ideological mystifications, institutional practices and concrete measures of control and surveillance organized around, and given intelligibility through, the amorphous notion of 'security'.[6]

In other words, with the declaration of the global 'war on terror', 'security' has become a kind of global signifier which authorizes measures and policies – both internally and externally – which would not hitherto have been seen as legitimate. Yet a number of paradoxes are central to this discourse of security: while the discourse of security takes as its seeming prerogative the protection of citizens from terrorist attacks, it provokes a permanent state of fear, vulnerability and insecurity; it is a (neo)liberal discourse, in the sense that it is driven, partly, by logic of capitalist globalization and the exigencies of liberal markets – and, at the same time, it is an authoritarian and highly regulatory post-liberal discourse which seriously violates the individual rights upon which any coherent understanding of liberalism is based; and while it is instigated by elected democratic governments in response, partly, to perceived democratic pressures and fears about terrorism, presenting itself, moreover, as being necessary to protect democracies against their external enemies – in its application and its potential, it is profoundly anti-democratic. We have, then, a discourse and politico-ideological paradigm which emerges from within the liberal-democratic space and yet which is profoundly hostile to liberal-democratic principles and practices.

The securitization of everyday life

The notion of 'security' is central to the 'war on terror'. This is a war, after all, that is being prosecuted to guarantee our security from future terrorist attacks: as President Bush is fond of reminding us, we must combat the terrorists abroad so that we do not have to do so on our own shores – a mantra that was echoed by his faithful 'deputy sheriffs' Tony Blair and John Howard when they were in power.[7] So the 'war on terror' is to be both an external and internal war to guarantee our security. Moreover, the 'war on terror', which was declared in the days following the 9/11 attacks, raised the idea of 'security' to an almost metaphysical level – protecting citizens from a terrorist attack has now come to be seen as the central function of government, perhaps even the only one given the privatization or abandonment of many of the state's traditional functions like the provision of services and welfare.[8] Moreover, a new ideological consensus has now formed around the priority of 'security', with politicians from across the political spectrum trumpeting their national security credentials. The claim to be tough on 'national security' – along with immigration and border control – forms the essential part of any political platform today. This consensus crosses party lines while, at the same time, reducing meaningful differences between opposing parties. Democrats and Republicans, social democrats and conservatives embrace the new security paradigm, evidence of the strength of what has become a fundamental feature of how the world is viewed (or allegedly viewed), explained and governed.

It is these measures and laws, moreover, which represent the most striking examples of the political transformation we are exploring here. The USA Patriot Act, which was passed rapidly through Congress in the weeks following 9/11, and which was renewed in 2006, allowed for widespread executive powers of electronic surveillance, detention without charge, immigration and border control, the regulation of financial transactions; searches without court warrants; as well as authorizing extra-judicial military tribunals and special powers of interrogation – undermining, in effect, existing legal precedents, notions of due process, rules of evidence and so on.[9] Moreover, the illegal NSA wiretaps on US citizens ordered by president Bush shows the willingness of governments to act outside the boundaries of their constitutional authority under the pretext of security. Other liberal democracies have seen their own similarly draconian counter-terrorism legislation. In the UK, various anti-terrorist bills enacted since the 9/11 and 7/7 terrorist attacks have allowed for the imposition of the infamous 'control orders', under which terrorist suspects can be detained without charge and without even the suspicion of having committed any crime – without, in many cases, even knowing the specific nature of the allegations against them. Legislation has also been introduced which criminalizes public statements that could be construed as an incitement towards terrorism, as well as giving the police and intelligence agencies widespread powers of search, arrest and surveillance.

While some of these laws and measures have provoked an outcry from civil liberties groups,[10] they have generally been accepted as normal, legitimate and necessary, and there has been little debate among the general public about the clear threat they pose to democratic rights and freedoms. Despite the unprecedented concentration of government and police powers, the restrictions on freedom of speech and protest, the constant intrusions into personal privacy, the undermining of centuries of legal tradition and the expansion of bureaucracy – developments in which liberal democracies become formally indistinguishable from authoritarian police states – the opposition to these security measures has been relatively muted. There seems to be a sort of ideological chimera of 'normality' here, as if what is utterly exceptional and previously unthinkable has now assumed an almost everyday appearance of normalcy and acceptability.

To understand this phenomenon we must look at the way in which the discourse of security has permeated society at all levels, functioning as an ideology which plays upon and deliberately incites people's fears and anxieties about terrorism. However, this fear is mingled, in a paradoxical way, with the fear of government itself. The discourse of security becomes internalized in the form of a self-censorship – the fear one experiences in passing through airport security; the awareness of the omnipresence of surveillance; the heightened climate of suspicion and paranoia; the sense of intimidation now felt by protesters and dissidents; the government messages encouraging us to spy on fellow citizens and report signs of 'suspicious activity'; the petty laws which restrict the freedom of speech, imposing severe penalties for statements that can be perceived as supporting terrorism; the reticence, even on the part of academics in the US, about not towing the official line in the months following 9/11 – and the persecution of those courageous enough to speak out.[11] Within this new security paradigm we have all become subjects of permanent risk – both as targets for terrorist attacks, as well as potential terrorists ourselves. Thus, we are subject to a constant suspicion and surveillance – positioned both as subjects requiring the overbearing protection of the state, and at the same time as potential threats to the security of the state.

As Ulrich Beck shows, the perceived threat of terrorism has now become the defining feature of risk societies – societies which see themselves as permanently threatened by uncontrollable disasters, such as global warming, nuclear accidents, mad cow disease or global financial meltdowns. What characterizes these risk-obsessed societies is an all-pervasive sense of distrust:

> The perception of terrorist threats replaces *active trust* with *active mistrust*. It therefore undermines the trust in fellow citizens, foreigners and governments all over the world. Since the dissolution of trust multiplies risks, the terrorist threat triggers a self-multiplication of risks by the de-bounding of risk-perceptions and fantasies.[12]

However, the logic of risk and security is more complex than Beck allows. Terrorism and the 'risk management' strategies that are applied to it, cannot be placed in the same category as other more genuine threats, like global warming for instance. To do so is to see the threat of terrorism as an objective reality that is beyond politicization and ideology – which of course it is not. This is not to deny that a certain level of terrorist threat actually exists – although this is grossly and quite deliberately exaggerated by the government and the media; nor is it to deny that issues like global warming are themselves politicized to some degree as well. However, what we are suggesting here is that the 'terrorist threat', because it is so heavily overladen with moral concerns, with the ubiquitous figure of the 'enemy', and with psychological states of fear and anxiety – consciously manipulated by the state – and with the spectre of unbearable violence, that it is bound up with state power and dominant political and ideological agendas in ways that these other threats are not. In other words, the 'terrorist threat' not only allows state power to be shored up and extended, in the ways we have been describing, but it also operates as a diversionary tactic and a 'substitute satisfaction' – to speak in psychoanalytic terms – taking attention away from other, much more serious and pressing concerns. While governments dither over global warming – some even disputing the gravity of the problem and its causes – they go into frenetic activity over security matters. However, this is also a kind of false activity: it has nothing to do with addressing the problem of terrorism in any real sense – many of the laws and counter-terrorist measures would do little to prevent terrorist attacks and, indeed, may even provoke them – and everything to do with creating the *appearance* of doing something, while at the same time legitimizing certain neoliberal political and ideological agendas both domestically and internationally. It is not, as Beck implies, simply that governments respond to the risk of terrorism with well-intentioned, though misguided, measures of control that are designed to allay our fears. It is, rather, that the security paradigm actually works by deliberately perpetuating a constant and ubiquitous sense of anxiety – in which the fear of terrorism blurs into an obscure fear of the anti-terrorist state itself. The constant directives issued by the Department of Homeland Security in the US, advising people on what to do in case of a terrorist attack, as well as encouraging people to report 'signs of suspicions activity' and to organize surveillance in their local neighbourhoods, had the deliberate effect of inculcating a certain level of anxiety and suspicion.[13] There can be little doubt that the state has a certain interest in maintaining this climate of fear, in promoting an all-pervasive sense of insecurity: at the most superficial level, one thinks of the government warnings about terrorism and the infamous colour-coded (and ultimately meaningless) terror alerts that were used so effectively in the run-up to the 2004 presidential election in the US; or the way that fears about security and terrorism were deliberately manipulated and played upon by both the US and UK governments to give legitimacy to the invasion of Iraq in 2003. Moreover, the enormous powers accrued by police and security agencies, the centralisation of security functions under new and enormously expensive super-bureaucracies like the Department of Homeland Security,[14] and the massive growth in military spending in the US since the declaration of the 'war on terror' suggest that certain vested interests are at stake here.

So there is something in the discourse of security itself which provokes insecurity, and even incites further terrorist threats. The danger with the principle of security becoming co-extensive with political life, as Giorgio Agamben argues, is that counter-terrorism and terrorism will merge into one deadly circuit of mutual incitement and provocation, in which terrorist attacks provoke an even more violent and terroristic response from the state.[15] Can we not see signs of this happening already? The interventions in Iraq and Afghanistan – undertaken in the name of combating the terrorist threat – seem only to have increased it, now serving as the ultimate recruiting tool for future terrorists around the world. Moreover, the state's response to perceived terrorist threats seems more and more violent and terroristic: the execution-style killing of de Menezes, along with the tortures in Abu Ghraib, the arbitrary detention of terrorist suspects, the indiscriminate killing of civilians in Iraq and Afghanistan, show that the state is in danger of becoming, or has already become, terroristic. This is a theme we shall pursue in subsequent chapters – but it is clear that there is a certain intrinsic relationship between state security and terrorism. Indeed, we could say that the very logic of securitization can only be accompanied by increased insecurity. Moreover, it actually works *through* this insecurity – acting upon it, but in doing so, sustaining and perpetuating it. The state project of security needs, and therefore actively sustains, a constant state of insecurity, a threatening external other which it seeks to control, and yet which at the same time constitutes its identity and legitimacy.[16] That is why security is always linked to insecurity – these two seemingly opposed dimensions are simply two sides of the same logic.[17]

The potential – and indeed actual – violence of the new politics of security is further evident in its targeting of certain groups in society as 'enemies'. While the discourse of security constructs everyone as subjects of risk (rather than as citizens with rights) it also isolates specific groups – particularly Muslim communities – subjecting them to constant police harassment and surveillance.[18] Indeed, a fragile sense of social unity is achieved through the production of the figure of the 'terrorist enemy', an enemy who is both external and internal, who must be combated abroad and rooted out at home. It is interesting to observe the metaphor of the virus at work here – the notion that the risk of terrorism and 'radicalisation' is spreading throughout certain 'high risk' communities (fuelled by those demonic Muslim clerics), infecting and endangering the body politic.[19] In other words, the figure of the terrorist enemy – with all the racial stereotypes attached to it – serves to unite the rest of society in opposition to it. The central ideological message of this discourse is the following: Western society – which stands for freedom, democracy, human rights, openness and tolerance – must stand firm against the fanatical, fundamentalist, violent, barbaric, women-oppressing enemies who 'hate our freedom and envy our prosperity', as Blair and Bush liked to remind us. Apart from questioning the hypocrisy, absurdity and childish simplicity of this message – pointing out that it is precisely these Western societies who are undermining their own much vaunted freedoms and openly violating human rights norms – it is also important to see its deeply racist undertones. It plays on, mobilizes and incites, in quite a deliberate although concealed way, racial prejudices and xenophobic anxieties in Western societies about immigration, multiculturalism and border control.[20] More will be said about this in the following chapters.

Neoliberal/post-liberal security

The construction of the figure of the enemy against which liberal societies must defend themselves, is also a way of more intensely regulating, controlling and policing the citizens of these societies. The way in which the 'war on terror' is used to mobilize people in support of their governments, and their supposedly liberal way of life against the terrorist enemy who threatens it, shows the utility that the discourse of war has in constructing social cohesion, disciplining people and deterring dissent. There is a general 'securitization' and even militarization of Western societies as a result of this discourse.

The 'war on terror' therefore presents us with a new theoretical terrain upon which to consider the relationship between security, liberalism and war. Michel Foucault, in his writings on governmentality and bio-politics, pointed to a certain intrinsic relationship between the idea of security and liberal modes of governmentality which started to emerge in European societies during the eighteenth century. Mechanisms of security, according to Foucault, unlike those of discipline which to some extent they supersede, function through a certain principle of *laissez-faire*, of 'letting things happen'. In other words, the apparatus of security relies on a certain freedom of economic movement, the circulation of goods, the flow of market forces – regulating and policing society precisely through this freedom.[21] What we would suggest is that today we are seeing a paradoxical splitting within the discourse of liberalism itself: the dominant articulation of liberalism today is that of neoliberal economics and the rationality of the market, while the political liberalism of individual rights and freedom has largely fallen away, leaving only a limited notion of the consumerist and economic freedom. Indeed, it would be no exaggeration to say that with the general obsession with security – and all the draconian policing and surveillance measures that come with it – we have moved into a *post*-liberal society, where the very concepts of political freedom, personal privacy and the right to dissent, are seen as things of the past.[22] A new, and somewhat amorphous political paradigm has emerged – one that is (neo)liberal at the economic level, yet deeply conservative at the political, social and ideological levels.[23]

The 'war on terror' is being used to promote a neoliberal economic agenda and a certain vision of globalization around the world, particularly in the Middle East. Neoliberal deregulation is carried out under the guise of 'fighting the global war on terror' and 'spreading democracy and freedom'. When George Bush talks about spreading democracy throughout the world as an antidote to terrorism, this usually equates with some notion of a free market – albeit one that favours primarily US economic interests. The almost total privatization of the Iraqi oil fields as one of the first decisions of the post-war interim administration is indicative of this, as is the suppression of independent trade union activity in the oil sector and the use of de-regulated contract labour. The invasion of Iraq, rather than having anything to do with combating terrorism or pre-empting supposed WMD threats, was more about violently integrating that country into the economic circuits of global 'free' trade.[24] Furthermore, as both Gordon Lafer and Naomi Klein show, the Bush Administration has used 'security' concerns and the 'war on terror' to push an aggressive neoliberal economic agenda within the US itself – for instance, denying the right to unionize to baggage screeners at airports and limiting union rights in other civil service sectors, privatizing and outsourcing security, surveillance and war-making functions.[25] This process can be most clearly seen, according to Klein, in the newly created super-bureaucracy, the Department of Homeland Security: this department is in reality a kind of empty shell whose sole purpose is to outsource security and surveillance to the private sector.[26] Homeland security, surveillance and war making have become the new frontier of the corporate world, the new growth industry, with the US government creating a new market and endless profits for private military and security contractors. Indeed, the imperative of security and the renewed trust in government following 9/11, rather than taking away the impetus for the neoliberal agenda of downsizing and privatizing the public sector, actually intensified it and provided it with a new ideological guise. As Klein says:

> Bizarrely, the most effective ideological tool in this process was the claim that economic ideology was no longer a primary motivator of U.S. foreign or domestic policy. The mantra '9/11 changed everything' neatly disguised the fact that for free-market ideologues and the corporations whose interests they serve, the only thing that changed was the ease through which they could pursue their ambitious agenda.[27]

In more general terms, the 'war on terror' has created a more conservative political and ideological climate, in which there is less resistance to deregulatory economic measures and the curtailment of collective bargaining rights.

Security and democracy

The neoliberal/post-liberal security project also raises major questions about democracy. This is for a number of reasons: the discourse of security in Western post-liberal democracies attempts to justify itself through the notion of democracy – that is, the idea that democratic states must use all available means to protect themselves against those who seek to undermine them. Furthermore, the 'war on terror' was seen – particularly by the neoconservatives in the Bush administration, but also by Tony Blair – as being part of a US-led mission to spread democracy around the world. Here, democracy is seen as an antidote to terrorism – 'give these people in the Middle East the Western style democracy and capitalism they have been craving and they will stop blowing things up', is essentially the message here. While it might be true, of course, that some form of democracy would be desired by those living under authoritarian regimes in the Middle East – such as those in Saudi Arabia and Egypt – the fact that the US continues to support these very regimes, in their open violation of democratic rights, as well as undermining the democratic claims of political movements like Hamas in Palestine, highlights the hypocrisy of this global 'democratic' mission. Nevertheless the point is that democracy somehow operates as the ideological standard bearer of the 'war on terror'.

Lastly, it is clear that the 'war on terror' and the politics of security are actually undermining, in a very real sense, the democratic rights that they claim their legitimacy from. The danger with this new security paradigm is that the exercise of democratic rights – particularly those of protest, dissent, public assembly, even militant trade union activity – are coming to be seen as threats to security which must be restricted. The only response to the mass protests in 2003 – where over a million people marched through London to demonstrate against the impending war on Iraq – was for the British government to ban protests within a 1km radius of Westminster. Security concerns have been used as a pretext to clamp down on protests and mass gatherings all around the world, including and especially anti-globalization demonstrations.[28] It would seem, moreover, that 'terrorism' is a mobile signifier which is being used to criminalize ever-wider forms of social protest. Counter-terrorist legislation in the UK and US, for instance, is so broad and vague as to include potentially any form of protest within the definition of 'terrorism' – indeed, such legislation has been used specifically against animal rights activists and militant environmentalist groups.[29] The repression of democratic dissent, and the deterring of mass political and social movements like the anti-capitalist movement, may well be the real aim of the security paradigm and the 'war on terror'.[30] So the politics of security is something which seriously threatens the full expression of democratic politics, leaving the largely meaningless ritual of voting once every four to five years as the only permissible democratic act.

So it is crucial to examine the relationship between security and democracy. However, the difficulty here is that while, on the one hand, the politics of security is limiting democracy, at the same time it emerges from a democratic space and is given impetus, to a large extent, by democratic electorates. In other words, it would be all too easy to suggest that the security measures which seem to so imperil democracy are instigated by governments entirely against the will of their own people: we have to acknowledge that there is also at some level a popular demand for intensified security, which is driven by fears and anxieties about future terrorist attacks. These anxieties coincide with and blend into more general fears about crime and illegal immigration. The politics of security is only possible in a climate of fear, and while it is true that this fear is deliberately manufactured and perpetuated by the politics of security itself, we also have to recognize the way it is partly legitimized by what is perceived by governments to be wishes of the electorate. The reason why the issue of 'national security' has become such a major part of any electoral platform – to the point where it would be almost impossible to be elected without appearing to take this issue seriously – is because the politics of fear and the desire for greater security has deeply permeated the psyche of democratic polities. The re-election of Bush in 2004, for instance, at a time of heightened fears about terrorism, shows the intense desire for security on the part of many people, and the appeal of conservative political forces which appear to respond to this desire with even 'tougher' security measures.[31]

The politics of security therefore works by constructing a climate of fear and anxiety, and then responds to this with ever more restrictive and draconian controls, thus creating a tenuous and largely illusory sense of public safety. We see a kind of infantilization of the democratic politic here: it is no longer a body politic composed of citizens with rights and liberties, but rather a Hobbesian body politic composed of subjects, driven by fears for their security into seeking the overbearing protection of the state. Tocqueville, in his study of American democracy in the early nineteenth century, perceived a new form of despotism there, one that could not be characterized as a tyranny of antiquity, but that had a distinctly modern and democratic character:

> Over this kind of men stands an immense, protective power which is alone responsible for securing their enjoyment and watching over their fate. That power is absolute, thoughtful of detail, orderly, provident and gentle. It would resemble parental authority if, fatherlike, it tried to prepare its charges for a man's life, but on the contrary, it only tries to keep them in perpetual childhood...Having thus taken each citizen in turn in its powerful grasp and shaped him to his will, government then extends its embrace to include the whole of society. It covers the whole of social life with a network of petty, complicated rules that are both minute and uniform...It does not break men's will, but softens, bends, and guides it;...it is not at all tyrannical, but it hinders, restrains, enervates, stifles, and stultifies so much that in the end each nation is no more than a flock of timid and hardworking animals with the government as its shepherd.[32]

What Tocqueville is describing here is a state of servitude that comes with an almost total dependence of people on their governments: the state exercises control no longer through an overt and tyrannical oppression, but by working itself into the social fabric at the most infinitesimal level. By facilitating their happiness and providing for their security, the state manages the lives of its people in the minutest detail. In the contemporary context, we see the myriad of petty rules, laws and policies that democratic governments implement, which are designed to regulate the conduct of people in virtually every social act and protect them against potential harms: one thinks of draconian rules against smoking in public places; laws to incarcerate the mentally ill, delinquent or 'problem' children, 'potential sex offenders', before they have even committed any offence; policies regarding 'health and safety' and 'sexual harassment' in the workplace; government programs designed to combat 'childhood obesity', etc. This is a democratic system of power and social control in which the state alone becomes responsible for our happiness and security, giving us succour and punishing our deviations. Securitization against terrorist threats is simply the latest and most intense articulation of this democratic despotism. The point is, however, that this sort of interaction between the state and society which characterizes modern societies, creates such a level of dependency of people on their government and erodes their autonomy and responsibility to such an extent, that there is demand for even greater government intervention and control, particularly when people are faced with an all-pervasive sense of threat.

Furthermore, as Tocqueville detected, there was a majoritarian impulse in democracies which threatened to become tyrannical and stifle the rights of individuals and minorities. Once again we can see this today in the 'war on terror': there is a willingness on the part of majorities to violate the rights and liberties of certain ethnic minorities because they are seen to pose a greater risk of terrorism. Muslim minorities have become the targets of police surveillance and harassment, and deliberate policies of racial profiling – measures that non-Muslim majorities in Western democracies generally tend to approve of. This readiness to sacrifice the rights of the few in order to protect and secure the many, has become one of the most disturbing features of the 'war on terror' and the obsession with security.

The desire for security that has emerged in modern democracies reflects a deepening political and ideological conservatism that has become all the more evident since 9/11. The increasingly social conservative agenda of governments, the influence of the religious Right on US politics, the growing hostility towards multiculturalism, the questioning of once accepted notions of human rights and secularism, all indicate a trend in Western democracies towards a conservative and even fundamentalist political paradigm – one that takes national security as its central value. Here David Domke has analysed what he calls 'political fundamentalism' – a politico-ideological discourse which has emerged with the Bush administration. This is a discourse which combines the socially conservative agenda of the religious Right with an aggressive reassertion of US national interests in international relations and the hubristic belief in the superiority of the American way of life. This discourse, moreover, is driven by the politics of fear, and uses this fear to mobilize support, national unity and patriotism. In return for offering some illusion of security from terrorism, this discourse demands unquestioning loyalty to the policies of the Bush administration – something that it was able to largely achieve due to a compliant media and a tamed Congress in the years following 9/11. As Domke shows, this is an authoritarian and fundamentalist discourse – one that draws on the fear of the public and their desire for security, as well as on religious and morally conservative sentiments and themes:

> The administration had created a national mood of spiritual superiority under the guise of a just sovereignty. It was a moral stance underpinned by threat, fear, and paranoia, and carried the connotations of the apocalypse; that is, of course, if Bush's prescriptions for deliverance were not followed. The ultimate irony is that in combating the Islamic extremists responsible for September 11, the administration adopted, pursued, and engendered its own brand of political fundamentalism – one that, while clearly tailored to a modern democracy, nonetheless functioned ideologically in a manner similar to the version offered by the terrorists.[33]

However, we should not imagine that this sort of political fundamentalism is limited only to the US. The UK, and other Western democracies, have become increasingly permeated with a political and social conservatism which works on along more or less the same lines.

Perhaps, as Jacques Derrida suggests, there is something in democracy itself which works against it – something in its own structural logic which threatens to undermine it from within. He refers to this suicidal quality of democracy as *autoimmunity* – a metaphor derived from the AIDS virus, where, in response to the virus, the body produces antibodies which at the same time attack its own immune system. As Derrida says,

> we see an American administration, potentially followed by others in Europe and in the rest of the world, claiming that in the war it is waging against the 'axis of evil', against the enemies of freedom and the assassins of democracy throughout the world, it must restrict within its own country certain so-called democratic freedoms and

the exercise of certain rights ... It must thus come to resemble these enemies, to corrupt itself and threaten itself in order to protect itself against their threats.[34]

In other words, in attempting to immunize itself against a terrorist threat, democracy undermines itself from within. One might, then, legitimately ask those governments who insist that the terrorists want to destroy our democratic rights and freedoms, why they are essentially doing the job for them. How democracy can respond to these challenges, including those that emerge from its own structural failings, is something that we will address in later chapters – but the point that Derrida is making is that there is a constitutive openness in democracy which is essential to it, and which at the same time leaves it vulnerable to attack. But if one tries to secure democracy against such attacks, one ends up undermining it. We would suggest, then, that the politics of security we have been describing is ultimately irreconcilable with democracy: while the latter embodies an openness, pluralism and indeterminacy, the former seeks only control, regulation and the delimitation of freedom. Securitization always does a certain violence to the very thing one is attempting to secure. For Dillon, 'securing is an assault on the integrity of whatever is to be secured'.[35]

Moreover, the anti-democratic tendencies which emerge from within the democratic space – including the growing conservatism of many people in post-liberal societies, and the demand for greater security at any price – is something that can only be resisted through a rigorous contestation of this very logic of security. Not only must its efficacy be questioned – the sense in which it creates only the illusion of security, while actually increasing insecurity – but also the way that it threatens the democratic spaces and institutions which it supposedly seeks to protect.

Here libertarian James Bovard is right to point out the failings of contemporary democracy, particularly in the US, to guarantee the rights of freedoms of citizens and to restrain the power of government. Indeed, his argument in *Attention Deficit Democracy*, is that while democracy was originally conceived as a way of maintaining a check on government power and safeguarding against tyranny, democracy today acts primarily to legitimize the growing authoritarianism of governments: uniformed, lazy and inattentive electorates are regularly duped, manipulated and browbeaten into supporting governments who violate their rights, exceed constitutional limits, spy upon them and engage in illicit torture and unjustified foreign wars of aggression. Elections are nothing more than 'reverse slave auctions' where the slaves get to elect their masters. So, according to Bovard, 'Modern democracy is far more effective at unleashing government than at protecting individuals.'[36] There is much in Bovard's argument that we would agree with – modern democracies have failed spectacularly in keeping governments accountable, and this is something that has become increasingly evident in the post-9/11 political paradigm we are analysing. Bovard is correct to highlight the limitations of contemporary systems of democracy in reigning in abuses of authority, and to show that democracy is not, in itself, a sufficient guarantee of individual liberty. Nevertheless we would argue that democracy is the *minimum condition* for liberty. Despite the contemporary failings of democracy, there cannot be any coherent understanding of individual rights and freedoms without at the same time a notion of democracy and political (and some level of social and economic) egalitarianism. What is needed to restrain the power of governments and to curb their growing authoritarianism and their disregard for individual rights is not *simply*, as Bovard suggests, a reduction in the size of government and a more rigorous enforcement of the rule of constitutional law – although these are important too – but a more radicalized and developed understanding of democracy itself, one that allows for much greater government accountability, more effective and direct representation and more citizen participation in power. The problem here is not democratic excess, but rather a *lack* of democracy; and the solution to the contemporary limitations of democracy is not necessarily to constrain it through law, but to have more democracy, or rather to have democracy of a different kind – one that is not simply confined to voting in infrequent and largely unrepresentative elections, but one that allows for greater power sharing among citizens. A protection and expansion of individual liberties and rights can only come about through a greater egalitarianism, as well as pluralism, of power. Here, democracy must be distinguished from simple majoritarianism: democracy itself would be the vehicle for the expansion of rights and liberties, not the thing that restricts them. We will expand on this idea in the final chapter.

Liberty and security

What must be questioned also is the notion of a *balance* between security and liberty/democracy. Western governments today claim that, after passing legislation which in actual fact severely limits civil liberties and democratic rights, that they have struck the 'right balance' between these two principles: that they have made some minor concessions in order that democracy and liberty may be better protected in the long run. In other words, the assumption here is that certain civil liberties and democratic rights can be restricted without affecting liberal democracy in its essence. This is the same argument that people like Alan Dershowitz and Michael Ignatieff have pursued. Dershowitz suggests that in a war on terrorism, it is justifiable to use even torture, given the right conditions and provided the right legal safeguards are applied.[37] In a more toned down argument, Ignatieff – who rejects Dershowitz's rationalization of torture – nevertheless claims that the sacrifice of certain rights and liberties can be justified as a lesser evil provided we get greater security in return. The suggestion here is that there are certain measures – such as preventative detention without trial, for instance – that can be justified in exceptional circumstances, without undermining liberal democratic principles, and that, moreover, it is precisely the liberal-democratic framework which applies such measures, that can best control them and prevent their abuse.[38] There are a number of problems with this argument, however, problems that will be fully addressed later in the book. For instance, it is at best questionable whether security measures actually give us greater security. Many security experts have suggested, for instance, that the majority of new security and surveillance measures are expensive, worthless and ultimately counter-productive.[39] Secondly, the idea that existing liberal democratic frameworks – because of the systems of checks and balances they enshrine – can adequately control and limit the coercive security measures that they implement, is also questionable: the US, which has the most developed system of constitutional checks and balances in the world, was patently unable to control executive power in its rounding up of hundreds of Arab Americans, its illegal wiretapping of US citizens and its administration of Guantanamo Bay. We cannot be so naïve as to imagine that when virtually arbitrary power is placed in the hands of security and military agencies, that this power can be controlled with constitutions.

What is really at issue here, then, is this idea of a trade off between security and liberty – the idea that certain rights and liberties can be curtailed while leaving intact the liberal-democratic paradigm which we are intending to secure. According to Jeremy Waldron, the very notion of a balance or trade-off between liberty and security must be questioned. It is doubtful whether any real gains to security ensue from sacrificing hard-earned rights and civil liberties like the right to due process, despite what our governments tell us, and despite the psychological sense of security that these sacrifices might bring.[40] Often the only thing that comes with such 'trade-offs' is an inordinate increase in the power of the state, something that any liberal should be worried about.

Therefore, the problem for liberal theory today is not how to strike a 'balance' between liberty and security in the 'war on terror' – it is obvious that there is no balance here, that the scales have been tipped too far in favour of security already. Rather, it is to develop ways of protecting, reinforcing and expanding the realm of rights, liberty, individual autonomy and personal privacy against the incursions by the state. Whether liberalism still has the conceptual language to do this, or whether this means inventing a new language of rights and freedoms, remains to be seen. We must remember that liberalism as an ideology has always been caught between the twin prerogatives of security and freedom – in which one cannot be realized without the other. However, we are faced today with a situation in which the very idea of security has become hostile and dangerous to that of liberty.

Conclusion: Security and the political

In its current articulation, the discourse of 'security' produces a deeply conservative politics – one that not only sees rights and freedoms as secondary to the prerogatives of order and stability, but also one that encourages the support of the status quo. In other words, the ideological message of this discourse is that the only alternative to fundamentalist terrorism and extremist violence is the increasingly authoritarian security state (with its own fundamentalism, terrorism and violence) – and that to criticize the existing order, to agitate for change, plays into the hands of the terrorists. By creating a sense of constant threat and impending catastrophe, by constructing the terrorist as an enemy out to destroy our very existence, the security discourse encourages us cling on to the existing system. In this sense, the politics of security is deeply anti-political – its function is to essentially ward off any form of politics which questions or challenges the status quo. The only thing the politics of security offers us is merely (in)security itself – the image of an empty, lonely landscape from which all hope of emancipation has vanished, and in which people are positioned as Hobbesian subjects whose only salvation is the authoritarian state.

At a more fundamental level, politics – particularly democratic politics – embodies the principle of openness and indeterminacy. Claude Lefort, for instance, describes the democratic revolution during the eighteenth and nineteenth centuries as the *'dissolution of the markers of certainty'*.[41] In other words, according to Lefort, the advent of democratic politics in the modern age introduces irretrievably into the social body the principle of indeterminacy and fragmentation – making visible, and indeed, institutionalising, the absence of foundations at the base of social identity. The logic of security, by contrast, attempts to reincorporate the social space, to establish fixed co-ordinates for social knowledge which are determined by the state and by its security apparatuses – to create some imaginary social unity through the construction of the figure of the terrorist enemy who threatens society. And yet, as we have seen, this attempt to stabilize the social body – to restore the social bond which has forever been severed – brings with it an all-pervasive sense of fear and insecurity. Security is, in reality, the attempt to securitize politics itself – to shut down an autonomous space for politics, and to control and police the conditions upon which genuine politics depends. By submitting social life to technical control and regulation, the discourse of security seeks an evacuation of politics itself. The idea of a life that can be completely secured against amorphous and ubiquitous threats is also a life without politics.

What is needed, then, is a reinvigoration of the body politic itself. As we have suggested, it is as much the fault of electorates, as it is of politicians, that the contemporary state has become so authoritarian, violent and intrusive, that the politics of security has become so ubiquitous, that rights and freedoms have become so circumscribed, and that governments have become so mendacious and unaccountable. Political leaders like Blair and Bush – both of whom, it must be remembered, were re-elected in the midst of scandals over cover-ups and the mismanagement of the war in Iraq – are as much a symptom of the malaise affecting democracy as they are a cause of it. The evisceration of democratic politics and the decline of a politically active, aware and engaged citizenry did not start with 9/11 and the neoconservative political climate that followed – rather they can be seen as making this latter phenomenon possible. In the final chapter, we shall explore how democratic politics might be reanimated and deepened. However, in order to understand how such political phenomena have become so entrenched today, it is important to understand underlying psychological factors which motivate things like prejudice, religious fundamentalism and violence, as well as foster a political culture of mendacity and authoritarianism. The following two chapters will be devoted to exploring these psychological factors and their political effects.

Notes

1. Ironically, in 2007, the same police commander, Cressida Dick, addressed a rally to protest against gun violence in London.
2. There have been subsequent shootings by police of terrorist suspects who turned out to be innocent – for example the non-lethal shooting of a Muslim man in a bungled police raid in East London in 2006.
3. One of the major threats to personal privacy resulting from the 'war on terror' has been the massive amount of personal information on citizens that is now collated on government databases, as well as the increased monitoring of electronic communication. See C. Northouse (ed.) (2006) *Protecting What Matters: Technology, Security and Liberty since 9/11* (Washington D.C.: Computer Ethics Institute, Brookings Institution Press).
4. For a comprehensive account of the lies, deceptions and misinformation that have characterized the Bush Administration, see D. Corn (2004) *The Lies of George W. Bush* (New York: Three Rivers Press).
5. Here we are referring to Foucault's idea that knowledge is ordered, in different historical periods, according to a certain set of rules that govern thought, language and discourse, that determine the truth of statements and the intelligibility of objects. See M. Foucault (2002) *The Order of Things: An Archaeology of the Human Sciences* (London: Routledge).
6. Barry Buzan et al., proposes an understanding of securitization in international relations: it is seen in terms of a linguistic framework of speech acts, which constructs a certain vision of a social order. See B. Buzan, O. Weaver and J. de Wilde (1998) *Security: A New Framework for Analysis* (Boulder, CO: Lynne Reiner), p. 32.
7. In 2003, President Bush caused controversy by referring to Australia as America's 'sheriff' in the South-East Asian region, echoing a statement some years earlier from the Australian Prime Minister John Howard that Australia could act as 'deputy-sheriff' to the US. The shameless obsequiousness of this statement reflects the broader willingness on the part of Australia, the UK and other countries around the world to accept their role as satellite states to a new global American hegemony.
8. Indeed, even many of the security and military functions of the state, particularly in the US, have been outsourced to private contractors – for instance the Revolution in Military Affairs (RMA) associated with the tenure of Defence Secretary Rumsfeld, saw many of the military's functions – from servicing and supplying the military abroad to conducting interrogations – outsourced to private contractors such as Halliburton and Blackwater. See N. Klein (2007) *The Shock Doctrine: The Rise of Disaster Capitalism* (London: Allen Lane), p. 285. Indeed, Klein's analysis of neoliberal economic orthodoxy, where societies are subjected to 'shock treatment' – rapid market deregulation and privatization – suggests a corporatist model akin to that of fascism: rather than a non-intrusive state, there is an expansion of the state's security powers coupled with a collaboration between big government and big business to use taxpayer money to outsource and privatize public services in the interests of the private accumulation of wealth and the concentration of power.
9. See R. Abele (2004) *A User's Guide to the Patriot Act* (University Press of America). See also K. Darmer, R. Baird and S. Rosenbaum (eds) (2004) *Civil*

Liberties vs National Security in a Post-9/11 World (Prometheus Books). For a comprehensive critical account of the way that the national security state has overridden and undermined basic civil liberties in the US, see J. Bovard (2003) *Terrorism and Tyranny: Trampling freedom, Justice and Peace to Rid the World of Evil* (New York: Palgrave Macmillan).
10. See R. Leone and G. Anrig (eds) (2003) *The War on Our Freedoms: Civil Liberties in the Age of Terrorism* (Public Affairs).
11. The White House Press secretary at the time, Ari Fleischer, said that people should 'watch what they do, watch what they say'. The terrorism of this statement is obvious.
12. U. Beck (2000) 'The Terrorist Threat: World Risk Society Revisited', *Theory, Culture & Society*, vol. 19: 4, pp. 39–55, p. 44. See also Beck (2003) 'The Silence of Words: On Terror and War', *Security Dialogue*, vol. 34: 3, pp. 255–267.
13. Such warnings were not restricted to the US. In a massively expensive – and, according to most security experts, ultimately useless exercise, the Australian government mailed out to every resident in the country glossy brochures encouraging people to be 'alert but not alarmed' and to report anything they thought was 'suspicious'.
14. The budget expenditure for the Department of Homeland Security in 2003 was $33.7billion dollars. See B. Schneier (2003) *Beyond Fear: Thinking Sensibly About Security in an Uncertain World* (New York: Copernicus Books).
15. G. Agamben (2002) 'Security and Terror', *Theory & Event*, vol. 5: 4. http://muse.jhu.edu/journals/theory_and_event/v005/5.4agamben.html.
16. See J. Huysmans (1998) 'Security! What Do You Mean? From Concept to Thick Signifier', *European Journal of International Relations*, vol. 4: 2, pp. 226–55.
17. See M. Dillon (1996) *Politics of Security: Towards a Political Philosophy of Continental Thought* (London: Routledge), p. 120.
18. In 2007 Muslim man in the UK, who was detained and then later released without charge in an anti-terrorism raid – a raid in which his house was broken into in the early hours of the morning by armed police officers – made the comment that the UK was becoming a 'police state for Muslims'. This comment was immediately shouted down from the highest levels of government – 'categorically wrong' said Blair; 'unacceptable' said Gordon Brown. Even that wily Jack Straw – who a while ago tried in a somewhat half-hearted way to launch his bid for the future prime-ministership race by attacking Muslim women for wearing the veil (something that proved *very* popular in the opinion polls) – chimed in and dismissed the claim as 'utter nonsense'. They doth protest too strongly, it would seem – as if stating what was blindingly obvious to British Muslims (subject as they are to constant suspicion, police harassment, surveillance etc) was somehow a violation of an unwritten rule that could not be tolerated. See BBC News website 8 February 2007. http://news.bbc.co.uk/1/hi/uk_politics/6342277.stm.
19. Continuing with this virus metaphor, M. D. Silber and A. Bhatt, in a report for the New York Police Department entitled 'Radicalization in the West: The Homegrown Threat' (2007) identify what they see as four stages of radicalization: (1) 'Pre-radicalization'; (2) 'Self-identification'; (3) 'Indoctrination'; (4) 'Jihadization'. Like different stages of a worsening disease, radicalization proceeds from the initial exposure of the subject right through to 'full blown' infection, where the subject apparently prepares to engage in jihadi attacks.

See http://www.nyc.gov/html/nypd/downloads/pdf/public_information/NYPD_Report-Radicalization_in_the_West.pdf (accessed 28 May 2008).
20. The ongoing debate about 'illegal' immigration, for instance, is often tied in with fears about terrorism, a link which is subtly encouraged by governments. As an example of this, the 2001 federal election in Australia, which was won by the incumbent conservative government, was dominated by fears about Australia being 'overrun' by asylum seekers and boat people arriving on its shores. The government deliberately manipulated the political discourse by suggesting that 'illegal' arrivals – particularly those from the Middle East – might be terrorists, playing upon the heightened hysteria about terrorism in the months following the 9/11 attacks.
21. See M. Foucault (2007) *Security, Territory, Population: Lectures at the College de France 1977–8*, ed., Michel Senellart, trans., G. Burchell (Basingstoke, Hampshire: Palgrave Macmillan).
22. Tony Blair, for instance, continuously dismissed certain civil liberties and legal precedents as 'outdated'.
23. For an excellent analysis of the way that the two quite disparate ideologies of neoliberalism and neoconservatism have come together to form the hegemonic political rationality in post-9/11 US, see W. Brown (2006) 'American Nightmare: Neoliberalism, Neoconservatism and De-Democratization', *Political Theory*, vol. 34: 6, pp. 690–714.
24. See N. Klein (2004) 'Baghdad Year Zero: Pillaging Iraq in Pursuit of a Neocon Utopia', *Harper's Magazine* (September).
25. See G. Lafer (2004) 'Neoliberalism by Other Means: The "War on Terror" at Home and Abroad', *New Political Science*, vol. 26: 3 (September), pp. 323–46.
26. Klein, *The Shock Doctrine*, p. 300.
27. Klein, *The Shock Doctrine*, p. 299.
28. The police response to these sorts of demonstrations, particularly at Gleneagles in 2005 and at the G8 summit in Germany in 2007, is ever more excessive. People travelling to these demonstrations have been arrested arbitrarily, violence and excessive force has been used and police with cameras photograph protestors as a form of intimidation.
29. For instance, anti-terrorism police powers have been used against environmental activists protesting outside Heathrow airport in 2007.
30. The highest ranking Muslim police chief in the London Metropolitan Police, citing concerns about Islamic 'radicalism', recently demanded that the UK Parliament pass even tougher laws restricting protests, including the banning of the wearing of masks or bandanas concealing the identity of protestors. It is clear that this is really directed at anti-globalization protestors who cover their faces to avoid police surveillance.
31. Survey after survey, in countries like the US and the UK, shows national security, terrorism and border control to be issues uppermost in people's minds.
32. A. de Tocqueville (1994) *Democracy in America*, trans., G. Lawrence. J. P. Mayer (ed.) (London: Fontana Press), p. 692.
33. D. Domke (2004) *God Willing? Political Fundamentalism in the White House, the 'War on Terror', and the Echoing Press* (London: Pluto Press), pp. 3–4.
34. J. Derrida (2005) *Rogues: Two Essays on Reason*, trans., P.-A. Brault and M. Naas (Stanford, CA: Stanford University Press), p. 40. See also Derrida in G. Borradori (2004) *Philosophy in a Time of Terror: Dialogues with Jürgen*

Habermas and Jacques Derrida (Chicago: University of Chicago Press), pp. 94–102.
35. Dillon, *Politics of Security*, p. 122.
36. J. Bovard (2005) *Attention Deficit Democracy* (New York: Palgrave Macmillan), p. 224.
37. A. Dershowitz (2002) *Why Terrorism Works: Understanding the Threat, Responding to the Challenge* (New Haven: Yale University Press).
38. Michael Ignatieff (2004) *The Lesser Evil: Political Ethics in an Age of Terror* (Edinburgh: Edinburgh University Press).
39. See B. Schneier, *Beyond Fear*, pp. 204–6. Here it is interesting to examine the debate over the introduction of ID cards in the UK: the government initially said that ID cards would be an important tool in the fight against terrorism. But after it turned out that the July 7 bombers were British citizens born and raised in the UK, the government now claims that the ID cards are really about cracking down on crime, identity theft and illegal immigration.
40. J. Waldron (2003) 'Security and Liberty: The Image of Balance', *The Journal of Political Philosophy*, vol. 11: 2, pp. 191–210.
41. C. Lefort (1986) *The Political Forms of Modern Society: Bureaucracy, Democracy, Totalitarianism* (Cambridge: Polity Press), p. 305.

2
Religion, Prejudice, Violence and Politics

When it comes to everyday discourse about political agency, there is a disturbing asymmetry between the kinds of explanation that tend to be offered of one's own group and those offered of foreign or enemy groups. The actions and motivations of political actors in one's own camp, say Western politicians, tend to be rationalized and understood in terms of straightforward, even if not always wholly lucid or laudable, cognitive goals. Beliefs and principles are generally assumed to be the chief motivating features here, and so explanations of actions, including acts of horrendous violence, have to refer to these. The underlying supposition of Western popular discourse on US policy in Iraq, for example, seems to be that no matter how ill-planned it has been, there could be no reason for the invasion of Iraq other than destroying weapons allegedly already present, or forestalling the development of weapons of mass destruction by an unwholesome and dangerous dictator or helping the Iraqis to free themselves of a tyrannical regime. These are often taken as laudable – or at least perfectly understandable – goals and as central to explaining, if not justifying, US action. Even if the strategy for achieving them is seen as misguided, the intention of the strategy at least makes sense.

However, the non-Western 'Other', as Wendy Brown,[1] Judith Butler[2] and others have noted, tends to be derationalized and dehumanized in an effort to push them beyond the pale of anything that affectively, morally or conceptually requires an equality of respect. This is a necessary first psychic step towards regarding the 'Other' as a morally and emotionally legitimate target of gross violence. The motivations of the 'Other' are seen as obscure and, when exposed to the cold light of reason, frankly ridiculous. Religion, as Brown argues, is seen as functioning one way in the West – as a force and artefact of culture and an embodiment of ethical values – but quite differently elsewhere.[3] In countries where Islam dominates, religion is seen as all the things that religion in the West is not. It is seen as a force at odds with rationality, culture, ethics, civilization and progress. This is not to deny that religious and racial prejudices lie behind the murderous acts perpetrated by the self-declared enemies of the West. It stands to reason that the same kinds of psychological forces, in particular prejudices and related phenomena, help account for violence and antipathy on all sides. The point is that these forces are at work in all moves to political violence. Any adequate understanding of terrorism and violence – including, crucially, state violence and state terrorism – has to be grounded in a general account of racial, religious and other prejudices and how they give rise to violence.

Our aim in this chapter, therefore, is to explore the link between racism, religious conviction and violence. We do so from a psychological perspective. Political violence is a complex phenomenon, and there is no easy route to an explanation of it. However, accounts of the psychology of racist and religious prejudice must play a role in any such explanation. Our focus is on the psychological underpinning of prejudice and related propensities to violence, which we explore through a psychoanalytic account of the nature of prejudice.

Racism and the prejudices

What, then, is the nature of prejudice, particularly in relation to violence? Prejudices, including racism, function in a variety of ways as modes of ego defence. They are attuned to specific character types and to the multitude of ways these types, often in combination, are manifest by individuals. This accounts for the strong motivational character of the prejudices as well as for their dangerous and often destructive nature.

Elisabeth Young-Bruehl says, 'we can define prejudices by saying that they are the reflections in attitudes towards groups (and individuals as members of groups) of characteristic modes (usually complex modes) of defense'.[4] She goes on to give a detailed account of these defences in which she relies on psychological and especially psychoanalytic concepts, theories and data. The key point in this account is that prejudices are modes of ego defence: they are ways in which we protect ourselves from perceived psychic threats of one sort or another, and as modes of defence they vary depending on character type. Note also the claim that social and political conditions function as triggers for prejudice by exacerbating the level of threat experienced by the ego. The ordinary affairs of life present us with many threats to our self-conception or our psychic ease. But particular social conditions can make things worse for us, and this is how virulent levels of prejudice and highly dangerous expressions of prejudice arise. It helps to understand what motivates strong prejudices like racism if one realizes that the quite ordinary dislikes or aversions one takes towards individuals are also products of prejudices of various kinds. Certainly, the wild indignation and repulsion that some non-smokers manifest towards smokers are prejudicially based. Often, when one kind of prejudice becomes socially unacceptable and so unavailable (e.g. anti-black racism), other prejudices will quickly be taken up to fill the defensive role that that prejudice plays. The objects of the prejudices matter very little so long as they can do the required psychic job: that of keeping one from oneself.

Psychoanalytic accounts of racism do not split theories of racism along cognitive and affective lines. They recognize that racism involves both cognitive and affective aspects, but deny that the source of racism or any prejudice is cognitively driven. According to Christopher Lane:

> '[The] ignorance and false consciousness' approaches to racism share ... an assumption that knowledge enhances cultural understanding while diminishing inter-and intra-group hostility. This emphasis often betrays a foundational hope that humankind, freed from alienation and political strife, would be wholly communitarian ... these approaches argue that a person's beliefs and assumptions, though determined by his or her class and racial background, can be altered simply by raised consciousness. Studies that aim to resolve urban strife and ethnic warfare often reproduce these assumptions: They anticipate that people locked in conflict want an end to struggle in order to secure the material gains they can achieve only in times of peace. To this perspective, psychoanalysis adds a difficult truth: When people and groups are locked in conflict, they are – beyond their immediate interest in securing sovereignty over another land or people – *already* experiencing intangible gains ... a group's 'gain' might consist in depleting another's freedom ... if we ignore these psychic issues, we promulgate fables about human nature, maintaining idealist assumptions while unexamined psychic factors fuel acrimony, resentment, and hatred.[5]

Neither racism and other prejudices nor the violence resulting from such states of mind can be adequately understood in terms of a cognitive approach. False beliefs alone cannot entirely account for the amount and type of violence, from any of the parties involved, that we are now witnessing in the 'war on terror'. A psychoanalytic approach is better equipped to satisfy explanatory demands. Furthermore, trying to morally assess such violence by recourse merely to normative ethical theory – out of historical, political, psychological, personal context – is hopelessly narrow. Nor does it help much to account for racism in explicitly normative terms, leaving aside the psychological and social complexities of the phenomenon in an attempt to capture the core moral truths of racism.

Garcia furnishes one such normative account of racism, an account directed at the affective components of racist attitudes. Racism, he thinks, is essentially a kind of wrong attitude to others. He writes that racism is

[1] ... fundamentally a vicious kind of racially based disregard for the welfare of certain people. In its central and most vicious form, it is a hatred, ill-will, directed against a person or persons on account of their assigned race. In a derivative form, one is a racist when one either does not care at all or does not care enough (i.e., as much as morality requires) or does not care in the right ways about people assigned to a certain racial group, where this regard is based on racial classification. [2] Racism, then, is something that essentially involves not our beliefs and their rationality or irrationality, but our wants, intentions, likes and dislikes and their distance from the moral virtues. Such a view helps explain racism's conceptual ties to various forms of *hatred* and contempt.[6]

There are reasons to be unhappy with Garcia's account of the moral wrong of racism. Garcia gives little account of how and why racial hatred comes about, and yet some such account is crucial to understanding racial hatred and its immorality. It is insufficient to note that racist prejudice is a 'vicious kind of racially based disregard for the welfare of certain people'. This is true, but any adequate discussion of the immorality of racism must take into account racism's causes. It must also take into account the nature of scope of personal responsibility for character and the unconscious operations of one's mind, the extent to which we can control aspects of our desires.

There is a tendency for moral philosophers to give psychologically superficial causal accounts of racism and to claim, in varying degrees, that such causal accounts are either otiose or relatively neutral with regard to the question of the nature of racism and its specific moral wrong.[7]

However, deeper causal accounts of racism are essential for both tasks. They are also necessary for any strategy to curtail or delimit racism. Coercive forms of social control, for example, may suppress the manifestations of racism up to a point, but no amount of social control is going to change the racist mind (much). Racism and other prejudices are either psychological structures or mental states themselves, or else grounded in such states. Under the right conditions, these states of mind result in prejudicial and often violent behaviour as well as lead to the formulation and acceptance of beliefs grounded in and produced by the self-deceptive and defensive strategies of the prejudiced mind.

Racism is not fundamentally about race at all but about psychic defence. Race is, as it were, an excuse for racism. This accounts for the bizarre nature of racism. On the face of it, it is extremely odd that a person would hate other people because of their skin colour. However, it turns out that racists are not really hating others because of their skin colour, but because of how these others are being psychically portrayed to them, and how these portrayals function in a system of ego defence. Prejudice may be exacerbated or quelled to a degree by the particularities of one's own personal, social, political, cultural and historical circumstances.

The scope of racism

Policies and practices can be unjustly discriminatory without being prejudiced or racist in the primary sense of being rooted in one or more of the psychological ways Young-Bruehl describes. Nevertheless where such discriminatory practices and policies persist, there is bound to be a significant connection at some level between such policies and genuine first-order racial hatred or contempt. Prejudicial and racially discriminatory policies, whether for example anti-affirmative action policies or the use of gross and unnecessary violence for allegedly political ends, will likely be grounded in racial hatred or antipathy. They are not just policy mistakes rooted in ignorance. For example, policymakers and citizens who extol the virtues of equality and human rights while claiming extraordinary rendition, preventative detention, torture, 'targeted assassination' and 'democratic' wars to be necessary and justified are not merely confused. A belief in the necessity of torture, for instance, can only be held together with a belief in one's own essential goodness at considerable psychological cost. It requires the capacity for robust denial, including denial about one's own sadistic impulses. Since imagined targets of torture are predominantly distinguished racially, this denial is itself a function of prejudice and racial antipathy.

Given that minorities and lower socio-economic classes bear a hugely disproportionate amount of the military burden, deaths and casualties in the current wars, there is reason to believe that prejudice underlies such inequality. This disproportionate representation is not to be explained away in terms of the fact that minorities and the lower socio-economic groups see the military as a way to make a living, although this too is the result of unjust discriminatory practices. Were prejudice not a determinative factor, policy formulation would see to it that such burdens were more fairly distributed, for example, by a universal military draft. Since relatively poor, non-white and poorly educated soldiers make up a disproportionate amount of those fighting in Iraq, the death toll – along with the incomparably higher death toll of the Iraqis themselves – is tolerable to a prejudiced (racist), relatively well off and powerful citizenry. Prejudice can be directed outwards towards others (towards Muslims) and inwards (towards non-white Americans) at the same time.

The absence of overt expressions of racism and other prejudices are hardly grounds for denying their presence, particularly when policies that target certain groups in racist or prejudicial ways gain our support or consent on grounds that are largely obscure to us. Prejudice is itself often seen as a rather mild form of immoral discrimination – even when it is recognized as a complex mode of ego defence. But prejudice can often be the source of terrible violence. Indirectly, it is also a cause – or a crucial part of the cause – of illicit political manoeuvrings and the rationalizations that cover them up. Practices such as blatant and sustained lying about important matters, obfuscation, subversion of democratic discourse and the like arise, in part, because there is much to be gained psychologically for all those tainted by them: for those telling the lies and for those relishing them. These are all features of contemporary political life necessary for perpetrating unjustified violence. The upshot of the psychoanalytic conception of racist prejudice, then, is that prejudice does its motivational work in many public arenas, often disguised as rational policy deliberation or the pursuit of national interest.

Looking for cures in all the wrong places

Some ailments can be treated successfully by addressing symptoms. However, given the truth of some deep psychological account of the prejudices, such as Young-Bruehl's, it is clear that attempting to substantially curtail racism or other prejudices by addressing symptoms such as racist behaviour – whether legally, socially or otherwise – is very unlikely to work. Certain political, social and economic structures at specific historical periods (such as *now*) do exacerbate the violent expression of prejudice. But racism, for example, cannot be adequately curtailed by simply seeking to alter those structures, since the structures are themselves the result of racism, and efforts to replace them are easily co-opted by rampant prejudice. The well-meaning moral exhortations one finds in so much of the philosophical and historical literature on racism are even more insubstantial as a basis for change. It hardly suffices to identify a wrong without any plausible proposal for redressing or forestalling the wrong.[8]

Another false hope is the faith many put in unmasking the grounds of prejudice and the falsehoods of one's ego constructions. An unmasking strategy assumes that a cognitive reappraisal will have profound effects on the underlying psychology of political agents. As we have shown, however, it is unlikely that such unmasking strategies work. In fact, they may even prove counterproductive. Prejudice is an ego defence, and attempts to unmask this defence directly tend only to exacerbate the ego threat. The unconscious mind has the resources to deal with exacerbated threats, but it tends to offer up just more of the same. Unmasking prejudice, paradoxically, can readily serve to entrench it. This is not to deny that the critical project of unmasking is important from an explanatory point of view or that it can play an essential role in disrupting complacency and combating hypocrisy. It is to suggest that unmasking prejudice is not a kind of cure of prejudice. So what possibilities of substantial change are we left with?

There are three possibilities left: change in the fundamental character of the citizenry, change in the conditions which exacerbate and generate prejudice (conditions, that is, which exacerbate the perceived need for psychic self-defence or the type of defence on offer) and change in the social conditions that allow the translation of prejudice into action. To entertain the first of these possibilities is to fantasize about a post-human future. The last of the possibilities presents us with a Sisyphusian task (but, of course, one we must undertake where we can). Let us consider the second in more detail. Prejudices are modes of ego defence. There is no eliminating the vulnerability to perceived ego threat that we all share, or our basic modes of dealing with threat. We will always be vulnerable to self-deception, denial, self-serving rationalization and projective defences of numerous kinds. Yet many perceived threats are social in nature: things such as a loss of status, say, or a dramatic, penetrative social signification of disrespect or contempt. To the extent that such social triggers can be ameliorated, the hold of prejudice can also be ameliorated.

Consider the US response to 9/11. 9/11 functioned not only as a signal of physical vulnerability, but, much more significantly from a psychological point of view, it functioned as a signal of profound disrespect and a threat to the (largely phantastical and narcissistic) ego constructions that dominate the US self-image (i.e. the ego constructions of average US citizens as they identify, to one degree or another, with their standing as citizens of the US). The message to US citizens was not, or not only: *you are vulnerable to us*; it was: *you are guilty; you are contemptible*. What traumatized the US citizenry was not that many people died, but that US citizens as a group were held so negligible or so guilty that the death of thousands of them was thought a reasonable price to pay to make a political point. 9/11 wasn't perceived as a tragedy, but as an affront and an accusation (and in spite of all denials, a deeply penetrative one). Intelligent people asked, with all the appearance of good faith: but *why* do they hate us? The point was not to have this answered. Plausible answers – they hate us because we hate them, are coldly contemptuous of them, have affronted and even harmed them in numerous ways and have been doing so for a long time – were not welcome. This was not puzzlement in search of an answer, but a lame attempt to reassert the great fiction of US innocence, to protect the ego by pretending that nothing really damaging had happened to it. But sturdier defences were also needed.

Given the ordinary way we erect ego defences, it is unsurprising that 9/11 unleashed a virulent wave of racism, one that paved the way for war and the death of hundreds of thousands. So what is the right critical response to 9/11 from a practical point of view? It is an accurate and often a welcome relief to respond to the racism implicit in the 'war on terror' by unmasking it, by pointing out how fake the narcissistic constructions of the orthodox US self-image is. But this is hardly likely to be an effective practical strategy for change. As we suggested earlier, this kind of response tends merely to ramp up perceived threat levels and exacerbate the problem. Speaking the truth to a person whose narcissistic self-construction is under attack is likely to push them towards a greater and more desperate defence, and to close them off from all critical voices. What is needed is the articulation of an alternative strategy of ego defence, not the naive insistence that no defence is needed or that none is deserved. The US could have responded to the psychological threat of 9/11 in more or less healthy ways. For example, it could have bolstered the (admittedly fake and narcissistic) US self-image of innocence and power by finding a less murderous demonstration of US power. The critical task, then, in the face of an incipient 'war on terror' was not only reactive – not just an unmasking of the hidden motives and illegitimate drivers of war and violence – but proactive. This is not a matter of articulating responses that accord with a critic's normative judgement. It is a matter of suggesting a response that might work: one that could avert the most egregious acts of violence and most extreme exacerbation of prejudice. The US was always going to do something large-scale to protect its narcissistic ego constructions in the aftermath of 9/11. The task – a very difficult task, but not an impossible one – was to imagine alternative, yet still powerful, avenues of ego defence. Imagine a US that responded to the affront of 9/11 by devoting itself to a non-horrendous demonstration of its power. For instance, taking world leadership on a range of real problems (Aids crisis in Africa, global warming and so on) might have functioned as an ameliorating, non-destructive form of ego defence. The very idea that this might actually have happened is perhaps risible, US politics being what it is. The point, however, is that there often are non-destructive avenues of ego defence available, and exploiting them might ameliorate prejudice and the violence it makes palatable. One crucial task for critics of the 'war on terror', therefore, is to articulate non-destructive avenues of ego defence.

This is one example of the role that an understanding of the psychological nature of prejudice could conceivably play in the attempt to limit or ameliorate the force and depth of prejudice and its expression in action. The key point is that the fight against prejudicial violence requires action in all sorts of indirect and unexpected ways. To fight racist violence, we must fight the conditions which generate perceived ego threats where we can, and hope that this takes the heat and violence out of prejudicial mindsets. Consider one of the most difficult cases of all: the Israeli–Palestinian conflict. This conflict is primarily about 'racial' and deep-seated prejudice on both sides. A disturbing feature of the conflict is the way in which the present Israeli government's leaders and propagandists hide behind charges of anti-Semitism to mask their own racist prejudices – prejudices that ultimately underwrite assassination, torture, lies and the infliction of constant misery and humiliation. This is odious in part for historical reasons, relying as it does on connections to anti-Semitism in manipulative and insidious ways. The past to which Israel refers is one on which they have no moral purchase. Given that they claim to have learned much from anti-Semitism, the question is how they could do such things to a virtually helpless, humiliated, desperate and oppressed – though by no means guiltless – minority. This barbarism is occurring despite the activity of citizens in the peace-movements, who are surely the one genuinely pro-Israel group, in stark contrast to those Jews and non-Jews, Israelis and US citizens who support Israel's brutal and politically unwise subjugation of the Palestinians.

Nonetheless, practical questions are much more difficult than explanatory. And they are more difficult than normative judgements of guilt or innocence. It is much easier to understand the prejudicial basis of Israel's oppression of the Palestinians than it is to suggest conditions for its amelioration. But it is just here that a psychological understanding of the origins of prejudice is crucial. The political tasks of building alliances, cultivating partners for peace, negotiating the division of disputed territories, etc. are to little avail if the population on both sides are unwilling partners in the peace process or consent passively or actively, in large numbers, to its being persistently undermined. The psychological task is to conceive of conditions under which the grounds of prejudice, on both sides, are diminished (they will, perhaps, never be removed).

Let us illustrate the kind of task here by making some rather drastic simplifications. (We make no pretence of offering a real solution.) Israel's oppression and humiliation of the Palestinians is not primarily a response to a perceived physical threat, but a form of ego defence. What threatens it is a form of self-hatred, and the continued contempt for the Palestinians is a way of rationalizing past outrages; it is a way of protecting a viable ego construction in the face of a dubious, barbarous history. It helps fend off the self-destructive realization that so much of Israel's recent history has been a betrayal of those who died in the camps. Palestinian hatred has a more straightforward source. It is grounded in the relentless signification of contempt that emerges from the daily humiliations of life inside the occupied territories and from the deracination of a people expelled from their homeland. It is also, among those committed to violent overthrow of the occupation, a projection that protects the ego from full self-understanding. A cult of martyrdom is another form of ego defence (a highly manipulative and murderous defence). It is forged in response to a fear of powerlessness and a guilt-ridden, blood-soaked and ineffectual history. How can the ground shift in this terrible situation? Only Israel, along with its US backers, can commence the task. This is not because Israel is primarily to blame for the conflict (or not only because of this) but also because of the differing grounds of prejudice that Israelis and Palestinians experience. Israeli prejudicial attitudes have primarily self-directed grounds; they are primarily grounded in Israelis' attitudes to themselves. Palestinian prejudicial attitudes have primarily other-directed grounds. It is possible for Israel to act unilaterally to deprive Palestinian hatred of some of its oxygen (and, by ameliorating reasons for self-doubt and self-hatred, also depriving Israeli hatred of the Palestinians of some of *its* oxygen). It is not at all clear how the Palestinians are to do likewise because the immediate conditions generating Palestinian and Israeli prejudice aren't amenable to Palestinian action.[9] There is a real psychological asymmetry between the two sides here. Before any peace settlement, there must come the disbandment of the apparatus of Palestinian humiliation. The defensive walls, the endless checkpoints, the blockades, the assassinations, the bombings, the culture of contempt must all somehow be eliminated. Israeli–Palestinian relations must be taken out of the hands of the military (even if, in the short term, this increases Israeli vulnerability to attack). Ameliorating some of the conditions of Palestinian prejudice will, in this way, also ameliorate some of the conditions of Israeli self-hatred and its defensive expression in anti-Palestinian prejudice and contempt. Somehow, Palestinians must come not to hate Israelis (or hate them less), and Israelis must, before anything else, come to hate themselves less.

Religion, prejudice and violence

Even if we were to articulate a psychologically plausible avenue towards the diminution of prejudice and its violent expression, there are roadblocks at every turn. The insidious logic of securitization, the vulnerability of citizenry to lies and mendacity, the exigencies of sovereignty and power, the creeping normalization of states of exception and the charms of empire are all roadblocks that we explore in this work. One oft-cited roadblock can be dealt with right now: this is the role that religious conviction plays in engendering and escalating prejudice and its violent expression. This is especially the case in the current post-9/11 political situation, where religion seems to increasingly intrude on the public sphere; where religious groups, particularly in the US, seem to have an inordinate and growing influence on public policy; and where the 'war on terror' is framed by our leaders in quasi-religious terms. The reason that religious conviction ought to be discussed in the context of racism and other prejudices is that religious conviction is itself a kind of prejudice.

It may seem odd to call religion a prejudice.[10] Nevertheless the way in which religion functions for the believer is as a prejudice. The needs that religion responds to are identical or similar to those that other prejudices temporarily assuage. Religious conviction functions as a kind of ego defence, at the heart of which is an attempt to recover the narcissistic ease of early childhood in symbolic form. However, there are important differences between religion and other prejudices. First, because religion is often introduced at an earlier age than other prejudices (sexism is a probable exception), it is likely to be deeply ingrained in character in ways that other prejudices need not be. Second, because religion, unlike other prejudices, feigns to regard itself as socially respectable and is generally taken to be so, it is able to mask certain reprehensible attitudes and behaviours that may be more difficult for other prejudices to sustain. Religious conviction is reinforced and legitimated at the levels of discourse, practice, community and institution. It manages this through every means at its disposal: self-deception, mendaciousness, hypocrisy, manipulation, force and others.

Of course, not all religious people are violent, and religion need not always function in prejudicial or immoral ways. For some people, religion in particular may sometimes be an overall positive feature of their lives. Tamas Pataki distinguishes between what he terms the religious and the religiose: 'between those for whom religion can be conceived, approximately, as a matter of opinion or belief; and those for whom it is a powerful expression of conviction and character'.[11] Pataki sets out the distinction in the following terms:

> The *religiose* are people for whom the relationship with God (or other supernatural beings) and with their religion is an intense and deep engagement. Their belief is tenacious, rooted deeply in the personality, and influences remote aspects of their lives. The religion of the religiose is *driven* by intense need articulated in rigid unconscious phantasies and dispositions, and this explains why their religious attitudes are, as a rule, mirrored in other attitudes – to politics, nationalism, gender issues, and so on.[12]

The most prominent needs that religion phantastically satisfies are those generated by narcissism, envy and guilt.[13] Such needs are present to a degree in all people, but they are prominent in the religiose, and religion finds special ways of satisfying them (this is religion's *raison d'etre*). As with other prejudices, the modes of satisfaction the religiose obtain are attuned to, or constrained by, their character types. These modes of satisfaction are general in many of their aspects and yet also individualized in respect to each person's psychic history and constitution. The religiose may think they believe what they do on the bases of reason, experience and evidence, but on a psychoanalytic account of religious conviction they do not.

What is the connection between the religiose and fundamentalists? As Pataki uses the terms, fundamentalism refers to the ideological or belief component of religion. Religious fundamentalisms tend to be assertive, often violent, counter-modernist movements in which the expression of religious conviction and group membership is fiercely controlled. They are characterized by dogmatic assertion of God's law (to which their group has special access) over secular law. Fundamentalists find it very difficult to accept something like the principle of secular reason, according to which public debate must be wholly carried out through the exchange of a common currency of non-religious reasons.[14] The principle of secular reason is a stark misfit with the ideological character of religious fundamentalism. It appears, rightly, to the fundamentalist to be a flat denial of God's sovereignty. Fundamentalists, with their penchant for Manichean world views, their suppression of sexuality (particularly female sexuality) and their revelling in the ersatz superiority conferred by the membership of an elected or a chosen lot are the most dangerous and destructive part of religion. But there would be no fundamentalists without the religiose; and it is the psychological vulnerability of our species to religiose formations of character that are our main concern here.

Religion caters to the intense unconscious needs and desires of people for self-esteem, superiority, belonging, relief from guilt, envy and shame. The idea that religion functions in ways that assuage the need for superiority and belonging suggests that the quest for ecumenicalism, tolerance or the acceptance of religious pluralism is much more difficult than is often realized – although not impossible.[15] Freud's hope in *The Future of an Illusion* that one day people would psychically outgrow the need for the very real satisfactions that religion delivers is itself illusory – driven by wish fulfilment. In the case of both, the religious and the religiose elements of narcissism and envy, rather than logic and argument, tend to generate beliefs. Those kind priests in the Hollywood movies of the forties and fifties (most prominently, Bing Crosby in *Going My Way* and *The Bells of St Mary's* – the top US box office attractions of 1944 and 1945, respectively) are motivated by narcissism and a need to feel superior, as are we who identify with them and love them to pieces. So too, with the kind old learned or imperious rabbis or imams. What we perceive are our own projections. No doubt many see religion as one of the most valuable and profound aspects of humankind. But on psychoanalytic accounts of religious conviction, such as Pataki's, this too is explicable. The idealizing of religious leaders involves projective or introjective narcissistic identification.

Once religion is seen as a prejudice rooted in narcissism, envy and a compelling need to feel special, the connection between religion and violence is easier to explain. Religion's connection to violence can be as direct as that of any of the other prejudices; even more so given the intensity of the needs it is constructed to address. Motivationally speaking, hatred of what is alien is only part of this. As Pataki puts it, 'Religion becomes especially dangerous and violent because of its deep roots in narcissism and omnipotence, in the frustrations and rage of relinquishing narcissism, and in the distorted and uncompromising internalized object-relationships in which these things are consolidated.'[16] In an effort to re-establish satisfying relationships with objects symbolically representative of important early relations (usually one's parents), violence is not only seen as unproblematic, it may also come to seem necessary.

If the account of religion sketched here is right, then the violence that has come to be associated with religion is not, as many of the religious would have it, a misuse or distortion of religion but part of its very nature. It is not just the violence associated with terrorism and war that is sourced from religion, but so too much of what has come to be termed institutionalized violence associated with our social and political fabric. The overall effects of religion are not predominantly good, and religion is not a source for what is good or just or valuable; on the contrary. However, it would be a mistake to conclude that *per impossible*, were religion to be eliminated, all would be socially, personally and politically well. There is every reason to believe that were religion not an obstacle to self-understanding and peace, various other psychological constructs and prejudices would rush to fill their place.

The future of an illusion

As the religiose know, numbers count. A significant part of the narcissistic satisfactions that religion delivers are had through group identity. The communitarian and institutional character of religions are central to their capacity to furnish the satisfactions requisite for religiose conviction in most people. Therefore, were the strength and pull of religions to wane, so too would their ability to provide the kinds of satisfactions they have traditionally provided. Were a critical mass of the religiose no longer dominant, religion would not only rapidly decline but may also come to be seen as largely illusory. A change in numbers may come about, in one place or another. However, no amount of criticism, no insight or future discovery of science, no play to the emotions and certainly no rational argument will ever be able to shake the religiose free from the needs that bind them or the way they perceive and experience the world.

One crucial way of restraining the religiose is essential to democracy in a pluralistic society; that is, the upholding of the principle of separation of church and state. Ideally, this would take the form of adherence to the principle of secular reason we mentioned earlier. The principle functions, among other ways, to prevent seepage of personal religious views into the social and political arena. It is not surprising, therefore, that this principle has not only come under attack wherever and whenever the religious have been able to exercise their power, but that for all intents and purposes, and despite it being enshrined in the US constitution, it has been overturned by all three branches of US government. Pataki explains the motives, predominantly fear, behind the refusal to adhere to so sensible and necessary a principle as that of separation of church and state:

> For all their front and bellicosity, the narcissistic states we are considering are, at bottom, frangible, precarious, and fearful. They are essentially states of withdrawal in which goodness is phantastically assigned to the self and the group with which it is identified, and most badness to the others. For this reason, amongst others, those of the religiose in whom narcissistic trends predominate are driven by fear: fear of autonomy and fear of other people. The only acceptable political organization in this circumstance is one governed by subjection to the authority of God, and under law proclaimed by God ... the idea of being ruled by divine law excludes the possibility of being ruled by other people; the religiose fear others because unconsciously they expect retribution for the effects of their own unconscious aggression, envy, and devaluation of others. Second, because it gratifies their grandiose self-conceptions: only God can rule over them! Third, because it affirms the special relationship or identification with God; Nietzsche, as usual, detected this element: 'By allowing God to judge, they themselves judge; by glorifying God they glorify themselves.'[17]

In practice, the attack on the separation clause of the US constitution seeks to legally enforce what the religiose take to be moral, even though they do not agree among themselves about what is moral. They insist that everyone must live, legally and morally, as they do – in accordance with *their* divine scriptural injunctions. We must do as *their* god tells them to do. They collapse any distinction between the legal and moral, insisting on a theocentric account of both ethics and law:

All fundamentalists agree that God alone is sovereign and God's commandments are law. The state or nation must also be under God's law, for the good religious life can be lived only in a society of coreligionists, in a political organization fashioned along religious lines. Hence the aims of religion and of constructing a national state converge.[18]

This attack on the principle of separation of church and state is bolstered by myths claiming that religion is the source of all morality and that apart from religion there could be no morality and moral chaos must ensue. Adjacent to this family of self-serving myths is the idea that, morally speaking, religious people are better people. Leaving history and hearsay to one side, in the case of the religiose at least, religion as a prejudice is likely to entail more rather than less unethical behaviour. Pataki spends some time addressing and refuting claims for religious moral superiority. The philosophical, rather than the psychological, issue that underlies these ways of thinking emerges in what has come to be known as the Euthyphro problem (from Plato's *Euthyphro*). Is the pious (τὸ ὅσιον) loved by the gods because it is pious, or is it pious because it is loved by the gods? Is some commandant moral because God commands it, or does God command it because it is moral? No proscription could be moral merely by virtue of God commanding it, since it is always possible to ask sensibly – non-tautologically – whether what God commands is in fact moral. Our notion of what is and is not moral precedes questions about the moral authority of God's commands.

While it is clear that there is no philosophically sound basis for the moral boasts of religion, the practical issue of how to address the dangerous and utterly destructive interference of religion in politics is not to be answered by philosophical refutation of the claims of religion. Since religious conviction is not at all based on reason, it is largely immune to the charms of philosophy. The urgent need, then, is to find ways of diminishing the influence of the religiose in the institutional and communitarian expression of religious conviction. The task is one of establishing a new form of religious pluralism and tolerance, one that is based on an understanding of the incorrigibility of religious doctrine, the intractability of religious conviction, and the native hostility of most religiose conviction to a cooperative politics of difference and tolerance. It is, in large measure, something that has to emerge from within religious contexts. There is little to be gained by winning the argument in secular terms. A key source of hope lies with the possibility of a non-threatening conformation of religious tolerance, one in which the consolations and satisfactions of religion come to rest less on the symbolic reassertion of infantile omnipotence and more on non-exclusionary narcissistic constructions. Religious conviction will always be rooted in the task of symbolically compensating for the lost narcissistic comforts of childhood; it will always be vulnerable to the projective satisfactions of envy, but not every conformation of the religious personality need be hostage to the Manichean hostilities of the religiose as they have emerged from the Abrahamic religions. Psychoanalytic accounts of religious conviction do not show that religious tolerance is entirely impossible – they show that religious tolerance is much more difficult, and more fragile, than is often supposed.

John Rawls famously suggested that secular principles of justice may become the object of an overlapping consensus of people whose personal convictions are anything but secular.[19] His thought was that a secular and pluralistic set of arrangements ought to be recognized as at least the second-best option by all, and the best achievable option, because it allows the social space in which everybody can pursue their private conception of the good, free from the threat of an imposition of other people's private conceptions of the good. Rawls made two mistakes. He misunderstood the determination of the religiose to control their own group (so that a second-best option for them would be a local, protected theocracy, not a universal liberal democracy). More fundamentally, he misunderstood what it is that drives the religiose. They are not after second-best options. They are not performing in game-theoretic mode or playing a role in a cooperative enterprise of any sort. They subject themselves to God's sovereign will – and God's sovereign will alone, when they have the courage – because they experience a determining need to. Without either the lasting political defeat of the religiose or a reformation of the kind we sketch above (as unlikely as that might be), the existence of the religiose will remain a perpetual source of hate and violence. It is one of the most intractable elements of the politics of violence, and plays a crucial role in a politics most unusual.

Conclusion

In this chapter we have examined the nature of prejudices – both racial and religious – basing our account on a psychoanalytic understanding of ego defence, envy and narcissism. This, of course, is not to ignore the way that religious violence, intolerance and racial prejudice are also motivated by social, political and economic factors, but rather to show how psychological motivations intersect with, sustain, and are sustained by such factors. Indeed, in the 'war on terror' we are seeing social and political mobilizations of intense prejudice and religious violence on both sides of the conflict, something that is achieved through a mutual incitement between psychically driven and latent intolerances, and violent and authoritarian political discourses and practices which play upon, and are played upon by, these intolerances. The idea, for instance, of one's identity – whether national, ethnic or religious – being under attack by hostile, alien forces is a powerful motivator for violent and intolerant reactions. Here we see, moreover, a certain collective or group unity being constructed through this illusory identification – groups (national, ethnic or religious) define themselves in contrast, and in many cases in violent opposition, to those who are outside and who may reject its shared convictions and values. An understanding of group identifications and dynamics is therefore important to an understanding of the forms of politics that have taken hold since 9/11. In particular, as we shall show in the following chapter, the psychodynamics of groups is central to explaining a political culture of mendacity – a culture of government lies, belief in or toleration of those lies, and the general absence of accountability.

Notes

1. See W. Brown (2006) *Regulating Aversion: Tolerance in the Age of Identity and Empire* (Princeton: Princeton University Press).
2. See J. Butler (1997) *The Psychic Life of Power: Theories in Subjection* (Stanford, CA: Stanford University Press); and (2004) *Precarious Life: The Power of Mourning and Violence* (London and New York: Verso).
3. Brown, *Regulating Aversion*.
4. E. Young-Bruehl (1996) *The Anatomy of Prejudices* (Cambridge, MA: Harvard University Press), p. 209.
5. C. Lane (ed.) (1998) *The Psychoanalysis of Race* (New York: Columbia University Press), p. 5. See Lane's discussion (pp. 5–7) of a major source of these ideas in Freud's *Civilization and Its Discontents*. People experience their neighbours, says Freud, not only as a 'potential helper or sexual object, but also as someone who tempts them to satisfy their aggressiveness on him, to exploit his capacity for work without compensation, to use him sexually without his consent, to seize his possessions, to humiliate him, to cause him pain, to torture and to kill him'. Freud (1929, 1930) *The Standard Edition of the Complete Psychological Works of Sigmund Freud*, trans., and ed., J. Strachey (London: Hogarth), vol. 21: pp. 59–145, p. 111.
6. J. L. A. Garcia (1996) 'The Heart of Racism', *Journal of Social Philosophy*, vol. 27: pp. 5–45, pp. 6–7.

7. See, for example, L. Blum (2004) 'What Do Accounts of "Racism" Do?', *Racism in Mind*, M. Levine and T. Pataki (eds) (Ithaca: Cornell University Press) pp. 56–77; and Blum (2002) *I'm Not a Racist, But ... The Moral Quandary of Race* (Ithaca: Cornell University Press).
8. The most valuable work in political philosophy over the last 30 years has been directed at deep controversies over the nature of such goals – for example the nature of political justice. This is part of the reason why the tradition of political philosophy, especially in Anglo-American philosophy, has had so little to contribute to the challenge of the 'war on terror'. The tradition has developed very few conceptual tools to deal in an informed and normatively well-grounded way with highly imperfect conditions. This is why so much discussion has fallen back on well worn and philosophically superficial versions of just war theory, and that is why so much of the discussion is mediocre at best. See, for example, J. Bethke Elshtain (2004) *Just War against Terror: The Burden of American Power in a Violent World* (New York: Basic Books).
9. A prediction emerging from this analysis is that unilateral Palestinian action – the oft-demanded moderation of Palestinian politics, for example – would prove ineffectual in altering the conditions of Palestinians' humiliation at the hands of Israel, at least in the short term.
10. This is not an attempt to define religion, but a claim about the fundamental character of religious (particularly 'religiose') conviction. For a recent attempt to define religion – broadly and flexibly – see B. Lincoln (2003) *Holy Terrors: Thinking about Religion after September 11* (Chicago: University of Chicago Press), pp. 1–8.
11. T. Pataki (2007) *Against Religion* (Melbourne: Scribe Publishers), p. 15.
12. Pataki, *Against Religion*, pp. 34–5.
13. The psychoanalytic idea of narcissism is of a 'self-reflexive libidinal relation' that serves to satisfy needs and protect one's fragile ego. It often does so by means of phantastic representation and the construction of prejudices. When we talk about narcissism underlying or motivating religion, we mean narcissism in this latter technical sense rather than in its ordinary meaning.
14. See R. Audi (2000) *Religious Commitment and Secular Reason* (Cambridge: Cambridge University Press).
15. See A. Plantinga (2000) 'Pluralism: A Defense of Religious Exclusivism', in P. Quinn and Kevin Meeker (eds) *The Philosophical Challenge of Religious Diversity* (New York: Oxford University Press), pp. 172–92; R. Swinburne (1983) 'A Theodicy of Heaven and Hell', in A. J. Freddoso (ed.) *The Existence and Nature of God* (Notre Dame: University of Notre Dame Press), pp. 37–54; and P. van Inwagen (1995) 'The Magnitude, Duration, and Distribution of Evil: A Theodicy', *God Knowledge and Mystery: Essays in Philosophical Theology* (Ithaca, NY: Cornell University Press).
16. Pataki, *Against Religion*, p. 82.
17. Pataki, *Against Religion*, p. 87.
18. Pataki, *Against Religion*, p. 33.
19. See J. Rawls (1993) *Political Liberalism* (New York: Columbia University Press).

3
Lying in the War on Terrorism

> Speak the truth, but leave immediately after.
> Slovenian Proverb

This chapter deals with an issue not much dealt with in the literature on terror – that of lying. It may at first seem a background or preliminary problem. It proves, however, to be very much at the centre of what has happened to politics as it responds to terrorism. It underpins a subversion of discourses on terror, tolerance and democracy, as well as means/ends thinking and a distortion of moral judgment. Lying and other forms of mendacity undermine freedom and democratic politics.[1] More than violence and terrorism itself (though deception and lying are directly related to these) it threatens the future viability of liberal democracy – not just as a polity but also as a way of thinking. It raises the question of whether so-called Western democracies, formally or substantively considered, can properly be regarded as democracies at all.[2] The overly insistent idea – used like some school motto – that it is terrorism and violence that threaten Western democracies rather than lies and deceit, is best seen as a subterfuge and projective form of defence. This kind of lying, like excessive self-deception and hypocrisy, is self-propagating and proliferate. Here on a local level at least, Kant's notion that the practice of lying as a matter of course is self-defeating in that it undermines the possibility of any meaningful discourse whatsoever seems to hold. Translated into political terms the claim is that when deceit – inimical to democratic institutions in the best of times – becomes rampant, it undermines and subverts both those institutions and the very possibility of meaningfully asserting anything political at all. At a recent government press conference in Poland a reporter asked the government spokesman if he was telling the truth? 'Is this the first time you've ever been to a press conference'? was his reply.[3] With Auden we need to ask: where is 'the conscious acceptance of guilt in the face of murder'?[4]

Lying in politics

In *Psychologie des foules* (1895) Gustave Le Bon says,

> groups have never thirsted after truth. They demand illusions, and cannot do without them. They constantly give what is unreal precedence over what is real; they are almost as strongly influenced by what is untrue as by what is true. They have an evident tendency not to distinguish between the two.[5]

What Le Bon and Freud both say about groups' utter disregard for truth – and so reality – is troublingly applicable today. It proves to be a good and perhaps even a necessary place to begin examining the sources of violence and terror in racial, religious, nationalistic and other prejudices.

There are those who simply deny that the leaders of the US, UK. and Australia repeatedly lie about fundamental domestic and international issues – particularly but by no means exclusively relating to post-9/11 claims like the presence of weapons of mass destruction in Iraq; US sanctioned torture; the role of the US and UK as being that of an 'honest broker' in the Israeli–Palestinian conflict in particular; or the need for the suspension of basic liberties and rights in what they (mendaciously) call 'the war on terror'. There are of course intermediate positions. Owens does not deny the lies but also says that,

> [n]eoconservatives are confident about the material and ideological power of the United States to, shape the human condition. In a vein similar to more optimistic, liberal-constructivist work, they believe in the power of ideas such as "freedom" and, "democracy" to change the world when allied with American power.[6]

Lying is compatible with such beliefs on the part of neoconservatives but the thrust of this chapter suggests that Owens has, at best, simplified what needs to be said about the neoconservatives' belief. Many believe no such thing at all though they purport to believe it. We must give some account for why those who do believe such things actually believe them and why others pretend to believe them or are self-deceived about what they believe. Owens attributes to Arendt the view that 'the origins of lying in politics are found in the nature of politics itself'.[7] As it stands, this assertion is vague. However, it seems more accurate to say that for Arendt the origins of lying in politics are found in the nature of lying itself. On our view, this is also simplistic and mistaken. The origin of lying in politics and turning away from reality – ignoring certain facts etc is to be found in group psychology. What Arendt clearly recognized was the significance of the gross lying in politics that we see today. It attacks both the substantive and procedural aspects of liberal democracy. And it is more about power and staying in power by attacking any and all opposition with lies, than it is about security or the adherence to ideals. She says:

> If it is the function of the public realm to throw light on the affairs of men by providing a space of appearances in which they can show in deed and word, for better and worse, who they are and what they can do, then darkness has come when this light is extinguished by a 'credibility gap' and 'invisible government', by speech that does not disclose what is but sweeps it under the carpet, by exhortations, moral or otherwise, that, under the pretext of upholding old truths, degrade all truth to meaningless triviality.[8]

Henry Giroux sees an explanation for the re-election of Bush in the face of flagrant and exposed lies in the administration's and media's successful attacks on critical thought. Echoing Arendt he says 'We are indeed living in dark times'.[9] But Giroux's explanation, like Arendt's, is at best superficial. What needs to be explained is what underlies the abandonment of critical thought.

There are those who minimize the history, extent and pervasiveness of the lies or lack of accountability, even while admitting that outright lying and routine deception has and is occurring.[10] In the face of overwhelming empirical evidence, however, such denials merely illustrate Le Bon's claims about group behaviour with regards to the truth. This is not the place to argue for the fact, nor the extent of the mendacity. That is well documented.[11] The obvious question is how in the face of such knowledge about lies and what has resulted from them, can leaders and citizens simply continue with things as they are? And how, in anything that purports to be an open and democratic society, can the citizenry seem to neither notice nor care? The remarkable fact that many people deny that such lying has occurred is as much in need of an explanation as the question of how Bush and Blair have managed largely to get away with lying outright and using transparent fabrications as grounds for extreme and reckless responses to terrorist threats. How can Bush's account of things, accounts known to be false, justify the Patriot Act let alone the US turning its back on the Geneva Convention and undertaking torture and extraordinary rendition?

Others quietly acknowledge the lies but regard them as justifiably driven by contemporary (and timely) incarnations of a necessary Machiavellianism. They conceive of a wedge between ethics and politics, and claim that while the two may overlap, as in a Venn diagram, aspects of political life (sound leadership in particular) are, of necessity, unethical. Just how dirty a leader's hands must be may be disputed, but that they have to be dirty is, on this view, a no-brainer. On this view, political leaders, at least wise ones, should *appear* to be virtuous (honest, compassionate, religious and trustworthy) because of a perceived expectation on the part of those they lead that they actually be so. All the while, however, due to some kind of moral or kindred necessity, leaders lie and engage in activities that are unethical. At its most basic, this is a view that political players respond to political imperatives that bear upon them independently of ethical concerns (or at least independently of the kinds of impartial concern that dominate standard ethical conceptions of political practice, i.e. conceptions – consequentialist or deontological – which insist upon the moral equality of all people). From a Machiavellian perspective, political players might sometimes 'justify' lying by appealing to national self-interest, but they are also likely to disguise it behind dishonest appeals to universal ethical concern: the march of freedom, American exceptionalism and so on. Then again, Machiavellian princes may not see themselves as required to articulate the greater good beyond securing peace (for the community or for themselves). It also is very much in the interests of Machiavellian princes that the ultimate 'justifier' of their practice remains obscure, yet authoritative for most people.[12]

Machiavellians would have it that it is on the altar of an alleged greater good, one perhaps unintelligible to mere mortals or even recognizable as a moral good, that the prince sacrifices his personal virtue and happiness. Their received wisdom has it that 'it is lonely at the top', and the prince travels more or less alone and to 'the beat of a different drummer'. In this case it is a drummer that allows or even encourages torture and routinely mitigates moral responsibility by presenting the problem of civilian causalities as regrettable, although often foreseen, but unintended consequences of war. The Machiavellian prince is here cast as a Kierkegaardian 'knight of faith' and defended as Kierkegaard did Abraham, in terms of a 'teleological suspension of the ethical'.[13] This time, however, in the case of the current conflicts and leaders, it seems that the knight of faith has run amuck – a hyped-up power junkie with media connections – albeit still claiming to do God's will. Abraham was silent about his action and his willingness to kill Isaac. And the way Kierkegaard tells the story this silence plays an important and necessary role in the suspension of ethical consideration. Abraham's actions could not be ethically understood let alone justified. No reference to some alleged greater good *could be* cited as it is possible to do in the case of the current conflicts. Bush and Blair, however, were not silent in invoking religious authority as an ethical justification for their actions, given that justification in terms of democratic processes and the will of the majority is simply not there. The empty gesturing towards some greater good, no matter how implausible it can be shown to be, is the stock in trade of a contemporary Machiavellian prince on the make.

If it is not alleged that some higher obligation, incomprehensible in any ordinary moral terms, justifies the prince's actions, then it is alleged that duty and duty alone – responsibility for the well-being and protection of the masses – prevents the political leader from exercising sincerity. The Machiavellian prince need not be a moral hypocrite. That is, the prince need not be faking their own moral self-regard. In effect, on one reading at least, the prince thinks there is nothing *genuinely*, morally wrong with what he is doing. This Machiavellian tactic – one remarkably still trotted out openly in these terms, and still, even more remarkably, seemingly effective – is a simplistic, misguided and allegedly utilitarian justification for mendacity in government. This is the well-worn tactic of demagogues and dictators, as well as presidents and prime ministers. It is a defence that is as immune to falsification in practice as it has proved to be in principle. One obnoxious feature of the Machiavellian arrogance of leaders is the flouting of a publicity requirement on political justification. The Machiavellian prince may think that certain courses of action are ultimately justifiable, yet may require that the grounds of its justification be kept secret from those affected by the action, i.e. those to whom justification is *owed*.[14]

Machiavellianism describes a cynical disregard for the basic requirement that political actions – particularly coercive political actions – be justified to those they affect (not just those nominally represented by political actors, but all those who fall under the umbrella of a state's coercive exercise of power). Understood this way, Machiavellian princes move easily between various forms of justification. At an extreme, the leaders can do no wrong merely because they are the leaders.

This Machiavellianism or quasi-Machiavellianism, or so-called dirty hands politics, is often combined with the view that political leaders have a secret or better knowledge, a privileged access to knowledge that no one else has. It is a view that leaders like Bush and Blair can be seen as having of themselves, when invoking religious justification and authority and in bypassing democratic procedure. But it is also a view that many citizens, due to wish-fulfilment driven by insecurity, fear and the mechanics of group psychology, have of leaders – Father knows best.

The idea is that what those in charge – working for the people – need to know and why they need to know it is too important to let you know about. Along with those who deny that politicians are manifestly lying or that lying in politics is any more of a problem now than it has been in the past, are those staunch and frightened defenders of the political status quo who insist that although there is serious lying, what is importantly not true is that the leaders are getting away with it, or that citizens *en masse* are untroubled by what they perceive to be the lies and lack of character displayed by their political leaders. For people with deep attachment to this picture of political health, it is probably of little use to point out just how little Bush, Blair and Howard, let alone their political underlings, have been held accountable – each re-elected, for example, and each with plenty of support in the media. The time-honoured tactic of dealing with moral failure – look to the future, don't become mired in endless bickering about the rights or wrongs of past decisions – is on full display in the politics of the US, UK and Australia.

It will likewise be of little use to point out that the political opposition that we might look to for change, and on which claims for accountability in government largely rest, are strikingly similar to those in power. Effective political opposition in US, UK, Australia, and so on, tends to have much the same Manichean views as Bush. Politically effective opposition insists on the fundamental righteousness of its own nation's actions. For example, Democrat opposition to the war on Iraq in the US is largely confined to prudential argument; the idea that a gross injustice has been perpetrated does not play in mainstream Anglo-American politics. This is not just because the issues are subtle and contested, but also because the charge of gross injustice strikes at a central, comforting myth. The myth is that nations such as the US, UK, Australia and Israel simply wish to live in peace, and have been acting (wisely or unwisely) in search of peace all the while. The view that democracy is working as it should, that all is relatively well and that there is more or less adequate accountability, can be seen as illustrating Le Bon's and Freud's point that groups readily give precedence to what is unreal over what is real and that they appear to be 'almost as strongly influenced by what is untrue as by what is true'. Our aim is not to convince adherents of this sanguine view otherwise – that ground is well trod – but rather to explain why they believe as they do; why it is so easy to neglect or avoid the truth.

Our task, then, is a search for explanation. Our basic issue is this: why do people buy the lies? Why did they not question official government explanations – about, for instance, the 'suicide' of weapons expert David Kelly in the UK, about the 'sexed-up' (and plagiarized) dossier about Iraq's WMD capacity or about the scandal over the UK government quashing an enquiry into the arms company, BAE and its illegal kickbacks to the Saudi monarchy?[15] Why did they accept the massive deception about the reasons for going to war in Iraq, or the claim that even though there were no WMD to be found, that the US still acted honestly and sincerely, in its own defence and for the protection of the innocent? There is the connected issue: even if people don't buy the lie – say they put down the war on Iraq as an attempt to shore up future US energy security – why don't they care that much? Bush's popularity remained low throughout much of 2007–8, but if his war on Iraq had been more successful, if, amazingly, unpredictably, it hadn't initiated a long and terrible insurgency and sectarian conflict, then Bush would probably be basking in high approval ratings. He would have gotten away with it whether or not people bought his lies about the justification for war. Success is its own justification, it seems. Failure is its own condemnation. Returning body bags have undermined the credibility of the Bush presidency, not the exposure of his deceit. The question is, why?

Arendt and the *Pentagon Papers*

The question is simply this. Given that we know politicians lie, that the lying is endemic, and that they know that they lie, how is it that they can get away with it? These are not, as we shall see, two distinct questions but rather two aspects of the same phenomenon. Why don't people (personally, politically, socially – nationally and internationally) seem to care, or care enough or appear interested in holding those responsible for lies to account in whatever ways they can? Note that this is not a question about why people lie. That question is relatively easy to answer. We know why people lie – at least we know this most of the time. We know why Clinton lied – not a political lie – about having sex with a White House intern. The real political lies he told, like those about the Iraqi embargo and the deaths it caused, seemed of relatively little concern.[16] The thing that is most puzzling is why lying is tolerated so readily, especially when it comes to political lying on a mass scale: high stakes lying where gross immorality may ensue.

These questions are similar to those raised by Hannah Arendt in her essay 'Lying in Politics' more than forty years ago. In this paper, among other things, Arendt gives a chilling synopsis, documented in *The Pentagon Papers*, of the incredible lies told by US government officials that, along with their extraordinary assumptions, hubris and cynicism and with little or no opposition, informed their policies in regard to just about every aspect of the Vietnam War. 'It is this remoteness from reality' Arendt says in a way clearly reminiscent of Le Bon and Freud's claims about the groups' disregard of reality, 'that will haunt the reader of the Pentagon papers'.[17] It is this seemingly utter disregard for truth and reality that requires explanation.

Introducing her account of these particular political lies, Arendt says:

> Secrecy...and deception, the deliberate falsehood and the outright lie used as a legitimate means to achieve political ends, have been with us since the beginning of recorded history. Truthfulness has never been counted among the political virtues, and lies have always been regarded as justifiable tools in political dealings. Whoever reflects on these matters can only be surprised by how little attention has been paid, in our tradition of philosophical and political thought, to their significance, on the one hand for the nature of action and, on the other, for the nature of our ability to deny in thought and word whatever happens to be the case. This active, aggressive capability is clearly different from our passive susceptibility to falling prey to error, illusion, the distortions of memory, and to whatever else can be blamed on the failings of our sensual and mental apparatus.... The deliberate denial of factual truth – the ability to lie – and the capacity to change facts – the ability to act – are interconnected; they owe their existence to the same source: imagination.[18]

The concerns Arendt sets out, and the distinctions drawn between 'the deliberate denial of truth' on the one hand and self-deception, 'distortion of memory' etc. on the other, are all relevant to the question about lying in politics. Her explanation, however, of capacities for the 'deliberate denial of factual truth', and for acting as if what one was asserting was true, in terms of 'imagination' is as opaque as it is wanting. Her explanation runs as follows:

> A characteristic of human action is that it always begins something new. And this does not mean that it is ever permitted to start *ab ovo*, to create *ex nihilo*. In order to make room for one's own action, something that was there before must be removed or destroyed, and things as they were before are changed. Such change would be impossible if we could not mentally remove ourselves from where we physically are located and *imagine* that things might well be different from what they actually are.[19]

As an explanation for the ability to lie (whether politically or personally), this account is difficult to understand. How and why does the ability to lie find its source in the imagination? On Arendt's account, imagination is needed for virtually every activity, and so its role in lying in particular requires a further explanation. What is it that motivates the imagination to take the course it does in the case of such deceptions?

In fact, Arendt leaves 'imagination' more or less aside in the rest of her account, where she bunches political lies with garden-variety lies and goes on to explain them all in terms of arrogance, self-deception, scientism, love of theory, claims to special knowledge, hubris, cunning and 'mistaken patriotism'. In addition to these explanations, the political lying she is discussing in relation to the *Pentagon Papers* also rests on the belief that 'politics is but a variety of public relations'. This results in the liars also being 'taken in by all the bizarre psychological premises underlying this belief'.[20] In short, she explains lying in terms of all of the usual, and some topic specific, accounts of why we lie. However, this discussion of the genesis of political lies is neither fully adequate on its own account, nor does it explain a phenomenon we especially have in view, namely, the apparent collusion between the liars and those lied to. If one seeks to address the problem of lying on the basis of Arendt's analysis, to seek solutions or means of redress, one barely knows where to begin. No doubt many political lies, lies in a political context, can correctly be attributed to the reasons Arendt cites. But is this enough to explain the kind of political lying we are witnessing?

Lying has many sources – which is not the same thing as saying that there are many reasons for lying. But what needs to be explained is what Le Bon, Freud and Arendt all call attention to – the lack of concern with truth and reality on the part of such liars and those who believe them.

Why does 'that simple everyday reality that sets limits to power and brings the forces of imagination down to earth'[21] fail to operate in the kind of widespread cases of political lying so bound up with politics in the age of terror? A different kind of explanation, one that takes the difference between ordinary and political lying as significant, can be sought. There are psychological processes that underlie and generate a lack of concern with truth and concomitant denial of reality – processes that account for a failure to rein in delusion. Arendt refers to 'varieties' of 'the art of lying'.[22] But the kind of radical and sustained falsehoods we are discussing, gross political lying, fall outside such artfulness or guile even though they are supported by these things. This is part of what makes the lies and those who believe or disregard them so disturbing and in need of a special sort of explanation. This is also what makes the focus of our discussion on lying in politics importantly different from Arendt's. In the final analysis, the lying that is endemic to politics is just another form of lying for Arendt – one requiring no special types of explanation. We, on the other hand, regard the lying as different – and not only because of the difference in consequences.

Arendt notes that political and philosophical thought has been remarkably unconcerned with these questions, though she does not seek an explanation for this lack of concern. Can the lack of concern, a relative blind spot, be a concomitant of the very problem it appears to ignore? The disinterest may partly be due to a history of under-psychologizing political philosophy and related philosophical issues. This in turn may be due to scientific and scientistic approaches by theorists seeking conceptual explanations for actions and events in terms of rational agents and historical, economic or political forces. Our claim is that other kinds of explanation, including fundamentally psychological ones, may at times be in order.

A central claim of our book is that there can be no adequate account of terrorism, violence, intolerance, prejudices or the role of religion in all of these things, without an informed psychological account. As we showed in the last chapter, it is not possible to understand racism or other prejudices, and the kinds of violence they produce, in terms of a purely cognitive account – one that sees racism as rooted in false beliefs or other cognitive defects, rather than in terms of underlying mental processes like ego defence, identification, fixation, projection and the like. Trying to understand seemingly inexplicable violence, racism and other prejudices, including those that are religiously grounded, independently of a psychological or psychoanalytic approach is like trying to understand motion without physics. Trying to morally assess the attacks on September 11 with recourse merely to just war theory, or any consequentialist or deontological normative theory (the sanitized approach) – focusing on that event out of context (historical, political, personal and psychological), and by itself – is hopelessly narrow.[23] The problem of lying in politics underlies all of these issues since it is intolerance, accounts of terror and prejudices that both fuel such lying and constitute much of its subject matter. In Arendt's essays, 'Lying in Politics' and 'On Violence', her ruminations on the relationship between lying on the one hand and violence and power on the other tend to regard mendacity as integral to political violence. To put the matter simply, on Arendt's account, political violence would not occur if the quantity and quality (i.e. significance) of the lies were not so prevalent.

The focus here is largely on the question why political leaders and the public seem oblivious to what are known to be outright and significant lies. Nevertheless accounting for the self-deception and hypocrisy of liars is a less difficult and less urgent explanatory task than explaining cases where outright and recognizable lies go relatively unnoticed or unremarked upon. What is the relation between leaders and groups such that neither seem interested in the truth and 'are almost as strongly influenced by what is untrue as by what is true'? An answer to this question can account for much of the self-deception and hypocrisy that seems to have enveloped politicians and leaders alike. It can also go some way to explaining the violence, curtailment of liberty in the name of peace and freedom, along with the subversion of truthful and insightful discourse about terrorism, tolerance, freedom and the like.

Accounting for lies

It is here that a resort to psychological explanation is needed. While there is no prospect of a simple, one-factor explanation of the phenomena we have outlined, we wish to draw attention to an often neglected avenue of explanation. Some of the most significant forces that both foster and maintain a pervasive culture of mendacity in politics are group psychological forces. In the politics of terror, processes that lead groups to shun truth are also exacerbated by the generalized inducement of fear, as the logic of securitization plays out. Prejudices and the hatred of others feed into processes of fixing and protecting delusions. Yet there is an explanatory factor that precedes appeals to fear and prejudice in explaining political cultures of mendacity. This is the propensity of members of groups – nations, peoples, political constituencies, religious communities, secular clubs, neighbourhood groupings, even families – to subordinate their cognitive independence to the demands of the group.

Groups involved in a culture of mendacity may be self-identified people, such as the people of the US, attacked on 9/11 as a group. It may be a group of neoconservative political figures and their supporters, designing war as political triumph; or a coalition of the religious right, envisioning a clash of civilizations, with God on their side and a perversion of God on the other side. The first of these groups is of particular interest because this is the group that was so easily sold the war on Iraq. Frank Rich demonstrates how successfully a largely mendacious campaign to promote the war on Iraq was mounted by the Bush administration in the US, commencing in the weeks following 9/11 and continuing until the start of hostilities against Iraq in March 2003.[24] Rich's is a compelling account of a largely mendacious campaign that succeeded spectacularly well in a domestic setting, but failed spectacularly in an international one. What is particularly interesting is the vulnerability of popular opinion in the US to the spin.[25] Why was popular opinion in the US so much at odds with popular opinion elsewhere in the world, including within its strongest ally, Britain? Of course the US was attacked on 9/11, not Britain or Germany, but a group explanation seems, *prima facie*, a highly plausible candidate for an explanation of why invasion and subjugation of Iraq recommended itself in the US as a response to 9/11.[26] There are a host of questions surrounding the issue of cultures of mendacity – the perpetrating of lies, half-truths, manipulative spin and so forth; the acceptance of mendacity; the vulnerability to mendacity – and group psychological processes have a role in answering many of them. But the question here sets out the kind of explanatory task at hand. Why should groups differ so markedly in their vulnerability to the mendacious promotion of war?

Here a number of platitudes about the way groups influence beliefs must play some role in explaining the emergence of political cultures of mendacity. Many beliefs, judgments, actions, reactions – including the politically important, foundational ones – are in some measure the product of our membership of groups; we only believe them (act this way etc.) because of our membership in the group. We are disposed to do what we have to do to remain comfortable in the group, including shunning criticism of the foundational ideas or ruling myths of the group. We are often frightened of ostracism from the group and are sometimes prepared to lie and dissemble in order to avoid this. Extravagantly foolish and implausible ideas – even downright delusional ideas – can sometimes be protected from serious criticism by becoming essential markers of group membership. Group membership can also essentially involve marking out others as non-members and this can be a source of prejudice and contempt: the most salient feature of a person is sometimes that they are not one of us. And these phenomena of group psychological formation are not purely cognitive phenomenon: they work through a sometimes disastrous economy of affect.

On any reasonable conception of how groups function in psychologically penetrative and manipulative ways (some groups more than others) the exchange of idiotic half-truths and blatant falsehoods is a permanent possibility. They may be, if nothing else, essential markers of group belonging. A person may believe that the US is a good international citizen, whose overriding concern is to live in peace in the world. To believe otherwise would be to alienate oneself from one's people; it would be to make one a stranger in one's own country, and a stranger to oneself, and that is too much for most people. This may explain in a very general way how it is that allegiance to various kinds of groups can have a distortional effect on a person's appreciation of reality and can diminish their actual concern for the truth at the very moment that they dogmatically assert their possession of it. Yet the platitudes themselves are in need of explanation. We have, to a large extent, merely redescribed the phenomena; but what stands in need of explanation is the psychological process of group identification itself and the kind of cognitive deficit this brings with it. Let us consider one particularly powerful and challenging attempt at a deeper explanation: Freud's. Our overall explanatory strategy does not depend upon the details of Freud's account, but is well illustrated by it. Freud describes an extreme form of group identification, one in which the psychological process of identifying with a group – and in particular with a leader or with a leading-idea – automatically brings with it diminishment of capacities to connect with reality.

Apart from concerns about unanswered questions, making suggestions for minor modifications, and claims about the inadequacy of Le Bon's account of the leader's function and 'prestige', Freud, in *Group Psychology*, largely agrees with Le Bon's 'brilliantly executed picture of the group mind' [GP, p. 81].[27] In addition to addressing some of these unanswered questions (e.g. the role of the leader), and relying on fundamental psychoanalytic concepts ('ego', 'ego ideal', identification, narcissism) Freud's group psychology provides a theoretical framework for Le Bon's observations; why, for instance, group members 'have never thirsted after truth'.

Here is Le Bon's description, as quoted by Freud, of key elements of group behaviour. Freud then goes on to explain these; how and why such behaviour comes about.

> [A group] has a sense of omnipotence...extraordinarily credulous and open to influence, it has no critical faculty...agreement with reality is never checked by any reasonable agency. The feelings of a group are always very simple and very exaggerated...a group knows neither doubt nor uncertainty....Anyone who wishes to produce an effect upon it needs no logical adjustment in his arguments; he must paint in the most forcible colours, he must exaggerate, and he must repeat the same thing again and again. Since a group is in no doubt as to what constitutes truth or error, and is conscious, moreover, of its own great strength, it is as intolerant as it is obedient to authority...What it demands of its heroes is strength, or even violence. It wants to be ruled and oppressed and to fear its masters. Fundamentally, it is entirely conservative, and it has a deep aversion to all innovations and advances and an unbounded respect for tradition....In order to make a correct judgement upon the morals of groups, one must take into consideration the fact that when individuals come together in a group all their individual inhibitions fall away and all the cruel, brutal and destructive instincts, which lie dormant in individuals...are stirred up to find free gratification....
> 'In groups the most contradictory ideas can exist side by side and tolerate each other' [Freud]...the truly magical power of words...can evoke the most formidable tempests in the group mind...Reason and arguments are incapable of combating certain words and formulas. They are uttered with solemnity in the presence of groups, and as soon as they have been pronounced an expression of respect is visible on every countenance, and all heads are bowed.[28]

Freud claimed that the notion of 'suggestion' or 'suggestibility' that Le Bon and others relied on to explain the relation of the individual to the group – specifically the 'intensification of the affects' and 'the inhibition of the intellect' [GP, p. 88] served no explanatory function. What needed to be explained is the urge to imitate itself – that is, one's susceptibility to suggestion.

Freud's account of group psychology is based on his account of an individual's psychology in relation to others:

> In the individual's mental life someone else is invariably involved, as a model, as an object, as a helper, as an opponent; and so from the

very first individual psychology, in this extended but entirely justifiable sense of the words, is at the same time social psychology as well.

[GP, p. 69]

Groups can be of any size. Thus, aside from political groups, family, friends, co-workers or lovers can all be groups. Freud discusses the church and the army as instances of 'artificial groups' before critiquing Trotter's interest in the 'herd instinct' (Chapter IX) and 'the most generalized form of assemblage in which man, that ... ["political animal" (Aristotle, *Politics*, 125b)] passes his life' [GP p. 119].

Central to Freud's account of group psychology, and what enables us to understand the individual in relation to the group, is the role of libido: ' ... libidinal ties [or "emotional ties"] are what characterize a group ... [or] constitute the essence of the group mind' [GP, pp. 91, 101]. Emotional ties are what hold a group together. It is the force behind individuals allowing themselves to be influenced by others, and 'the need of being in harmony' [GP p. 92] with others,

> individuals in the group behave as though they were uniform, tolerate the peculiarities of its other members, equate themselves with them, and have no feeling of aversion [or intolerance] towards them. Such a limitation of narcissism can ... only be produced by one factor, a libidinal tie with other people. Love for oneself knows only one barrier-love for others, love for objects.
>
> [GP, p. 102]

The group's emotional ties are made possible through a form of 'identification' – the way an individual ego identifies with an 'ideal type', usually a father figure, or in the case of the group, with the group's leader, who is a sort of substitute father figure: 'Identification endeavours to mould a person's own ego after the fashion of the one that has been taken as a model' [GP pp. 105–6].

Along with the emotional ties generated by 'identification' with both the leader and other group members, another source of emotional connection is based on the illusion that the leader loves all members of the group equally. Freud focuses on those that have a leader and those that do not. In the Catholic Church and army, both artificial groups, there is a leader (Christ or the commander) 'who loves all the individuals in the group with an equal love' [GP p. 94]. Whatever other ties there may be, it is the 'illusion' of such a leader and their love, and the individual's unity with the leader – a 'substitute father' – that holds the group together. Freud explains the 'alteration and limitation'

[GP p. 95] on the individual's personality in the group in terms of these two 'intense' emotional ties. When a group's emotional ties languish, 'panic' in the sense of 'neurotic fear or anxiety' [GP p. 97] results. The reaction is natural since what the individual must now face (psychically) alone he could previously face with the group as a whole.

In the case of religion – whose relation to violence, intolerance and prejudice we are particularly interested in – dissolution results not in fear but in 'ruthless and hostile impulses towards other people ... which owing to the equal love of Christ, they had previously been unable to do' [GP p. 98]. (Freud is discussing the Catholic Church in particular but the points are easily generalized.) And further:

> But even during the kingdom of Christ those people who do not belong to the community of believers, who do not love him, and whom he does not love, stand outside this tie. Therefore a religion, even if it calls itself the religion of love, must be hard and unloving to those who do not belong to it. Fundamentally indeed every religion is in this same way a religion of love for all those whom it embraces; while cruelty and intolerance towards those who do not belong to it are natural to every religion. ... If today that intolerance no longer shows itself so violent and cruel as in former centuries, we can scarcely conclude that there has been a softening in human manners. The cause is rather to be found in the undeniable weakening of religious feelings and the libidinal ties which depend upon them. If another group tie takes the place of the religious one ... so then there will be the same intolerance towards outsiders as in the age of the Wars of Religion; and if differences between scientific opinions could ever attain a similar significance for groups, the same result would again be repeated with this new motivation.
>
> [GP, pp. 98–9]

Here then is an argument for intolerance and worse as being intrinsic to the nature of that which holds the group together.

A leader seems indispensable to a group, but Freud suggests that an idea might take the place of leader (i.e. a 'leading idea'):

> The leader or the leading idea might also, so to speak, be negative; hatred against a particular person or intuition might operate in just the same unifying way, and might call up the same kind of emotional ties as positive attachment.
>
> [GP, p. 100]

Although Freud does not explicitly address the issue of why leaders lie, part of the answer can be gleaned from *Group Psychology*. First, as mentioned earlier in connection with Arendt's account, they lie for the usual reasons people lie. Such lies are engendered by, and further engender, self-deception, hypocrisy, weakness of will and a full array of other psychologically grounded strategies integral to a mendacious character with little integrity. Second, there is an aspect of group psychology where the leader can himself be regarded as part of the group and so is subject to the same dynamic. An account can also be given of how the group picks the leader it needs at the time, incorporates him and the leader responds to these needs at an unconscious level, as well as in all the usual political ways. This may result in part from projective identification: the leader is manipulated into playing out the worst impulses of the members of the group.

Another feature of 'group feeling' is that it can 'replace' jealousy among members – and along with it provide instinctual satisfaction otherwise stifled. 'Originally rivals, they have succeeded in identifying themselves with one another by means of a similar love for the same object' [GP, p. 120]. Group spirit is derived from envy. 'No one must want to put himself forward, every one must be the same and have the same' [GP, p. 120].

The kind of political lying and disregard for truth and reality we are seeking an explanation for can be shown to have its sources in the same psychic economy of the group mind that intolerance and cruelty do. None of this is hard to discern in evangelical Christianity and other religious fundamentalisms. Pat Robertson, Jerry Falwell and much of the fundamentalist religious right were smugly self-satisfied after 9/11. With God on their side and their ready-at-hand explanations, they blamed not only homosexuals, but basically everyone who disagrees with the Robertson/Falwell world view. These feelings (hate in the guise of love, intolerance made to look like tolerance) were satisfied again and again with the violent responses to 9/11, even misdirected responses like the attack on Iraq.

So how do the libidinal ties that unify groups result in a lack of concern with truth and reality? Idealization 'falsifies judgment'. This is what happens in love – a tendency towards 'overvaluation' of the sexual object. We tend to overlook the faults of the objects we love and idealize. Freud says:

[T]he object is being treated in the same way as our own ego, so that when we are in love a considerable amount of narcissistic libido overflows on to the object ... in many forms of love-choice ... the object serves as a substitute for some unattained ego ideal of our own. We love it on account of the perfections which we have striven to reach for our own ego, and which we should now like to procure in this roundabout way as a means of satisfying our narcissism.

[GP, pp. 112–3]

In a case of even greater sexual overvaluation, and love, where sexual satisfaction is 'pushed into the background', one's ego runs the risk of being 'consumed'.

> [T]he ego becomes more and more unassuming and modest, and the object more and more sublime and precious, until at last it gets possession of the entire self-love of the ego, whose self-sacrifice thus follows as a natural consequence. The object has, so to speak, consumed the ego ... the functions allotted to the ego ideal entirely cease to operate. The criticism exercised by that agency is silent; everything that the object does and asks for is right and blameless. Conscience has no application to anything that is done for the sake of the object; in the blindness of love remorselessness is carried to the pitch of crime. The whole situation can be completely summarized in a formula: *The object has been put in the place of the ego ideal ... A primary group of this kind is a number of individuals who have put one and the same object in the place of their ego ideal and have consequently identified themselves with one another in their ego.*
>
> [GP, pp. 113–6] [italics are Freud's]

Freud goes on to suggest that it might be the ego itself rather than the ego ideal that the object is put in the place of and he says that one of the functions of the ego-ideal is testing the 'reality of things' [GP, p. 114]. He attributes this function to the ego in his later 1923 work *The Ego and the Id*.[29] Either way, whether it is the ego or the ego-ideal, one's faculty for testing reality is rendered inoperable with its replacement by the object. Freud says 'No wonder that the ego takes a perception for real if its reality is vouched for by the mental agency [the object that has replaced the ego or ego ideal] which ordinarily... [tests] the reality of things'. As in hypnosis or love 'the ego experiences in a dreamlike way whatever he [the hypnotist, lover, leader] may request or assert' [GP, p. 114].

An important difference between hypnosis and loss of ego in relation to a group leader is this:

> It is noticeable that, even when there is complete suggestive compliance in other respects, the moral conscience of the person hypnotized

may show resistance. But this may be due to the fact that in hypnosis as it is usually practised some knowledge may be retained that what is happening is only a game, an untrue reproduction of another situation of far more importance to life.

[GP, p. 116]

In the case of a group, however, any such knowledge is likely to be confused or lost since on the surface at any rate, one is going about one's business as usual and one's sense of reality is reinforced by other group members (who are likewise deceived or deluded).

Not only does Freud explicitly connect group psychology to prejudices, intolerance, stereotyping and the 'herd instinct' generally, he also argues that these phenomena are widespread. Much as in neurotic behaviour, such phenomena govern activity and is largely definitive of who we are:

> We are reminded of how many of these phenomena of dependence [and suggestibility][the individual upon the leader and equally other members of the group upon each other] are part of the normal constitution of human society, of how little originality and personal courage are to be found in it, of how much every individual is ruled by those attitudes of the group mind which exhibit themselves in such forms as racial characteristics, class prejudices, public opinion, etc.
>
> [GP, p. 117]

There may be a tendency to think of groups as discrete entities focused around a single leader or leading idea. But groups (like Wittgenstein's language games) overlap and individual members of groups may belong to many with significant similarities that reinforce particular prejudices on behalf of ego defence.[30] A variety of groups with many members in common may form around a leader like Bush who 'may only possess the typical qualities of the individuals concerned' [GP, p. 129], for example, an infantile Manichean, 'us against them' view of good and evil. The violence that this view or idea is seen as ultimately justifying will thus be bolstered and grounded in multiple sources. The justification for violence is thereby overdetermined and attenuated by fear-mongering – subtle and overt. This is done relatively easily and naturally, by exercising and exacerbating already present group prejudices and hate formations. Politicians play to the home crowd by lying to the home crowd. And the home crowd loves it and they lie right back.

Conclusion

However, while we need to be aware of the political dangers of group dynamics – the way they can foster a political culture of authoritarianism, violence, racism, mendacity and the abrogation of individual responsibility and critical reflection – it is entirely unrealistic to expect political action, or social action of any kind, to occur independently of groups and their inevitable dynamics. Some groups undermine capacities for critical reflection more deeply than others; some groups involve their members in greater complicity than others. Rather than do away with the group as a field of political action and political reflection, we need to think of ways of undermining the tendency of groups to overwhelm the capacity of their members to participate in critically reflective political action. One way of contributing to this goal is to break down the monolithic power of large-scale groups and their leading ideas. Such monolithic group formations flourish in the absence of a genuine plurality of political discourse and political participation. It is therefore important to explore the other side of this question: the way that the *breakdown* of certain social groups and collective identities can also lead to critical deficit and failure to deal effectively with political mendacity. The economic and political logic of neoliberalism, which has become dominant over nearly the past three decades, has not only led to privatization, deregulation and the withering away of the welfare state, but has, more fundamentally, contributed to a culture of egoistic individualism, economic competition, consumerism and a 'culture of contentment' as Galbraith[31] would put it, in which collective political action becomes increasingly absent. As Brown says, 'The model neoliberal citizen is one who strategizes for herself/himself among various social, political and economic options, not one who strives with others to alter or organize these options'.[32] Moreover neoliberal rationality and the atomization of the citizen discourage critical thought and ethical judgement: 'Thinking and judging are reduced to instrumental calculation in this "polar night of icy darkness" – there is no morality, no faith, no heroism, indeed no meaning outside the market'.[33] Certain modes of group politics – collective bargaining and militant trade union activity, social movements and organized political dissent of all kinds – have tended to become more and more deracinated and restricted in the face of both state coercion (now intensified post 9/11) and the general climate of political apathy we have been describing.

One could say that the effective use of populist politics to mobilize people around a national identity in the US after 9/11 – the unquestioning loyalty to Bush and the lack of critical reflection on his policies – is perhaps symptomatic of the erosion of independent group identities at the level of civil society, identities which might have functioned as effective sites of resistance. Indeed, this aggressive and paranoid nationalist populism actually worked to deter protests and dissent, as well as gave impetus to further attacks on trade union power and collective bargaining rights.[34] We see the way in which a certain mobilization of group politics – one that is sanctioned by the government and operates at a national level – works to undermine other forms of group politics. In the war on terror, the only legitimate form of politics that seems to be on offer is a Hobbesian one, where our collective loyalties are to our political leaders and to the nation: at the level of the state, people are brought together around a largely fictional national identity – one that is seen to be under attack from external and internal enemies; and therefore the group must cohere even more tightly and loyalty given even more unquestioningly. At the level of civil society, however, people are individualized, atomized, isolated and fearful, encouraged by official security propaganda to distrust other people, spy on their neighbours, be constantly alert to 'security threats'. This is a political climate that is hostile to group allegiances other than to those sanctioned by the state or to conservative social and religious affiliations which support the state.

So one way of countering uncritical and mendacious politics might be to actually foster more political and social groups, not less – in other words, to generate greater political pluralism. Group politics and collective identification are not in themselves the problem – the problem is with forms of group politics on a mass scale, endorsed by the state, and where the dynamics of identification are unconscious: for instance, identification with the nation, as a group, has a kind of dreamlike and phantasmatic quality, where critical capacities are suspended, and where there is a greater likelihood of hysterical and violent patriotism and loyal devotion to the leader. There are, however, other kinds of groups – community action groups, protest groups, for instance – where involvement is more conscious and engaged, where activity is more direct and 'hands on', and where, although certain dynamics of identification still operate, they operate in a different way: not so much the slavish adulation for a leader, but rather a mobilization around a particular worthy goal or ideal. We should not imagine that small, non-state groups are always like this, of course: think of vanguard revolutionary groups, terrorist groups or right wing militias, which can be violent and highly authoritarian in structure. But the point is that when there is a plurality of small groups, with porous and overlapping identifications, rather than an all encompassing mass group where identification is turned into unquestioning loyalty and devotion to the leader, there is a greater possibility of critical political engagement and less risk of the complete abrogation of individual ethical responsibility and rational reflection.

We will explore this question of political pluralism further in the last chapter, but our goal here was to diagnose what we see as a political culture of mendacity which has become apparent since 9/11 – where government lies, cover-ups and dissimulations have become more blatant and breathtaking, and where, more worryingly, there appears to be, on the part of the public, a greater tolerance of (and even appetite for) these lies. This absence of accountability and critical reflection can be seen as part of a certain political condition – enabling it as well as being symptomatic of it – in which state power becomes excessive, and where governments increasingly act outside the boundaries of law and constitutional authority. This is the political condition that Carl Schmitt formulated as the 'state of exception', and it is that we will explore in the next chapter.

Notes

1. Indeed, Norberto Bobbio sees the *visibility* of power as being the crucial element of democracy. See (1989) *Democracy and Dictatorship: The Nature and Limits of State Power*, trans., P. Kennealy (Cambridge: Polity Press).
2. See D. Beetham for a discussion of the relationship between the formal and substantive aspects of democracy. You cannot have one without the other. Being a democracy may be a matter of degree, but on Beetham's account, and so many others, it is seriously questionable, not merely rhetorical, as to whether Western democracies are democracies at all – whether they have even attained a threshold. (1999) *Democracy and Human Rights* (Cambridge: Polity Press), Chapter 5, pp. 89–114.
3. *The New York Times Sunday Book Review*, 11 February 2007.
4. W. H. Auden (1977) *The English Auden: Poems, Essays and Dramatic Writings, 1927 39* (ed.) E. Mendelson (New York: Random House), p. 212.
5. Quoted by Freud (1921) in *Group Psychology and the Analysis of the Ego, The Standard Edition of the Complete Psychological Works of Sigmund Freud*, vol. 18, p. 80. Henceforth, in this chapter, *Group Psychology* will be referred to in the text as [GP].
6. P. Owens (2007) 'Beyond Strauss, Lies and the War in Iraq: Hannah Arendt's Critique of Neoconservatism', *Review of International Studies*, vol. 33, pp. 265–83, p. 266.
7. Owens, *Beyond Strauss, Lies and the War in Iraq*, p. 268.
8. H. Arendt (1983) *Men in Dark Times* (New York: Harcourt Brace), p. viii.
9. H. A. Giroux (2006) 'Dirty Democracy and State Terrorism: The Politics of the New Authoritarianism in the United States', *Comparative Studies of South Asia, Africa and the Middle East*, vol. 26: 2, pp. 163–77, p. 172.

10. Jean Bethke Elshtain specializes in this kind of denial, alongside an attempt to mask the poverty of her case with aggressive displays of contempt for her opponents. 'So those who claim that the WMD threat was "made up" or that the intelligence was hyped or, as is commonly heard these days, at least in allegedly scholarly circles, that the president, the secretary of State, the national security adviser, and all other spokespersons for the Bush administration "lied" about WMD, just do not know what they are taking about. The core around which a justification for war [i.e. the war on Iraq] was based is uncontroverted, namely, the materials and weapons that were catalogued and that Iraq itself admitted it possessed as of 1998. If we add to what they admitted having produced what intelligence suggested they were in the process of producing, you have a threat of serious proportions'. Elshtain, *Just War against Terror*, p. 187.
11. See F. Rich (2006) *The Greatest Story Every Sold: The Decline and Fall of Truth-The Real History of the Bush Administration* (New York: Viking); also L. Cliffe, M. Ramsay and D. Bartlett (2000) *The Politics of Lying: Implications for Democracy* (Basingstoke and London: Macmillan).
12. For a discussion of various interpretations Machiavellianism as a justification for lying see M. Ramsay (2000) 'Justifications for Lying in Politics', in Cliffe et al., *The Politics of Lying*, pp. 3–26. Again one sees excellent accounts of the political lies told and an account of the scope of the problem. But the reasons given for the extraordinary lying are invariably rational. The reason for lying in politics is to knowingly (consciously) achieve some desired end. Whether this is viewed as moral or immoral or some kind of necessary political expediency that is supra moral varies. See, for example, Ramsay's discussion of the causes of government deception (Cliffe, 2000: 44). On our account, the four kinds of reasons listed are superficial, and so inadequate, or else just false.
13. S. Kierkegaard [1843] (1983) *Fear and Trembling*, H. Hong and E. Hong, eds and trans. (Princeton; Princeton University Press).
14. Perhaps this attitude might explain the Bush Administration's obsession with secrecy: the way it has used a variety of means – FOIA exemptions, weakening judicial and Congressional oversight, undermining and delaying the automatic declassification of official documents and records, conducting secret wiretaps, claiming 'executive privilege' – in order to limit public scrutiny and access to government information. See 'Secrecy in the Bush Administration' (House of Representatives Committee report prepared for Rep. Henry A. Waxman, 14 September 2004). http://oversight.house.gov/features/secrecy_report/pdf/pdf_secrecy_report.pdf (accessed 26 February 2008).
15. The British High Court later found that the Serious Fraud Office had acted unlawfully in dropping its inquiry into BAE's dealings with the Saudi government, as it had done under pressure from the Blair government supposedly in the interests of 'national security'.
16. See J. Gordon (1999) 'Economic Sanctions, Just War Doctrine, and the "Fearful Spectacle of the Civilian Dead"', *Cross Currents*, vol. 49: 3 (http://www.crosscurrents. org/fall_1999.htm); also J. Gordon (1999) 'Sanctions as Siege Warfare', *The Nation* (22 March) http://www.thenation.com/doc.mhtml?i¼19990322&s¼gordon.

17. H. Arendt (1969) *Crises of the Republic* (New York: Harcourt Brace Jovanovich), p. 20.
18. Arendt, *Crises of the Republic*, pp. 4–5.
19. Arendt, *Crises of the Republic*, p. 5.
20. Arendt, *Crises of the Republic*, p. 11.
21. Arendt, *Crises of the Republic*, p. 8.
22. Arendt, *Crises of the Republic*, p. 10.
23. See, for example, Elshtain's crude, reductive explanation of Islamic terrorism: '…Islamist ideology is promoted in textbooks, including one mandated for use in Saudi tenth-grade classes that declares it compulsory for Muslims "to consider the infidels their enemies". That is why I argue that such persons hate us for *what we are and what we represent and not for anything in particular that we have done*'. *Just War against Terror*, p. 23.
24. Rich, *The Greatest Story Ever Sold*. Especially valuable in Rich's work is a timeline setting out what we know the Bush Administration knew, when they knew it, lined up against what they said, when they said it (pp. 227–307).
25. In a Washington Post/ABC News Poll conducted 6–9 February 2003, 63% of respondents answered 'enough' to the question: 'Do you think the Bush Administration has or has not presented enough evidence to show why the United States should use military force to remove Saddam Hussein from power?'; 69% agreed that the US has presented strong evidence showing that Iraq has chemical and biological weapons; and 62% agreed that the US has presented strong evidence showing that Iraq is trying to develop nuclear weapons. In a 17 March Washington Post/ABC News poll, 58% of respondents supported the statement 'The Bush Administration says it will move to soon disarm Iraq and remove Saddam Hussein from power, by war if necessary, working with the countries that are willing to assist, even without the support of the United Nations'. http://www.usiraqprocon.org/pop/Resources-Polls.html#F; (accessed 30 July 2007.) In Western Europe, at the same time, there was dramatically less popular support for an invasion of Iraq without UN approval. In January 2003 this ranged from 69% disapproval in Britain to 89% disapproval in Germany (Sylvia Kritzinger (2003) 'Public Opinion in the Iraq Crisis: Explaining developments in Italy, the UK, France and Germany', *European Political Science* Autumn. http://www.essex.ac.uk/ECPR/publications/eps/onlineissues/autumn2003/feature/kritzinger.htm (accessed 30 July 2007).
26. An obvious competitor to this kind of explanation makes appeal to a difference in media cultures between the US, Britain and, say, Germany. The US media were particularly gullible in their response to the Bush administration's promotion of war, as Rich makes clear (Rich 2006). However, this kind of explanation – appealing to the lead taken by media organizations in development of popular opinion – is either too superficial or too implausible. How the media plays out a story is at least as much a reactive as a productive phenomenon. Fox News, for example, is vastly popular because it tells people what they want to hear, the way they want to hear it. The question is why did a preponderance of people in the US, and only in the US, between September 2001 and March 2003, want to hear a story of an inevitable march to war with Saddam Hussein's Iraq?

27. Whatever compliments Freud gives with one hand he quickly takes away with the other. He denies for instance that there is anything at all new in what Le Bon has to say, and he claims that Le Bon focused selectively on certain kinds of groups and neglected the more positive aspects of groups (p. 82).
28. Le Bon (*Psychologie des foules [1895]*), quoted by Freud [GP, pp. 77–81].
29. See [GP, p. 114n2].
30. Freud says, 'Each individual is a component part of numerous groups, he is bound by ties of identification in many directions, and he has built up his ego ideal upon the most various models. Each individual therefore has a share in numerous group minds–those of his race, of his class, of his creed, of his nationality, etc. ...The individual gives up his ego ideal and substitutes for it the group ideal as embodied in the leader. ... He [the leader] need often only possess the typical qualities of the individuals concerned in a particularly clearly marked and pure form' [GP, p. 129].
31. J. K. Galbraith (1992) *The Culture of Contentment* (New York: Houghton Mifflin).
32. Wendy Brown (2003) 'Neoliberalism and the End of Liberal Democracy', Theory and Event, vol. 7: 1. http://muse.uq.edu.au/journals/theory_and_event/v007/7.1brown.html.
33. Gordon Lafer (2004) *Neoliberalism by Other Means*, p. 15.
34. Brown, *Neoliberalism and the End of Liberal Democracy*, p. 20.

4
Sovereignty, Violence and the State of Exception

So far we have considered a number of dimensions to what we have seen as a new political paradigm that is emerging with the 'war on terror'. The first of these has been the politics of security – that is, the overwhelming obsession with security that has come to dominate our societies. As we have shown, however, not only does the deliberate vagueness and permeability of idea of 'security' lead to greater insecurity – in both real and psychological terms – it also seriously undermines democratic politics by restricting spaces for autonomy, freedom and political agency. The second of these dimensions has been the resurgence – or at least a re-articulation – of religious fundamentalism and racial intolerance, not only in the Islamic world, but also here in our supposedly secular West. Thus, it also poses a threat to liberal democratic politics, which relies upon a clear separation between the political and the religious. The third element of this paradigm has been the cynical manipulation of the truth – or downright lying – that has come to be a feature of contemporary political life. This lack of accountability – and, more worryingly, people's apparent complacency in the face of the lies and distortions of their political leaders – also suggests a profound debilitation of democratic politics.

This seemingly paradoxical coexistence of religious moralizing on the one hand, and a cynical and mendacious Machiavellianism on the other, is in fact wholly consistent. It is not simply that men (and women) of God can be shameless liars when it comes to pursuing their political and ideological objectives (here it makes little sense to ponder whether George Bush and Tony Blair are either sincere believers or cynical liars – clearly they are both) but rather that both positions draw upon a certain idea of sovereignty. The idea, in other words, that what is at the heart of politics is absolute and unconditional power, that governments and political elites must at times be able to rule in an unquestioned manner, that they must at times be able to exceed their constitutional authority and even distort the truth and manipulate electorates if it is in the national interest or for the purpose of preserving the social order, is central to understanding the series of mutations that politics is undergoing at the moment. It is no wonder that the neoconservatives in the US – those who, for a while at least, had such a decisive impact on the direction of US foreign policy – were disciples of Leo Strauss, whose notion of the 'noble lie' justified the deliberate manipulation of the masses by 'enlightened' political elites, the proliferation of religious beliefs for the purpose of maintaining the social order, and the engagement in permanent warfare in the name of preserving the health of the nation state.[1]

The concept of sovereignty is therefore a crucial terrain upon which the various dimensions of post-9/11 politics must be considered: the predominance of the politics of security, for instance, is only intelligible through the idea – going back to Hobbes – that the basic function of the state is the protection and security of its citizens, and that this justifies extra-judicial, authoritarian and even violent measures. The dissimulations and distortions of the truth that have characterized the decision for war in Iraq, the official denials and prevarications over the use of torture, the treatment of detainees and secret rendition flights, as well as the censoring of certain public utterances, can only be made sense of through the idea that the preservation of the state trumps all other considerations, and that in the interests of 'national security' the sovereign has the right to manipulate truth, to control the flow of information, to decide what statements are permissible and impermissible.[2] Furthermore, we must also consider the way that the idea of political sovereignty has its roots in religion – in the notion of God as the ultimate and indivisible authority – and that the 'return' of religious fundamentalism into the political domain can partially be explained by the theological stain which continues to haunt modern, democratic forms of sovereignty.[3] Religion and political sovereignty are bound together in intricate ways. These links, while they are formally disavowed in liberal democracies, are exposed not only in the overt religiosity of our political leaders, but also in the sovereign violence that is exhibited in the 'war on terror'.

This chapter will explore the question of sovereignty in contemporary politics. To what extent does the 'war on terror' suggest a new paradigm of sovereignty, one that increasingly operates outside of legal constraints, accepted notions of democratic accountability and human rights norms? What is the relationship between sovereignty, law and violence? Central here is the notion of the 'state of exception' – derived from the Weimar legal theorist Carl Schmitt – which suggests that the sovereign must be able to stand outside the law and suspend it through a unilateral decision. Sovereignty therefore exists in an ambiguous relationship to the law, and the law is grounded on a sovereign violence which always exceeds it. Our contention is that this secret of politics, this disavowed sovereign violence, is increasingly becoming its explicit condition. In other words, there is a tendency today for political executives in liberal democracies to act outside the law both domestically and internationally or to use legislation itself to limit and undermine fundamental civil liberties and constitutional safeguards. These developments – which governments try to justify through the notion of a terrorist emergency – suggest that the state of exception is becoming the dominant and explicit paradigm in politics today, that it is no longer the exception but the rule.[4] This tendency presents a fundamental problem for liberal democracies, which define themselves according to the rule of law, checks and balances on government power and constitutional safeguards of the rights of their citizens. Furthermore, it is by acting in this extra-legal sense that governments share a paradoxical complicity with the terrorism they seek to counter. This is not *simply* to say that torture, detention without charge, illegal invasions and secret renditions risk placing governments, security agencies and military apparatuses on the same moral level as the terrorists, or undermine the very things they claim to be defending against terrorism; nor is it *simply* to say that such measures actually incite and provoke further terrorist attacks or serve at the very least as recruitment tools for terrorists.[5] More so, it is to say that both terrorism and the anti-terrorist state share the same sovereign logic of exception – that is, they both embody a form of violence and exceptionalism which is beyond the law and which has little or no regard for human rights. This violence, moreover, occupies a spectral dimension in which the borders between state and non-state are blurred, and in which the fundamental question of how political authority justifies itself is posed.

States of exception

To understand this paradoxical link between terrorist and anti-terrorist violence we must understand the logic of exception that lies at the heart of sovereignty. In *Political Theology*, Schmitt defined the sovereign as 'he who decides on the exception'.[6] Central to the concept of sovereignty, according to Schmitt, is its ability to decide on, and to determine the coordinates of, an emergency – a situation of 'extreme peril' in which the very existence of the state is in question. In other words, what defines sovereignty is the ability to determine what is in the interests of the state in a situation of national emergency or conflict. What is crucial here is the way that the exception – the situation of emergency and the sovereign response to it – is outside the law. It is not codified in the legal order, and in this sense represents a genuine exception in opposition to which the norm is constituted. It is impossible for the law to account for every eventuality, and therefore there will always be a situation which requires the sovereign to act in ways that are not strictly legally circumscribed. Therefore, according to Schmitt, it is at times necessary for the sovereign to act in ways that might exceed his constitutional authority. The sovereign must therefore not be constrained by the legal order:

> If such action is not subject to controls, if it is not hampered in some way by checks and balances, as is the case in a liberal constitution, then it is clear who the sovereign is. He decides whether there is an extreme emergency, as well as what must be done to eliminate it.[7]

However, for Schmitt, this ability to step outside the law, to suspend the constitutional order in 'emergency' situations, is precisely what guarantees the legal order. In other words, the very existence of the legal order depends upon the sovereign being able to defend it in an emergency, whether this be an external attack, or civil war or some other form of domestic disturbance. Such situations would require the sovereign to have the authority to act outside the law. The legal order must at times be suspended in order for it to be saved. In this way, the state of exception is a sort of limit concept: the legal order is not based on the norm – the regular, everyday application of laws – but on the sovereign decision which exceeds the norm. The decision to suspend the legal and constitutional order becomes, paradoxically, the very condition for its survival: 'The state suspends the law in the exception on the basis of its right of self-preservation'.[8]

For this reason, Schmitt has little regard for liberal constitutionalism which sought to impose limits on sovereign power by attempting to regulate the exception, to define it in law. For Schmitt, this was not only misguided but actually disingenuous and caught in a kind of logical contradiction: 'The tendency of liberal constitutionalism to regulate the exception as precisely as possible means, after all, the attempt to spell out in detail the case in which the law suspends itself'.⁹ In other words, the exception always exceeds the law, and so by trying to define and regulate the exception through law, liberal constitutionalism is in effect attempting to define the conditions under which the liberal legal order may be suspended. Put simply, there is always a limit to the law and to the law's ability to deal with emergencies of state – and at this limit appears the sovereign. The paradox is, however, that while the sovereign's power to suspend the law poses a threat to liberal constitutionalism, it is also its fundamental guarantee. The survival of any legal order – even a liberal legal order – depends upon the survival of the state, and it is for this reason that the sovereign must in the last instance be able to do whatever it sees fit to ensure its survival. That is why, what ultimately characterizes the exception is 'unlimited authority, which means the suspension of the entire existing order. In such a situation it is clear that the state remains, whereas law recedes'.[10]

This limit situation that Schmitt describes seems to uncannily reflect many of the 'exceptional' measures governments have taken in recent years in the name of fighting the 'war on terror'. Indeed, many have acknowledged the usefulness of Schmitt's ideas in understanding these developments.[11] Since 9/11, we have seen governments in liberal democracies using the idea of a terrorist emergency to justify exceeding their constitutional authority in all sorts of ways: for instance, the rounding up and detention of thousands of Arab Americans in the months following 9/11; the kidnapping of terrorist suspects on foreign soil and their indefinite and extra-judicial detention in offshore prison camps, in contravention of both domestic and international law; as well as the Bush Administration's authorization of illegal wiretaps on US citizens. There has been an unprecedented accumulation in the power of the state and, in particular, the intelligence and security apparatuses, as well as a suspension of the usual constitutional limitations and checks and balances. Here we appear to be witnessing the aggressive reassertion of the Schmittian sovereign, with an expansion of state power and the retreat of the law.

However, it is not simply a case of a zero sum game, where when the sovereign speaks the law is silent. The dialectic between sovereignty and law is more complex: the law is used to suspend and weaken itself. For instance, the various pieces of counter-terrorism legislation that have been passed through democratic parliaments – the USA Patriot Act (2001), for instance, and the Prevention of Terrorism bill (2005) in the UK – have seriously undermined constitutional rights, as well as existing legal precedents concerning civil liberties and due process.[12] In other words, rather than the law imposing constraints on sovereignty, the law increasingly operates as its instrument or weapon. Through this 'state of exception', then, the law embodies its own lack, its own suspension – and thus there is a paradoxical relationship between law and lawlessness, between the rule of law and its abrogation.[13] As Schmitt showed, the exception is both inside and outside the law simultaneously. So it is not simply the case that sovereign power in the 'war on terror' operates in a domain which is entirely extra-legal or outside the law (although sometimes it does), but rather that there is a kind of grey zone – or zone of 'undecidability'[14] – between sovereignty and law, in which the limits of each become indistinct and blur into one another. The sovereign decision on the exceptional situation refers not just to the ability to act unilaterally outside the law in response to a real or perceived terrorist threat, but also to work through and use the law to suspend and limit the legal constraints that would normally be imposed on sovereign power. Indeed, an attempt was made by Bush's legal advisers to explicitly and formally legalize his sovereign exceptionalism under the concept of 'unitary executive' presidential power.[15]

Moreover, as we have seen with Schmitt, the sovereign's power to decide on the exception also refers to its being able to define it, interpret it and determine its coordinates – in other words, it is the sovereign who decides whether or not the state of exception exists, whether a particular emergency actually constitutes an exceptional situation. Again we see this sovereign logic being reflected in the 'war on terror'. Governments decide not only what powers they need to deal with terrorist emergencies and what the appropriate response should be, but also whether there is a particular threat or emergency in the first place and how serious it is. The government decides, for instance, when to issue warnings about 'impending' terrorist attacks, when to increase threat levels and implement more intense security measures. There is very little transparency or accountability in these decisions: governments might raise the threat level seemingly arbitrarily, claiming at the same time that they have no specific information, or that if they do, it must be kept secret for security reasons. Thus, an overwhelming and all-pervasive sense of fear and vulnerability is created, without any specific information about the nature of the threat or without any evidence that a threat actually exists in the first place. We hear, for instance, of obscure terrorist plots being foiled all the time, without any details being made public. Furthermore, we have seen governments deliberately manipulate these terrorist threat levels in order to gain political advantage: the use of the colour coded terrorist alerts and obscure and vague warnings about terrorist attacks in the run up to the 2004 presidential election in the US; or the mobilization of troops and army personnel carriers at Heathrow airport in 2003 while the UK government was trying to make the case for invading Iraq. More generally, governments claim that the threat they are facing in the 'war on terror' is new and unprecedented – that it actually constitutes an 'exceptional' situation for which exceptional measures and powers are required to combat it. In this way, the emergency is discursively constructed. This does not necessarily mean that a real terrorist threat does not actually exist, but rather that the extent and level of the threat, the way it is defined both legally and operationally, the way it is used ideologically, the levels of media attention it receives, and what are deemed to be appropriate responses to it, are all determined unilaterally through the sovereign decision. By the sovereign designating a particular situation as 'exceptional' – a situation which, statistically speaking, may represent no more risk or gravity than other situations (in many cases much less)[16] – it *becomes* exceptional.

In this way, the sovereign state of exception refers not only to the way governments expand their power and act outside their constitutional authority – or deform the law in such a way that they can do so 'legally' – but also to the way that they decide the truth itself. In other words, the 'war on terror' is not simply a series of security and military measures, but also a series of discourses and speech acts in which truth is manipulated, distorted and constructed to suit the ideological and political prerogatives of Western governments. The 'war on terror' has its own language, and the sovereign decision on the exception is something that determines the rules of this discourse and, thus, what is considered true and false. The very way in which terrorism is officially defined, and who are actually identified as 'terrorists' would be an example of this: terrorism is defined strictly as violence committed by non-state actors, whereas any serious reflection on terrorism suggests that it is actually impossible to define in these terms and thus impossible to distinguish from state violence. We shall return to this point later. Another example would be the deliberate designation of terrorist suspects held at Guantanamo and elsewhere as 'illegal enemy combatants' so as to exempt them from both US law and international legal protections for POWs. Here also one could point to the way that the rules have been completely rewritten by the US government in such a way as to make it virtually impossible for detainees to prove their innocence, and where they are guilty simply by association or because they were in the wrong place at the wrong time. In other words, in order for the US government to make its case against terrorist suspects, the very 'facts' of the case must be predetermined by the government. A further example would be the infamous 'torture memo' approved by Alberto Gonzales, the then White House legal counsel to Bush, and who went on to become US Attorney General. This memo sought to redefine torture so narrowly as to permit anything (psychological abuse, physical pressure, 'waterboarding' or worse) short of actions leading to 'significant organ failure or death'. There was a similar distortion of discourse when the UK and US governments were making their case to go to war in Iraq, with the term 'Weapons of Mass Destruction' becoming a sort of talismanic signifier, the continual invocation of which was evidence enough – for a while at least – of their actual existence.[17] There was a deliberate construction of a 'reality' here, where overwhelming evidence to the contrary was ignored, and where the flimsiest of 'evidence' in the affirmative was presented as a sign of incontrovertible truth. The facts were quite simply made to fit the sovereign's decision to go to war – a decision taken long in advance, probably before 9/11 itself. As Devin Zane Shaw argues:

> Since in the war on terror fact and law are increasingly confused, we can see a double movement where decisions or justifications shift according to facts, and where the facts shift according to the decisions ... Or, as Donald Rumsfeld put it, 'the absence of evidence is not the evidence of absence'.[18]

Such government distortions and manipulations of language and truth are of course facilitated by the mainstream media, which – despite a slightly greater degree of scepticism now, post-Iraq – continues for the most part to act as an echo chamber for the government. By adopting the language of the 'war on terror', by referring unquestioningly to 'Islamic extremism', 'Islamic fundamentalist terrorism' and so on, the media simply perpetuates this official discourse and, through this, advances the ideological and political objectives of governments. Government control and manipulation of information, the distortion of facts, the proliferation of new meanings and terminology, the arbitrary designation of certain enemies as 'terrorist' etc, can be seen as a way of ruling on the exception, of constructing the truth in support of the sovereign's objectives.

The liberal democratic exception

What consequences does this universalization of the state of exception in the 'war on terror' have for liberal democratic politics? We have to remember that while the sovereign state of exception would seem to be antithetical to liberal democracy, it nevertheless emerges from within liberal democratic regimes. As Schmitt has pointed out, as much as liberal democracies try to constrain sovereign power within constitutions and legal orders, there is still a moment of exception at their base which exceeds them and through which they can be suspended. For Schmitt, the state of exception is the condition of any state's existence, including a liberal one. However, while it is true that the sovereign state of exception has always remained the permanent yet disavowed possibility of liberal democratic regimes, what is different in the contemporary situation is that the state of exception has become both explicit and permanent.[19] In other words, where previously the state of exception was the hidden condition of liberal democracies – invoked periodically perhaps in times of national crisis[20] – the 'war on terror' now suggests a permanent state of emergency. The 'war on terror' is seen as a permanent war: we are told that the threat we face from terrorism is ongoing, and therefore the authoritarian measures that have been put in place to combat it, and the new powers accrued by governments, are here to stay. There is no suggestion, for instance, that practices such as detention without trial, and intensified surveillance and control measures, will ever be discontinued, or that the laws which authorize them will ever be repealed. On the contrary, the laws are becoming more and more draconian, and surveillance is becoming more widespread.[21] The claim made by governments that the powers they have gained are exceptional is belied by the sad reality that these powers have become a permanent feature of the political and legal structure.

Furthermore, there is also an explicitness to the state of exception: rather than being a secret place of detention, for instance, Guantanamo Bay presents to the world a highly visible spectacle of absolute power and the sovereign exception. The existence of this prison camp, and the incarceration of detainees there, is designed to send a signal to the world about the impunity of US power and its haughty disregard for international law and human rights norms.[22] Despite limited access, the media nevertheless reports on the conditions in the camp, and the photos of detainees clad in orange overalls, in kneeling positions behind masses of barbed wire are familiar images in the public's imagination. Even accusations of torture and prisoner abuse are winked at by the US authorities rather than simply denied. Indeed, we have seen that the Bush Administration, while piously stating that torture is contrary to American values, has done everything in its power to facilitate torture, including working to prevent legislation that would make recognized practices of torture such as 'waterboarding' illegal. We should not make the mistake, moreover, of thinking that Guantanamo Bay is simply an aberration: even if recent Supreme Court decisions place in doubt the military tribunals that the US government proposes to hold there, there is no sign that the camp itself will be closing down or that the practice of indefinite detention will be stopped.

So, if the state of exception has become permanent and visible, where does this leave liberal democratic regime? Here it is not sufficient to claim, as Michael Ignatieff does, that a state of emergency may be a necessary temporary response to a terrorist crisis, containing series of exceptional measures which can be controlled and regulated through liberal checks and balances and judicial review.[23] Even though Ignatieff is somewhat sensitive to the risks posed to liberal democracies (although from our perspective, not nearly enough) by exceptional security and anti-terrorist measures, he nevertheless contends that such regimes can remain intact provided the proper constitutional safeguards are enforced. We would suggest, on the contrary, that liberal democracy is in a state of crisis, and that these exceptional measures have not, and perhaps cannot, be contained by existing liberal institutions. The US, for instance, has the most elaborate system of checks and balances in the world, but these were patently unable to constrain the excesses of the Bush Administration following 9/11. Of course, having a tamed and submissive Congress, a compliant media and a Supreme Court largely unwilling to exercise its judicial independence, not to mention a public whipped up into a paranoid and hysterical nationalism, did not help. But the ease with which the political executive was able to exceed its constitutional authority and violate the rights of US citizens, points to serious structural flaws in the system of checks and balances. Even though recently the Congress and the Supreme Court have reasserted some degree of independence and have called into question, for instance, the military tribunals in Guantanamo and the illegal NSA wiretaps, the exceptional security and surveillance powers largely remain in place and have become part of the apparatus of the state. This is even more the case in other actually existing liberal democracies such as the UK and Australia. What we are suggesting, then, is that we can no longer talk about liberal democracies as though they still exist in an untainted form – the state of exception, so far from being an exceptional situation which can be reigned in by liberal democratic structures, has become the permanent paradigm of liberal societies.[24] Liberal democracy is undergoing a series of transformations under the 'war on terror' – and as we have suggested in the first chapter, it makes more sense to refer to a post-liberal political paradigm.

However, while Schmitt's concept of the state of exception is useful in explaining the actions of certain Western governments post 9/11, we would disagree with his normative justification of this state of exception, and in this sense our approach is anti-Schmittian. Rather than the state of exception being necessary for the survival of societies, we have attempted to show that it may actually endanger them further, alienating certain ethnic and religious minorities, inciting further attacks and, perhaps most importantly, undermining the moral credibility of Western democracies. Rather than responding to emergencies and threats to national security with extra-legal and violent actions in both the domestic and international arenas, it may not only be more morally desirable but actually more effective in the long term to insist upon a rigorous application of the rule of law and human rights norms. Moreover, if Schmitt is correct in seeing the state of exception as being at the heart of state sovereignty, then maybe what is needed is a new way of thinking about state sovereignty – in which state power is checked, fragmented, democratized and pluralized through a series of sub-national, transnational and international politico–ethical–legal structures. We shall return to this point later in the book.

Sovereign violence

However, in order to explore the problem of the state of exception further we must first address its relationship to violence. The sovereign state of exception – which as we have argued is becoming increasingly visible in the 'war on terror' – not only articulates itself through an intensified securitization and surveillance of everyday life, but also through a certain violence which lurks at the margins of the legal and political order. The fundamental decision of the sovereign is the right to decide on life and death, on who shall be killed and who shall be spared. Foucault characterized sovereign power as the right to kill, as having the power over life and death: 'The sovereign exercised his right of life only by exercising his right to kill ... Its symbol was, after all, the sword'.[25] Violence, then, is at the heart of sovereign state of exception. Today, this sovereign violence might be seen not only in the illegal wars launched on Iraq and Afghanistan, with their total disregard for civilian life, but also in the humiliation, torture and mistreatment of detainees in US run facilities, through to the reckless slaying by police of an innocent commuter on the London subway system. To take the example of Abu Ghraib, the ritualized and sadistic humiliation and torture of detainees there can be seen as a symbolization of sovereign power: it is well known that such practices – so far from being isolated instances – were widespread and systematic, and that similar techniques applied in Guantanamo had been personally authorized by the Defence Secretary Rumsfeld. Abu Ghraib can be understood as a kind of *mise en scène* or theatricalized staging of the excessiveness of American power and its disregard for human rights – an excessiveness which takes a highly perverse and bizarre form, as if in a kind of parody of itself.[26]

A similar point could be made about Guantanamo Bay: this may be seen as a site of a sovereign power which is unlimited and unconstrained, and where a total domination and the threat of arbitrary violence is exercised over the lives of those detained there. Detainees incarcerated there are deprived of any legal status, and are placed beyond the rights and protections of national and international law. This means that they are subject to an unrestricted, unlimited sovereign power: literally *anything* could (and has) happen to them.[27] Those incarcerated there are reduced to the status, as Agamben would say, of 'bare life' – a subject defined purely by his biological existence, without any legal or political recognition, and whose life is therefore completely indeterminate and at the mercy of sovereign power.[28] As Judith Butler points out, sovereignty in GITMO is diffuse, fragmented and embodied in those who administer the camps – the bureaucrats, guards, military judges and officials who have the power to decide on the fate of the detainees; the power to interrogate, humiliate, torture and kill more or less with impunity. These are the 'petty sovereigns' who administer a power that they are also at the same time caught up in and do not fully understand or control.[29]

For Agamben, these spaces of indefinite detention which have emerged in the 'war on terror' are a crystallization of the sovereign state of exception. They highlight the sovereign's intimate relationship to violence – its suspension of legality; or, to be more precise, its folding together of law and lawlessness. Sovereignty is, for Agamben, '...the point of indistinction between violence and law, the threshold in which violence passes over into law, and law passes over into violence'.[30]

Terrorism and the state

That state sovereignty has an intimate relationship with violence and extra-legality[31] has important implications for any consideration of terrorism. For instance, what makes state violence any less terroristic and illegitimate than non-state or anti-state violence? Where are the grounds to determine which is legitimate and which is illegitimate?

Why is flying planes into the World Trade Centre an illegitimate act of terrorism, whereas bombing Fallujah or firing a missile into a crowded apartment block in Gaza are considered legitimate military actions? What is the essential difference between these forms of violence, other than that one is committed by a stronger power? It simply does not hold to say that one is an action taken by a state actor and therefore legitimate, and the other by a non-state actor and therefore illegitimate. There is nothing from our point of view that morally separates state from non-state terrorism. Moreover, the outrages committed by terrorists, while often spectacular, are trivial in scale compared with the crimes of sovereign states. To object here that liberal democratic states cannot be put in the same moral category as authoritarian states who might be said to engage in 'state terror', is also questionable. Not only is this distinction increasingly dubious, as we have suggested, but the US and UK military violence against civilians in Iraq and Afghanistan, not to mention the decades of US support for authoritarian state terrorist regimes in Latin America and elsewhere, is evidence enough of the violent nature of states which pass themselves off as democratic. Furthermore, we can point to the way that democratic states such as Israel were, in a very real sense, founded on acts of terrorism – from the bombing of British hotels in Jerusalem to the violent ethnic cleansing of Palestinian populations in Deir Yassin.

Moreover, both forms of violence occupy the same logic of exception, and in this sense they are both reflections of the problem of sovereignty. Indeed, anti-state and state (counter)terrorism are part of a complex and paradoxical dialectic in which their own violence is both instantiated and disavowed in its relationship to the other. Both forms of violence are really a fascination with the abyss, with the ontological gap at the basis of sovereignty. Non-state terrorism has the effect of exposing this abyss, of calling attention to the illegitimacy of sovereignty; by eliciting a violent response from the state, it shows that the state engages in the same sort of terroristic and illegitimate violence, that it has little or no respect for human rights, and that its much vaunted liberal–democratic superiority is ultimately a sham.[32] Terrorist violence always threatens to expose the emptiness and indeterminacy at the base of the symbolic authority of the law and the state. It unmasks the violent and mysterious foundations of this authority.[33] Counterterrorist state violence, on the other hand, by claiming to enforce the law, functions to cover over its own emptiness, to disavow the lack of legitimacy at its own foundations. However, as we have said, this has precisely the opposite effect of exposing its own violence. And yet, the anti-terrorist state needs its terrorist other to legitimize its continual expansion and permanent militarization. The state of exception cannot be justified, as Schmitt showed, without an enemy which threatens the existence of the state. The picture, however, is even more complex than this. Sovereign state violence and religiously inspired terrorism also share in the same desire to cover over their own groundlessness, to hide the ontological gap in their foundations. Religious fundamentalism, which motivates a certain form of anti-state terrorism – as well, in a more oblique way, motivating state (counter)terrorism – may be seen as the attempt to disavow, through acts of violence and professions of faith and religious conviction, a kind of lack or emptiness at the heart of religious authority. As Derrida shows, the ontological ground of religion is something that cannot be represented, and that is why it is depicted as a kind of ineffable and sacred mystery, a veiled secret that cannot be disclosed, that is beyond human experience.[34] What this mystery hides is a void, an unbearable nothingness which must be kept hidden. In this sense, there is a parallel between religious authority and political authority – both are ultimately dependent on a moment of exception without legitimate ground. Religious fundamentalism can therefore be seen as an attempt to violently disavow this lack, to reaffirm or shore up the authority of religion by insisting, in a hysterical fashion, on the literalness of the word and the purity of the message. In this sense, Islamic fundamentalism – or Christian fundamentalism for that matter – cannot be seen as simply a return to religious tradition, a tradition whose coherence and purity are largely imaginary in any case. Rather, it is a distinctly modern reaction to the perceived loss of a religious identity, due to the economic, social and technological pressures of modernity. In the same way that the 'war on terror' might be seen as a violent reaction to the crisis of the nation state in the context of globalization – a point we shall return to later – so too might religious fanaticism, and particularly militant Islam, be seen as a violent reaction to the crisis of religion in the face of hypercapitalism and late modernity.

Theology and politics

Here we are saying more than simply that religion motivates and intensifies both sides of the conflict in the war on terror, or that religious references are used by democratically elected political leaders and terrorists alike to justify their actions. More fundamentally, we are referring to the way in which state sovereignty and anti-state terrorism are deeply intertwined and related, not only through the violence that they both entail, but also through religion. The 'war on terror' reveals the deeply theological nature of sovereignty itself. Indeed, Schmitt sees political sovereignty as a 'secularized theological concept', and the state of exception equating with a 'miracle' in the religious sense.[35] The sovereign or lawgiver, for Schmitt, is a secularized God, who authorizes himself and who rules on the exception with the same unilateral and unquestionable will. For Derrida too, there is a clear link between the indivisible authority of God and that of the political sovereign.[36]

While the rationalist Enlightenment rejection of religion was accompanied by the rejection of the political absolutism of the sovereign, and while modern liberal regimes claim to be secular and based on the separation of the religious from the political, the continued existence of sovereignty represents a religious trace, a kind of theological stain which is often in tension with liberal democratic principles. The theological roots of sovereignty are repressed and disavowed, and yet form part of the political unconscious of liberal democracies. What we are witnessing now might be seen as a 'return of the repressed'. It is not simply that religious conservatives in countries like the US have gained more influence on politics than they should – although this in itself is a significant problem – but that religious references and ideas have become much more prominent in political discourse generally, to the point where the political domain is constructed in quasi-religious terms. It is perhaps no wonder, then, that political leaders like Bush and Blair were not only believers themselves, but regularly called upon religious ideas to justify their policies and actions.[37] Moreover, when Bush couched his 'war on terror' in terms of a metaphysical struggle between Good and Evil, we see this close interweaving between religion and sovereignty: he was not only drawing on religion to defend certain political and strategic goals, but was also enacting the sovereign decision, one that determines the coordinates of a particular situation, that violently divides and reconstructs the political field in Manichean terms, positioning the sovereign as the embodiment of the good and the enemies of the sovereign as a figure of evil. Here we not only see the predominance of religious obscurantism, but also a kind of *political obscurantism* – a lack of democratic scrutiny and accountability, and a public which is prepared, for the most part, to accept the lies told to them by their political leaders and, worse, to not react when these lies are later found out. Thus, we see the way in which religious authority and religious mysticism parallel, and are closely bound up with, political authority and political mysticism; that the return to religious conservatism in liberal societies corresponds with a growing political conservatism – and indeed fundamentalism – in which the decision of the sovereign is not to be questioned or scrutinized too closely, and people are happily prepared to sacrifice their liberty for the illusion of security.

It is therefore absurd and obscurantist to see the world in terms of a 'clash of civilisations' in which Western liberal democratic secularism is pitted against Islamic theocracy. Rather – to invoke the title of Tariq Ali's book[38] – it is much more accurate to describe the 'war on terror' as a clash of fundamentalisms, in which religion, social conservatism and political authoritarianism infuse both sides of the conflict, and in which the language of jihad is closely mirrored by the crusading terminology of US neo-imperialism and global capitalism. Indeed, so far from there being a conflict of values as Huntington imagined, there is if anything a natural *affinity* between Islamic and Christian fundamentalists: both endorse socially conservative, patriarchal values, and are rabidly opposed to what they see in liberal permissiveness, in particular, homosexuality and abortion; both insist on a strict, dogmatic interpretation of religion; both seek a much closer integration of religion with political life; and both support (albeit somewhat different) models of the capitalist market. What essentially unites these two politico–religious and ideological positions is their rejection of secularism, their contempt for liberal institutions and human rights, and, above all, their political authoritarianism – their insistence on a strong state and an unconditional sovereignty, provided it reflects their values.

Friend and enemy

Central to this resurgent sovereign political theology that we have been trying to explore is a certain conception of the political field based on a violent opposition between friend and enemy. In this paradigm, the world is divided between antagonistic forces – and politics is seen as a life and death struggle between friend and foe. Indeed, Schmitt sees the friend/enemy distinction as being at the heart of the political, and thus fundamental to the existence of the state.[39] This antithesis between friend and enemy is, for Schmitt, a sort of existential condition for politics: any political identity is always defined by an other, something which is existentially different, and which therefore presents a potential threat to this identity. It is for this reason that war – or the possibility of war – is always at the basis of politics: 'The friend, enemy, and combat concepts receive their real meaning precisely because they refer to the real possibility of physical killing. War is the existential negation of the enemy'.[40] This antagonism seems to have become explicit in the 'war on terror', in which – from the perspective of both the US and other Western powers, as well as from militant Islam – the world is carved up into friend and enemy: thus we see the Bush administration's rhetoric of good versus evil being exactly mirrored in the terrorists' distinction between believer and infidel. When, in the days following 9/11, President Bush addressed the world declaring 'you are either with us, or with the terrorists,' he was reflecting this Schmittian political logic, in which the sovereign decides who is the friend and who is the enemy from a purely partisan position. Moreover, to invoke the language and means of war to frame the United States' response to the terrorist attacks – where a judicial and police response, although in itself problematic, would have been more appropriate and effective – also makes this violent antagonism explicit.

However, the 'war on terror' also represents a certain destabilization of the friend/enemy distinction. Rather than the enemy being fixed and identifiable, the enemy is ambiguous, almost spectral. The figure of the terrorist enemy is constructed in various and contradictory ways: he is both outside our Western societies – 'out there' in the Middle East, having values and beliefs which are entirely alien to ours; yet also, at the same time, he is 'in here' – the internal enemy, already within our societies, having infiltrated our communities, living imperceptibly among us, adopting Western habits etc; Al Qaeda is seen at the same time as a distinct organization, with a strict chain of command, and as a loose, decentralized social and ideological movement with adherents all over the world. In the conceptual paradigm of the 'war on terror' the enemy is everywhere and nowhere, shifting, imperceptible yet identifiable, territorialized and deterritorialized. Moreover, as we have seen, the amorphousness and ambiguity of the designation 'terrorist' means that it can be applied to different enemies as it suits the shifting political and strategic objectives of Western powers. This ambiguity reflects a crisis in the concept of the sovereign nation state after the collapse of Communism and an increasing integration of the global economy: here the nation state attempts to reassert itself in a hysterical and paradoxical fashion by trying to pin down and construct a new enemy. The changing nature of the international system, and the emergence of new modes of sovereignty and neo-imperialism, is something that we shall discuss in the following chapter – but it is clear that the 'war on terror' articulates the Schmittian friend/enemy distinction in a radically new and dangerous way.

A further departure from the Schmittian friend/enemy model can be seen in the way that the 'war on terror' – while it reflects for the most part crude national and neo-imperialist interests – at the same time styles itself as a universal war on behalf of all humanity. The proponents of the 'war on terror' see themselves as fighting a war on behalf of humanity and universal human rights against a terrorist enemy which is the complete antithesis of these values: indeed, political leaders like Bush and Blair saw themselves as being on a civilizing mission to bring these values, of which their countries are said to be shining examples, to the rest of the world, particularly to the Middle East and Afghanistan. Indeed, the invasions of these countries were seen partly as 'humanitarian interventions'. In his State of the Union speech in 2003, Bush claimed that freedom was not America's gift to the world, but God's gift to humanity. This is more than simply rhetoric, however: the 'war on terror' is ideologically organized around the idea and discourse of liberal humanism – even though in its effects it is anything but liberal or humanistic – and one of its aims is to impose a certain Western model of social and economic organization on other parts of the world.[41] The 'war on terror' is being partially expressed through a kind of pumped up (and deeply perverted) Wilsonianism, claiming to being fought on behalf of all humanity. According to Schmitt, however, the notion of a humanitarian war is deeply problematic: not only is humanity often invoked to disguise imperialist expansion, but the idea of a humanitarian war actually denies any human dignity to the enemy. Here Schmitt's words become disturbingly prophetic:

> To confiscate the word humanity, to invoke and monopolize such a term probably has certain incalculable effects, such as denying the enemy the quality of being human and declaring him to be an outlaw of humanity; and a war can thereby be driven to the most extreme inhumanity.[42]

Do we not see precisely this dehumanization of the enemy in the current 'war on terror'? The figure of the terrorist – deeply overladen with racist stereotypes – is depicted as barbaric, primitive, uncivilized, intolerant, violent, women-oppressing, obscurantist and unenlightened, indeed as the other of humanity. The imagery of the monstrous is often invoked here.[43] The Islamic terrorist is seen, moreover, as embodying a violent rejection of the secular, liberal and enlightened tolerance the West apparently represents. When, as Schmitt predicted, a war styles itself as humanitarian – as the current 'war on terror' partially does – the enemy is reduced to the level of the subhuman, and can therefore be more easily terminated. This was brutally articulated by the then Defence Secretary Donald Rumsfeld when he said that the aim of the US incursion in Afghanistan was to capture or kill as many Taliban fighters as possible; or when the naked bodies of suspected insurgents were grotesquely humiliated, mocked and tortured on camera in the bowels of Abu Ghraib. However, we could say that this 'war on terror' represents the paradoxical intersection between the strictly political sovereign dimension of friend/enemy, and the apolitical notion of an abstract universal humanitarian war. Both logics are brought together here, one blurring into the other. Humanity itself becomes the field for the violent intervention of the sovereign state; the identity of 'humanity' is defined arbitrarily through the hyperpoliticized sovereign decision and through the elimination of a subhuman enemy.

Conclusion

In this chapter we have explored the question of sovereignty in the 'war on terror'. Specifically, we have defined sovereignty through the state of exception, suggesting that this hidden possibility of liberal democratic states has now become their permanent and explicit condition and a new paradigm through which political power is conceived. We have also explored the threat this poses to the idea of liberal democratic politics through the link between sovereignty, violence beyond the law and religion.

However, this discussion has thrown up a number of central questions, questions which will be addressed in subsequent chapters. Firstly, what is the future of liberal democratic politics? If, as Schmitt says, liberal democratic politico-legal orders are always conditioned by the sovereign exception, and if, as we have shown, this moment of exception has now become their permanent expression, then how can liberal democratic politics reinvent itself – if indeed it can at all – in ways that escape or at least limit the dangers of sovereign exceptionalism? Secondly, what is the future for secular politics, for liberal notions of the separation of church and state? As we have shown, secularism is increasingly under threat – not only from the resurgence of religious fundamentalism in all societies, but also from the more intricate interweaving of religion and politics which is itself an expression of the theological roots of sovereignty. Thirdly, in what ways does the 'war on terror' suggest a reconfiguration of the traditional concept of nation state sovereignty; how and to what extent is it transforming the international system? The last question will be explored in the next chapter.

Notes

1. See S. Drury (1999) *The Political Ideas of Leo Strauss* (New York: Palgrave Macmillan) and (1999) *Leo Strauss and the American Right* (New York: Palgrave Macmillan).
2. Hobbes himself maintained that the sovereign had the power to decide on matters of truth and should be the judge of all opinions and doctrines. T. Hobbes (1968) *Leviathan* (ed.) C. B Macpherson (London: Penguin, 1968) Part II Chapter 18, p. 233. Indeed, in 2001 Donald Rumsfeld set up within the Defence Department, an 'Office of Strategic Influence', whose specific aim was to spread disinformation and propaganda against US enemies, including deliberately falsifying information to the US media. See Chalmers Johnson's discussion of 'information warfare' in Johnson (2004) *The Sorrows of Empire: Militarism, Secrecy, and the End of the Republic* (New York: Metropolitan Books), Chapter. 10.
3. See J. Caputo (2003) 'Without sovereignty, without being: Unconditionality, the coming God and Derrida's democracy to come', *Journal for Cultural and Religious Theory*, vol. 4: 3 (August), pp. 9–26.
4. Here I am referring to Giorgio Agamben, who invokes Walter Benjamin's famous aphorism from his 'Theses on the Philosophy of History' that the state of exception is *no longer the exception, but the rule*. [W. Benjamin (1982) *Illuminations* (ed.) H. Arendt and (trans.,) H. Zohn (London: Fontana) p. 259]. See G. Agamben (1998) *Homo Sacer: Sovereign power and bare life*, trans., D. Heller-Roazen (California: Stanford University Press).
5. In 2005, the Pentagon moved to block the release of new photo and videotape evidence of prisoner abuse at Abu Ghraib, conceding that it would serve as a recruiting tool for insurgents and terrorist groups.
6. C. Schmitt (2005) *Political Theology: Four Chapters on the Concept of Sovereignty*, trans., G. Schwab (Chicago: University of Chicago Press), p. 5.
7. Schmitt, *Political Theology*, p. 7.
8. Schmitt, *Political Theology*, p. 12.
9. Schmitt, *Political Theology*, p. 14.
10. Schmitt, *Political Theology*, p. 12.
11. See, for instance, G. Agamben (2005) *State of Exception*, trans., K. Attell (Chicago: The University of Chicago Press); and William E. Scheuerman (2006) 'Survey Article: Emergency Power and the Rule of Law After 9/11', *The Journal of Political Philosophy*, vol. 14: 1, pp. 61–84.
12. For instance, habeas corpus – or the right to be brought before a court if detained so that the legitimacy of one's detention can be examined – is one of the oldest and most fundamental principles in common law, preceding even the Magna Carta of 1215. However, this right has been seriously undermined with the introduction of preventative detention in the UK and Australia, where terrorist suspects can be detained without charge, without the presentation of evidence and without legal redress for a certain period of time. The period of detention is currently 28 days in the UK, but the government has sought to increase this.
13. As Agamben shows, for instance, in most existing constitutions there is always some sort of legal provision which allows the entire legal order to be suspended in times of national emergency and crisis. See *State of Exception*, p. 1.

14. See Agamben, *Homo Sacer*.
15. See C. Johnson (2006) *Nemesis: The Last Days of the American Republic* (New York: Metropolitan Books), p. 39.
16. For instance, there is little evidence to suggest that the risk of terrorist attacks is necessarily higher now than prior to 9/11. Moreover, in comparison to the annual figure for car deaths (42,000 in the US alone) the actual risk of dying in a terrorist attack, at least in the West, is trivial. See David Colt, 'Terrorism in the Context of Other Threats: Assessing Risks and Solutions,' *Security Policy Working Group paper* – Proteus Fund. http://www.proteusfund.org/spwg/pdfs/Terrorism%20In%20The%20Context%20of%20Other%20Threats.pdf (accessed 28 May 2008).
17. Indeed, the inability of the UN weapons inspectors to find WMD in Iraq prior to the invasion was perversely twisted into a reason for going to war: according to the US Administration, it signified the deceptiveness of the Iraqi regime in hiding its weapons, as well as the failure of the UN to do its job properly.
18. D. Z. Shaw (2006) 'The Absence of Evidence is Not the Evidence of Absence: Biopolitics and the State of Exception', *Philosophy Against Empire* (ed.) T. Smith, *Radical Philosophy Today*, vol. 4, pp. 123–38, p. 127.
19. Here John Armitage refers to a 'hypermodern' State of Exception, which is based on a certain conception of the political: what is perceived as global lawlessness and lack of order can only be met with an application of excessive military force and political control which itself often exceeds the rule of law. See Armitage (2002) 'State of Emergency: An Introduction', *Theory, Culture & Society*, vol. 19: 4, pp. 27–38.
20. For instance, one might think of President Roosevelt's suspension of habeas corpus during the Second World War.
21. Even though the USA Patriot Act contains a 'sunset' clause, it was renewed by Congress in 2006. The various pieces of anti-terrorism legislation in other countries have no sunset clause at all, which means that they have become permanently part of the legal structure.
22. A. Kaplan (2005) 'Where is Guantanamo?' *American Quarterly*, vol. 57: 3 (September), pp. 831–1001.
23. See Ignatieff, *The Lesser Evil*.
24. See J. C. Paye (2007) *Global War on Liberty: Anti-terrorism, dictatorship, permanent state of exception*, trans., J. H. Membrez (Telos Press Publishing).
25. M. Foucault (1978) *The History of Sexuality VI: Introduction*, trans., R. Hurley (New York: Pantheon Books), p. 136. See also Achille Mbembe's (2003) essay 'Necropolitics', *Public Culture88*, vol. 15: 1, pp. 11–40.
26. As J. Baudrillard says, this was a power that 'no longer knows what to do with itself, and cannot stand itself' (2005) 'War Porn' (*'Pornographie de la guerre'*) *International Journal of Baudrillard Studies*, vol. 2: 5. http://www.ubishops.ca/baudrillardstudies/vol2_1/taylor.htm#_edn1.
27. There have been constant allegations of torture, mistreatment and humiliation of detainees. There have also been several suicides. On 11 June 2006 three detainees – being held indefinitely for some three years with no recourse to normal legal representation – hung themselves at the Guantanamo prison. New York Times Editorial: The Deaths at Gitmo, 12 June 2006. 'The news that three inmates at Guantánamo Bay hanged themselves should not

have surprised anyone who has paid the slightest attention to the twisted history of the camp that President Bush built for selected prisoners from Afghanistan and antiterrorist operations. It was the inevitable result of creating a netherworld of despair beyond the laws of civilized nations, where men were to be held without any hope of decent treatment, impartial justice or, in so many cases, even eventual release'.
28. See, Agamben, *Homo Sacer.*
29. Butler, *Precarious Life*, p. 78.
30. Agamben, *Homo Sacer*, p. 15.
31. The paradoxical relationship between sovereignty, violence and law is something that has been explored by thinkers such as Walter Benjamin [(1985) 'Critique of Violence', *One Way Street and Other Writings*, trans., E. Jephcott and K. Shorter (London: Verso)]; and Jacques Derrida [(1992) 'Force of Law: The Mystical Foundation of Authority,' in D. Cornell (ed.) *Deconstruction & the Possibility of Justice* (New York: Routledge)].
32. Ignatieff sees the strategy of the terrorists as being one of provoking liberal democracies into greater atrocities, and into violating their formal principles and institutions. See *The Lesser Evil*, p. 62.
33. This idea of the violent and mysterious foundation of authority is also to be found in Derrida. See *Force of law*, pp. 3–67.
34. J. Derrida (1995) *The Gift of Death*, trans., D. Wills (Chicago: University of Chicago Press). See also C. Venn (2002) 'World Dis/Order: On Some Fundamental Questions,' *Theory, Culture & Society*, vol. 19: 4, pp. 121–36. More generally, the intrinsic connection between religion and the sacred, and violence, is explored by Hent de Vries in (2002) *Religion and Violence: Philosophical Perspectives from Kant to Derrida* (Baltimore: The Johns Hopkins University Press). A similar link between terror and the sacred is also found by Terry Eagleton in (2005) *Holy Terror* (Oxford: Oxford University Press).
35. Schmitt, *Political Theology*, p. 36.
36. J. Derrida, *Rogues*, p. 75.
37. George Bush apparently claimed that God told him to 'end the tyranny' in Afghanistan and Iraq, and to bring peace to the Middle East; while Tony Blair proclaimed in a TV interview that God alone would judge him in his decision to go to war in Iraq. Both statements are profoundly anti-democratic – particularly the last, because it suggests that political leaders are not judged by the people but judged by God. It seems the old doctrine of divine right of kings has made a comeback.
38. T. Ali (2003) *Clash of Fundamentalisms: Crusades, Jihads and Modernity* (London: Verso).
39. C. Schmitt (1996) *The Concept of the Political*, trans., G. Schwab (Chicago: University of Chicago Press), p. 26.
40. Schmitt, *The Concept of the Political*, p. 33.
41. See J. Reid (2007) *The Biopolitics of the War on Terror: Life Struggles, Liberal Modernity and the Defence of Logistical Societies* (Manchester: Manchester University Press).
42. Schmitt, *The Concept of the Political*, p. 54.
43. See J. K. Puar and A. S. Rai (2002) 'Monster, Terrorist, Fag: The War on Terrorism and the Production of Docile Patriots', *Social Text*, vol. 20: 3, pp. 117–48.

5
American Empire and its Discontents

In the last chapter we explored the state of exception in terms of its implications for domestic politics. The moment of exception referred to the way that the sovereign defines a state of emergency and decides unilaterally on how to respond to it, suspending the legal framework which would otherwise limit it. The state of exception is therefore a crystallization of the power of the state, a strange no-man's-land beyond the law in which the sovereign can act with violent impunity. We found that this situation applies increasingly to political life in contemporary Western societies, societies which define themselves as formally liberal and democratic but which implement 'security' measures that are more akin to those of authoritarian police states.

If offshore detention, extraordinary rendition and generalized surveillance represent a transformation of liberal democracy and an internalized state of exception, they also point to an external or global state of exception. Indeed, Guantanamo Bay, as Amy Kaplan points out, is a space of exception which is neither exactly internal to the US – being offshore and outside the jurisdiction of the US court system – nor exactly external to it – being under the direct control of the President and the Department of Defense, on a piece of territory which is geographically part of Cuba and yet politically part of the US, and operationally removed from international human rights and POW conventions. In other words, it is the symbol of a new form of US sovereignty which is no longer restricted to its national borders, which spills out over its geographical edges and permeates a liminal space between nation states, and between the nation state and the international system. Guantanamo Bay might therefore be seen as a blurring of two states of exception, a moment in which the territorialized sovereignty of the US nation state and the deterritorialized logic of US empire intersect.

According to Kaplan, Guantanamo's 'legal – or lawless – status has a logic grounded in imperialism, whereby coercive State power has been routinely mobilized beyond the sovereignty of national territory and outside the rule of law'.[1] The practice of extraordinary rendition – in which terrorist suspects have been kidnapped by CIA agents on foreign soil and detained in offshore prisons situated around the world – represents a similar blurring of the borders of sovereignty, a global yet deterritorialized permeation of US power. Here there is a double exception in operation: a practice which goes beyond not only US law, but also the law of other countries, to say nothing of international law and human rights norms. While Schmitt located the state of exception within the discreet boundaries of the nation state, what we are seeing today is precisely the blurring of these borders and the globalization of the exception.

However, while Schmitt believed that the globalization of conflict – enshrined in the notion of a universal humanitarian war – would lead to the breakdown of the friend/enemy distinction and the nation state polity upon which it was based, the dialectic between the national and the global, between territorialized and deterritorialized sovereignty, is in fact far more complex and paradoxical. As we shall see, the global state of exception – as well as the economic and technological processes and transactions that go by the name of globalization – coincide with an aggressive reassertion of national sovereignty, particularly that of the US. Meanwhile, what styles itself as a global war of all humanity against terrorism and in the name of democracy and freedom, masks the ruthless pursuit of US national interests. The only way to understand these contradictory phenomena is through a notion of US (neo)imperialism. This is a political configuration defined by a number of features: an explicit exceptionalism – the violation or opting out of a series of international laws, treaties, institutions and human rights norms, as well as ignoring world opinion on matters such as the invasion of Iraq; a violation of the sovereignty of other countries, particularly those that are sufficiently weak, as well as being of strategic interest to the US – such countries are defined as 'rogue states' or members of that metaphysical formation known as the 'axis of evil'; implicit threats to the sovereignty of other countries – when President Bush declared a 'global war on terror', stating that countries around the world had a choice of either being 'with us or with the terrorists', he was effectively consigning them to a kind of virtual or conditional sovereignty – a sovereignty that could be arbitrarily removed if they did not toe the line; the building and extension of international security, intelligence sharing and surveillance networks led by the US, right up to the cooperation of countries like the UK with the covert renditions undertaken by the US agencies; and the shameless recruiting of ideas about democracy and universal human rights in the service of narrow imperialist interests, where they are twisted, traduced and robbed of any meaning. This chapter will be devoted to exploring the contours of this new and more explicit form of US imperialism, and its consequences for the international system.

Globalization and the crisis of sovereignty

The question of US imperialism must be situated in the broader problematic of global developments over the past two decades: the collapse of the Communist state systems and the shift from a bipolar to a unipolar world; as well as the emergence of the global economy and the hegemony of the neoliberal model of capitalism. These developments have led a kind of crisis in the concept of the sovereign nation state. The often forceful and violent integration of countries into the global economy, and the instantaneous flows of finance and investment capital across national borders, has led to an erosion of the state's ability to regulate its national economy – although this loss of autonomy and sovereignty is more the case in poor rather than wealthy countries. Economic globalization also partly explains both terrorism and the counterterrorist security state. Rather than the latter simply responding to the former, it can be seen in terms of an aggressive and somewhat desperate attempt to reassert the authority of the nation state – as if the last area of life that the state can control (or at least claim to control) is policing and security: thus we have seen not only the intensification of counterterrorist measures, but also a more draconian policing of borders and crackdowns on illegal immigration. Such measures are driven not simply by anxieties about security, but also by a renewed racism and xenophobia directed towards immigrants, as well as the deliberate – although veiled and coded – manipulation of these sentiments on the part of governments. Police and security action, as well as fighting permanent wars such as the 'war on terror', are a way for the state to redefine itself and reassert its sovereignty in the ambiguous world of globalized capitalism.[2]

The emergence of Islamic fundamentalist terrorism might also be seen as a reaction to globalization, particularly to the way that economic globalization brings with it a cultural imperialism, consumerism and a perceived displacement of traditional identities by Western values. However, this antagonism cannot be reduced to the simple conflict between tribalism and globalism – as in Benjamin Barber's *Jihad vs. McWorld*: there is a more complex dialectic between these two forces, in which fundamentalist terrorism is as much a symptom of globalization as a reaction against it, and where, as we have suggested, the division between the supposedly secular capitalist West and the religion-steeped Islamic world is never clear-cut.[3] Rather, the antagonism between Jihad and McWorld, between Western capitalism and fundamentalist terrorism, is a tension internal to global capitalism itself.

This antagonism has a precise ideological and political function – which is to allow the dynamic of the Western neoliberal model of capitalism to perpetuate itself and to extend its reach. It is here that the 'war on terror' must also be situated within the context of the post-Cold War era. Since the end of the Second World War up to the collapse of the Soviet system in the late 1980s/early 1990s, the world had been dominated not only by a geopolitical conflict between the two superpowers, but also by a conflict between two rival economic systems and two opposed ideologies: it was easy, in other words, to imagine a simple split between democracy, liberalism and capitalism on the one hand, and communism and totalitarianism on the other. Moreover, even though Communism was an impediment to Western capitalism – its external limit – it was also its *constitutive* limit: that is to say, the existence of a different and hostile economic, political and ideological formation outside capitalism allowed capitalism to define itself, to achieve an ideological coherence and to align itself with notions of democracy and liberal freedom, with the idea of 'the Good' in other words. The collapse of this distinction had the dual effect of allowing capitalism to spread around the world – thus constituting a truly global economic system – and yet, at the same time, denying it an external limit, a barrier to work against and to define itself in opposition to. For all the triumphalism of Fukuyama's 'end of history' pronouncements and his notion of liberal capitalist democracy as the highest political form that can be aspired to, capitalism lacked a coherent ideological project – other than that of dismantling whatever was left of the welfare state, privatizing whatever was left of publicly owned utilities and forcefully opening up poorer countries to the barbarism of the global market. Global capitalism, in other words, increasingly displayed the empty nihilism of accumulation without end. The 'global war on terror' – declared by the US and signed up to by the rest of the 'civilized world' – shows that capitalism as an economic system needs to be supplemented with a coherent ideology. Global capitalism is not sufficient on its own as an economic form – it also needs a political form. In this new paradigm, fundamentalist terrorism has replaced Communism as the enemy of the capitalist West – its new constitutive limit – and thus global capitalism can organize itself around a new ideological project, that of defending Western civilization against fundamentalist obscurantism, and spreading democracy and human rights around the world, especially to the Middle East. We see this reflected in the discourse of Bush and Blair, who saw themselves as being on a civilizing mission – with all its religious and imperialist overtones – to rid the world of terrorism. Of course, in this discourse democracy and freedom are defined in the narrowest terms, equating simply with the free market – and thus the project of exporting democracy and freedom boils down to little more than opening up every corner of the world to Western corporations. We shall return to this point later, but we see here the way that the 'war on terror' not only provides Western capitalism with a definitional limit – upon which its dynamism and coherence depend – but also allows the neoliberal market model to be extended to places in the world which had been resistant to it. In this new discourse, 'terrorist' increasingly applies to anyone who opposes Western hegemony and the free market.

The question of empire

If there is a crisis of the traditional model of sovereignty in the post-Cold War world, what new forms of sovereignty are emerging in its place? Sovereignty can no longer be confined to the traditional model of the nation state – although there are still, of course, nominal nation states which comprise the international system. On the other hand, we go too far if we subscribe to Michael Hardt and Antonio Negri's thesis of a fully transnational Empire. Hardt and Negri propose that with capitalist globalization, the sovereign nation state has given way to a transnational form of sovereignty which is dispersed and no longer controlled by any particular country or countries. Rather, they argue, this is an Empire of capital, comprised of supranational institutions, legal structures and organizations, and where power structures reflect the post-Fordist and deterritorialized flows of the global economy.[4] While Hardt and Negri might have been describing certain trends which seemed to be emerging throughout the 1990s – the decade of multilateralism, 'humanitarian' interventions, NGOs and the hegemony of global financial institutions like the IMF and WTO – the aggressive reassertion of US national sovereignty and unilateral military action post 9/11 seems to have at least partially discredited their thesis.[5] This is still a world dominated by major powers – in particular, one major power, the

US. Rather than a supranational Empire, it seems more accurate to talk about a renewed US imperialism.

However, we must still take account of what is the central insight in Hardt and Negri's thesis – the deterritorializing logic of global capitalism. Here the Marxist geographer David Harvey provides the most convincing account of the current situation: imperialism can be seen as the point of intersection between two contradictory logics – the deterritorializing flows of capitalism, which cannot be confined to a fixed location, and the territorial, spatial logic of the nation state. In other words, the contemporary condition of capitalist imperialism – that is, imperialism in the service of capitalist accumulation, as opposed to simply territorial expansion – can be characterized by the fusion of two contradictory forms of power: the molecular, deterritorialized forces of capitalism which flow across spaces, borders and which compress time; and the traditional spatial power of the state, defined by its political, diplomatic and military institutions. Even though there are obvious tensions between these two logics, there is also a reciprocal relationship between them – each resonates with and sustains the other: the state is required to stabilize and regulate the global flows of capitalism; moreover, the endless accumulation of profit required by capitalism also depends upon an endless accumulation of political power.[6]

It is clear that today this role is primarily played by the last remaining superpower, the US. As a global hegemon it influences and determines the shape of global politics, leading other countries through a combination of coercion and consent. Its function is to sustain, stabilize and extend the reach of global capitalism – particularly the neoliberal 'free market' model of it that is dominant today; and yet it does so largely to its own benefit. In other words, the US directs the global economy in its own self-interest – although this also has economic benefits for other wealthy countries. Throughout the 1980s and 1990s, the US had dominated the global economy through international 'free-trade' agreements and US-influenced financial institutions, as well as the infamous IMF 'structural adjustment programs' that were more or less forced on poor countries – programmes which demanded the deregulation and privatization of their domestic economies, opening up their markets to heavily subsidized foreign goods, thus devastating local industries. Through mechanisms such as these – where the economy was wielded as a weapon, backed up with political and even in some cases military power – the US was instrumental in extending the neoliberal market model around the world, while at the same time heavily protecting and subsidizing its own industries. The US, through its economic, diplomatic and military power, acts to sustain and expand global capitalist accumulation, while at the same time pursuing its own economic interests.

The dominant position of the US in the global economy is sustained not only by its economic power, but also by its military power, in which it has been unrivalled since the end of the Cold War, and for some time before. Indeed, even with the end of the Cold War and the absence of any major military rival, American military spending has never fallen below 85% of the highest levels of spending during the Cold War (currently it is around 12% *higher* than average Cold War levels). The US spends on average between $332 and $513 billion annually on its military machine, more than the combined budget of the next fourteen biggest military spenders.[7] Behind this is the idea which America projects both to the world, and to its own people, that there can be no competitor to American power – that its military power is infinite and unrivalled, something that no other country can possibly hope to match. Central here is the concept of 'full spectrum dominance' – the idea that US military power must be supreme in all theatres of operation, on air, land, sea and even in space.[8] This idea is clearly outlined in the 2002 National Security Strategy of United States (otherwise known as the Bush doctrine) which not only enshrines the idea of pre-emptive strikes, but also states that 'Our forces will be strong enough to dissuade potential adversaries from pursuing a military build-up in the hopes of surpassing, or equalling, the power of the United States'.[9] The expressions of concern by the US Defense Department over the relatively modest build-up of China's antiquated army, and the diplomatic pressure being exerted on that country over this matter, can be seen as an example of this paranoid obsession with maintaining US military supremacy at all costs. Moreover, the US promotes nuclear non-proliferation around the world, threatening countries over their nascent nuclear programmes, while at the same time developing a new range of tactical 'bunker-busting' nuclear weapons to be used, it is claimed, as an effective weapon against terrorists hiding out in caves.[10]

This military machine is an important – perhaps the most important – mechanism in securing the economic interests of the US. The world's richest and most powerful nation acts to sustain a way of life – based on the idea of limitless consumption – that was, as President George HW Bush informed us back in 1992 in response to modest calls to limit the damage of industry to the natural environment, 'not negotiable'. In particular, its profligate consumption of oil has led to the conviction that ensuring a steady flow of this ever-dwindling resource is a matter of vital strategic importance and a major national security concern – a conviction that has meant an ongoing and predatory interest in the Middle East. Indeed, America's growing dependence on foreign oil imports has been the overdetermining factor of its foreign policy for several decades – and the so-called war on terror, despite its lofty democratic rhetoric, may be seen as a war to sustain the American 'way of life'.[11] The war in Iraq had nothing to do with any supposed WMD threat, still less to do with liberating the Iraqi people (the fallback justification now that no WMD have been found). Rather it was to gain a strategic foothold in a vital region, and to have a friendly government in power in a country with the second largest proven oil reserves in the world in order to ensure the steady flow of that resource to the US – or, perhaps more importantly, to control the flow of oil to other parts of the world, especially Europe.[12]

The renewed strategic focus on the Middle East and its oil resources began during the Carter administration in the 1970s, in the wake of the world energy crisis, and was pursued under successive administrations. Indeed, as Bacevic suggests, World War IV – the war over the Middle East – began concurrently with the Cold War (World War III): from Reagan's interventions in Lebanon and Afghanistan; to Bush the elder's Gulf War; to Clinton's (and Blair's) enforcement of crippling UN economic sanctions on Iraq; to Bush the younger's military adventurism in Afghanistan and Iraq. In this context, the 9/11 attacks can be plausibly seen as a defensive reaction to these imperial interventions.[13]

The new imperialism: The gloves come off

Given this background, what can we say has changed in the current course of US imperialism? To make it clear, the US has always been an imperialist power: from the inward expansion of the early American settlers, and the genocide of the Native American Indians; to the outward colonial expansion during the Spanish–American war in the late nineteenth century; to the dirty wars, covert operations and CIA-backed coups in Latin America (Chile, El Salvador, Nicaragua, Panama, Grenada, Haiti); to the war against the North Vietnamese; to the so-called humanitarian interventions in Kosovo and Somalia; to the persistent meddling in the Middle East – the long list of wars and interventions, both overt and covert, are evidence enough of the imperial ambitions that have coloured the history of the US. These interventions have not been primarily about seizing territory – although territory was seized in Guam and the Philippines during the colonial war with

Spain – so much as extending the reach and influence of US power, particularly its economic power and interests, in different regions: one thinks here of the CIA-backed military coup in 1954 against President Arbenz of Guatemala, who had threatened land reforms which would have gone against the interests of the American multinational the United Fruit Company; or the CIA-funded coup against Mossadegh, the Iranian prime minister who nationalized the Iranian oil fields; or, perhaps most notoriously, the CIA's role in the military coup against Allende in Chile in 1973, a coup in which the telecommunications company ITT was implicated, and which led to over a decade of military dictatorship and bloody repression in that country.[14] That the US has always sought to extend its power and influence beyond its borders – supporting authoritarian governments who were amenable to its interests, and overthrowing democratically elected governments who were not – is beyond question.

However, with the declaration of the 'war on terror' following 9/11, the US can be said to have entered a new phase of imperialism, one that is more overt and explicit. According to George Steinmetz, the latest phase of American power is best seen as a moment of both continuity and discontinuity with the past: while American hegemony is still based on a post-Fordist mode of production and capitalist accumulation, it has now taken on an explicitly imperialist and authoritarian political framework. In other words, previous forms of US hegemony relied on and took the form of an expanding neoliberal market model, which stressed economic deregulation, globalism and multilateralism. Yet this lacked a coherent political and ideological framework. In other words, even though US hegemony in the past could be said to be capitalist–imperialist, it lacked a clear and explicit imperial form. With the post-9/11 'war on terror', the US has been in the process of defining for itself a more forthright imperialist ideology and politics – one that is more structurally suitable for its dominant position in the world economy.[15]

This change is reflected in a number of different ways. Firstly, there is a shift from multilateralism to unilateralism. Under the Clinton, and even the first Bush administration – even though the US still engaged in unilateral military strikes – the emphasis was more on multilateral action and coalition building: one thinks here of the multinational coalition in the Gulf War, or the NATO actions in Bosnia and Kosovo during the 1990s. Following 9/11, the Bush II administration favoured a policy of unilateral action: the US declared that it would act multilaterally where possible, but unilaterally where necessary, with or without the approval of the international community. This is spelled out explicitly in

Bush's National Security Strategy document, which stresses the right of the US to act alone and, if necessary, pre-emptively, against its enemies. Indeed, the neoconservatives in the Administration made it quite clear that the US was ready to go it alone in Iraq – without even the rickety 'coalition of the willing' – and certainly without the endorsement of the UN.[16]

Secondly, there was an even greater emphasis on the military power in defining the direction of US imperialism. This was signified by the immediate war footing that the US was placed on following 9/11, the declaration of a global and permanent 'war on terror', the invasion and military occupation of two countries within the space of two years and massive increases in military spending. One can also speak of a militarization of cultural and public spaces, something that Giroux sees as a sign of the growing authoritarian and even fascist tendencies in American society,

> the state is being radically transformed into a national security state, increasingly put under the sway of the military-corporate-industrial-educational complex. The military logic of fear, surveillance, and control is gradually permeating our public schools, universities, streets, media, popular culture, and criminal justice system.[17]

This increasingly militaristic culture can be seen, according to Giroux, in everything from the marketing of Humvees to a military aesthetic in fashion shows. While, as Bacevic argues, militarism has always been central to American culture and identity, recent tendencies in American politics and society seem to suggest an aggressive intensification of what C. Wright Mill's termed a 'military metaphysics'.[18]

The third aspect of the new phase of US imperialism would be the pre-eminence of neoconservative ideology in US politics – neoconservatism has become the dominant ideology of empire.[19] Neoconservatism has gone from being the obscure ideology of Straussian intellectuals, disaffected hawkish liberals, policy analysts, Defense Department hacks and right wing think tanks, to becoming the more or less official ideology of the White House under the Bush presidency.[20] Indeed, the influence of the 'neo-cons' – such as Paul Wolfowitz, Dick Cheney, Richard Pearle, Douglas Feith – on Bush's foreign policy, particularly on his decision to invade Iraq, should not be underestimated.[21] While neoconservatism shares with the traditional Right a social conservatism – a belief that American society had become decadent and corrupt, weakened by liberal permissiveness, secularism and welfarism – it departs from this in the sense of being outward looking and interventionist. The central theme of neoconservatism is the idealistic notion of worldwide capitalist democratic revolution: indeed, it was America's God-given role to export the capitalist democratic revolution to the rest of the humanity, even – indeed preferably – through the use of military force. In the words of Michael Leeden, the 'best democracy program ever invented is the U.S. army'.[22] Thus, we see the strangely idealist and utopian revolutionary fervour of neoconservatism: like Trotskyists of the Right, they saw a global capitalist revolution being exported on the back of an Abrams tank. Indeed it was America's moral mission to remake the world in its own image, and in this America should not be hampered by international law, human rights concerns, world opinion or even by realpolitik. This endorsement of US exceptionalism and unilateralism could be seen in the policy papers put out by organizations such as Project for the New American Century (PNAC) which called for a foreign policy defined by 'military strength and moral clarity,' for increases in defence spending, as well as for a high-tech revolutionizing of the military, pre-emptive strikes against America's adversaries and regime change.[23]

Yet for all its seeming idealism, neoconservatism also embodies a hard-nosed, cynical Machiavellianism: while it likes to distinguish itself from realist foreign policy – proclaiming high-sounding notions about spreading democracy and freedom, rather than containing and 'appeasing' rogue states – it also encourages the ruthless pursuit of US national interests. However, for neoconservatives there is no contradiction here between US strategic and economic interests and the global democratic revolution – indeed the two things are the same. What is good for America must also be good for the rest of humanity. For Robert Kagan, 'A successful intervention in Iraq,' something the neoconservatives had been calling for since the 1990s, 'would revolutionize the strategic situation in the Middle East, in ways both tangible and intangible, and all to the benefit of American interests'.[24] So we see in the delusional – and at the same time cynically aware – mindset of the neoconservatives, the happy coincidence between democratic regime change in the Middle East and the American national interests. And yet, if democracy starts to become a threat to these strategic interests, if democratic rumblings start to create problems for American power – as was the case in Palestine with the election of Hamas and as is currently the case in Saudi Arabia – then democratization must be put on hold, and authoritarian, yet strategically important, regimes must be propped up with financial and military aid.[25] Nevertheless, its hypocrisy aside, neoconservatism as an ideology that espouses US exceptionalism, aggressive nationalism mixed with military interventionism, regime change and pre-emptive strikes, became the dominant belief system of the Bush administration, at least in its first term.

The move from covert to overt imperialism can also be reflected in another ideological shift, one that is reflective of the hegemony of neoconservative ideas: empire-talk has now become acceptable.[26] While the US has always in effect been an empire, it has in the past refused to acknowledge itself as such. 'Imperialism' was in the past a dirty word, and to talk about US imperialism meant you were on the radical Left.[27] Now, however, it is not only the Left that describes the US as an imperial power – this mantle is cheerfully acknowledged by not only neoconservatives on the Right, but also by some liberals like Ignatieff, who sees the US as essentially a benign empire of liberal humanitarianism. We shall return to Ignatieff's argument later, but the point is that this new openness, and indeed enthusiasm, about the imperial role of the US signifies an important change not only in the politics and ideology of the US empire, but also in public perceptions and discourse. Many now accept the idea that the US has an imperial role to play in the world today, stabilizing capitalism, overthrowing dictatorships, spreading democracy and freedom and enforcing a global Pax Americana. In the words of the neoconservative columnist Charles Krauthammer, 'People are now coming out of the closet on the word empire'.[28]

The lonely empire

If America is an empire – and if it increasingly sees itself as such – what sort of empire is it; what sort of peace will this new Pax Americana be? In opposition to those like Ignatieff and Niall Ferguson, who see America's role in the world as basically benign – bringing peace and stability into war zones, overthrowing corrupt dictatorships, building liberal democratic institutions and so on – we would argue that the US is a solitary and self-interested empire, one whose overriding goal is the pursuit of its own economic and strategic objectives and whose interventions around the world lead only to greater instability and disorder. The bloody anarchy in Iraq created by the invasion – barely diminished now, despite official claims about the success of the 'surge' – threatens to destabilize the whole region, dragging surrounding countries into a conflagration whose consequences no one can predict. Moreover, its recent interventions cannot be taken as a sign – as it is by some – that the US has awoken from its isolationist slumber and is now taking a greater interest in the world outside its borders: it remains a self-enclosed power, and its new outwardly focussed militarism is simply the other side of inward-looking isolationism; both are driven by a narcissistic self-interest and an obsession with preserving the 'American way of life'. In its lonely isolation, it cannot tolerate even the most minor challenges to its sovereignty: Pat Robertson's call a while ago for special forces to be sent to Venezuela to assassinate Hugo Chavez because he posed a threat to US national interests, reveals – in its extremity – the truth of US imperialism.[29]

Furthermore, while the US is a global empire, the Pax Americana is anything but universal – it is divided into different peripheries and spheres of interest and strategic importance. The US can devote its entire military and political energies on the Middle East, spending countless billions on the invasion and occupation of Iraq, meddling in the affairs of the broader region; while at the same time being completely unconcerned with the fate of millions of Africans afflicted by poverty, disease and inter-ethnic war. In other words, rather than US imperialism bringing a stable Pax Americana, a prosperous liberal democratic world, as some liberal and conservative proponents of empire like to imagine, it is in actual fact an empire of disorder, an uneven and chaotic imperial space comprising different peripheries of either special interest or complete disinterest, wealth and extreme poverty, stability and extreme instability and violence – wastelands of genocide, barbarism, economic ruin and repression.[30] Areas of the world become the (usually unwelcome) focus of US attention, while other parts of the world are consigned to total abandonment. As Alain Badiou puts it:

> In truth, the USA is an imperialist power without an empire, a hegemonic power without territoriality or front line. To designate its relationship to the world, I propose the term 'zoning': any part of the world may be considered by the American government to be a zone of vital interest or a zone of total disinterest, subject to their shifting judgement about what comprises their 'democratic' comfort. Death may occur *en masse* without America raising an eyebrow (as has been going on for years with the African AIDS crisis), or, on the contrary, you may be subjected to be being piled up in the middle of the desert by a colossal army.[31]

However, rather than suggesting that US imperialism is imperialism without empire, without sovereignty, it might be more accurate to describe it as a deterritorialized empire – a form of sovereignty which is everywhere, and yet cannot be localized. It is an empire which is limitless and borderless, pervading different regions and blurring national borders. The US has a troop presence in 156 countries, with permanent military bases in 63 countries; moreover, since 9/11 it has established 13 new bases in seven countries.[32] Despite claims to have handed sovereignty back to the Iraqi people, the Pentagon has plans to build four permanent 'superbases' in that country, each one capable of holding 55,000 troops, and which come complete with shopping malls, fast food outlets, swimming pools, gymnasiums, cinemas and cyber cafes. It is an empire which is both external and internal, which is directed outward and inward. Here Kaplan makes the point that this borderless empire becomes at the same time obsessed with policing its own borders, the concept of homeland security and fortress America becoming the predominant signifiers of US politics.[33] Indeed, current anxieties about border control and illegal immigration in the US are simply an extension of this. However, this notion of fortress America – while it conjures up an image of a secure bastion of freedom protected from a hostile world of tyranny and violence – actually entails an internalized empire, an imperialism turned inwards as well as outwards: in the discourse of 'homeland security' borders are seen as permeable, civil society is seen as being threatened by a ubiquitous and imperceptible terrorist enemy who is already among us, and therefore citizens must be subjected to constant surveillance, policing and control.[34]

As we have shown, the security state operates by sustaining a certain level of insecurity, thus justifying ever greater levels of control and surveillance. Thus, US imperialism also turns its gaze inwards: indeed, its very logic demands a heightened level of fear and insecurity in the domestic population, because this allows not only increased domestic control, but also produces an aggressive nationalism and permanent militarization. War is an excellent way of creating internal order and rallying support for the government – and a permanent war against an invisible and shifting enemy is even more effective. Indeed, the stifling climate of patriotic loyalty in the US following 9/11, in which Americans rallied around the flag, and where expressions of dissent were silenced, was one of the major factors enabling the invasion of Iraq.

An empire of liberty?

Moreover, this aggressive nationalism and militarism of US empire is at the same time justified in the language of freedom and democracy. While, as we have shown, the 'war on terror' is largely the imperialistic pursuit of self-interest, this is sold to the world, and to the American people, as a civilizing mission to spread democracy, freedom and human rights around the world. Bush has been persistent in the claim that it is America's role to defeat terrorism through the spreading of freedom and democracy:

> I believe that God has planted in every human heart the desire to live in freedom ... America is a nation with a mission, and that mission comes from our most basic beliefs. We have no desire to dominate, no ambitions of empire. Our aim is a democratic peace – a peace founded upon the dignity and rights of every man and woman. America acts in this cause with friends and allies at our side, yet we understand our special calling: This great republic will lead the cause of freedom.[35]

This claim was echoed by Tony Blair, who invoked a war between civilized humanity and its enemies: 'This is not a clash *between* civilizations, it is a clash *about* civilization.'[36] Just as the imperialists of old justified their expansionism in racist terms of 'the white man's burden,' and bringing Christian civilization to the dark regions of the world, so the new imperialism invokes a new kind of missionary zeal.

For an empire of human rights and democracy, it would seem, moreover, that the US empire is remarkably inconsistent in its application of these principles. When it suits its strategic interests, the US is only too happy to support authoritarian and repressive regimes around the world – or at least to turn a blind eye to their flagrant human rights abuses – as it did for years with Saddam Hussein's regime in the 1980s and with the Taliban in the 1990s and as it continues to do so with Saudi Arabia, Egypt, Uzbekistan,[37] to say nothing of its ongoing support for Israel and its brutal occupation of Palestine. The US has little interest in democracy and human rights, unless they also happen to coincide with its strategic interests. Furthermore, it is totally hypocritical of the US to claim to be fighting wars for freedom, democracy and human rights, when it is itself a major violator of those principles – both at home and abroad. The US, as well as the UK, and other countries fighting the 'democratic war on terror', have been consistently criticized by human rights groups for practices such as indefinite detention without charge, extraordinary rendition, the torture of terrorist suspects (as well as the outsourcing of torture to other governments) and the general undermining of civil liberties, as well as its opting out of international human rights conventions.[38]

Moreover, even if we chose to ignore the hypocrisy of the US and other countries and took at face value their claims to be serious about liberty and human rights, one must ask whether war is ever an effective means of implementing these ideals. In other words, can wars ever be liberal; or are their consequences – economic devastation, massive loss of human life – so severe as to cancel out, and indeed make ultimately impossible, any benign or liberal intentions that may have motivated them in the first place? It is difficult to see how the deaths of – as is estimated – 650,000 Iraqis as a result of the invasion could have furthered the cause of liberty and democracy in the Middle East. Indeed, such destruction and suffering is itself so obviously *illiberal* as to make one sceptical of any claims about liberal military interventions. As Lawrence Freedman argues: 'The problem with liberal wars, I argue, lies less with the ends than the means. Wars are inherently illiberal in their effects and their consequences.'[39]

In examining the new American imperialism, then, it is important to look at the way that 'democracy' is used as the ideological signifier around which this imperial project is organized. What sort of democracy is this that is being exported, and what sort of example of democracy is the supposedly 'democratic' West setting for the rest of the world? This is a remarkably narrow, limited understanding of democracy that is being foisted on the rest of the world – even as inconsistently as it is – a model of democracy that is always equated with the free market, and sometimes implies nothing more than the free market. In every reference that Bush and Blair have made to democratization in the Middle East it is always to 'free-market democracy'. What does this mean? As Naomi Klein has shown, the planned post-invasion reconstruction of Iraq was more about turning Iraq into a perfect model of the neoliberal free market than it was about building a functioning and effective democracy. Iraq was seen by the neoconservatives and those in charge of the reconstruction effort as a sort of fantasy projection of a free market utopia, as well as the Middle East testing ground for the same sort of economic 'electric shock therapy' that wrought such devastating consequences in Russia after the fall of Communism. Thus, in Iraq, state run industries were privatized overnight; trade barriers were removed and the economy was completely opened to foreign investment and ownership; the public sector was dramatically cut; flat taxes and low levels of corporate tax were introduced; and the repressive laws of the old regime curbing independent trade unions were retained.[40] The imposition of this extreme free market formula on Iraq – which had disastrous consequences and seriously hampered the reconstruction effort – reveals the true message of this 'free-market democracy' pursued through other (military) means. The initial unwillingness of the interim government in Iraq to build genuine democratic institutions showed that the US was interested in little more than furthering the commercial interests of its multinational companies.

Furthermore, the fact that democratic rights are being seriously eroded at home and that Western democracies suffer so many structural problems – inadequate representation, massive wealth and power inequalities, low levels of voter interest etc – shows perhaps that we care as little about democracy back home as we do about the exported variety. Just as Freud showed that the surface symptom was the key to unlocking the deeper neurosis, we must understand that even though 'democracy' is an ideological mask of imperialism, it is a mask that reveals a deeper truth. In other words, even though 'democracy' is the surface ideology of imperial domination, even though it is not taken seriously by the imperial masters who claim to be acting in its name, we cannot ignore it: we have to ask why empire takes this particular ideological form, why it *needs* to take this form. What does this say about empire, and, more importantly, what does this say about democracy itself? Indeed, the fact that democracy is used as the imperial standard bearer in this way gives us an opportunity to re-examine what democracy means today, and how it might be radically expanded and transformed. This will be explored in the final chapter.

Liberal defenders of empire

Nevertheless the idea that the US exports democracy, freedom and human rights around the world is the key component in the argument that a number of liberals and conservatives make in defending American imperialism. The American empire, they argue, is an empire of liberty – an imperial project that can be instrumental in bringing stability and democratic and liberal institutions to areas of the world afflicted by instability, poverty, violence, tyranny and corruption. These defenders of the imperial project claim not to be naive in their assessment of US imperialism: they know – or claim to know – that the US is acting in its own self-interest, but that this can also have beneficial consequences for the rest of the world. In other words, the argument being made here is a consequentialist one: if good outcomes ensue from American imperialism, then its motives and intentions are unimportant; if there is a happy coincidence between US strategic self-interest and a world consisting of stable liberal and democratic institutions, then why worry? Pointing to the US involvement in nation-building and peacekeeping efforts in Bosnia, Kosovo and Afghanistan, and later, defending the idea of regime change in Iraq,[41] Ignatieff argues that the American empire, despite acting out of self-interest, can also be a humanitarian empire. Indeed, according to Ignatieff, the problem is not that the US is an empire, but that it is an empire in denial, that it is not committed enough to its own imperial project, that it has a tendency to withdraw and leave failed states in its wake. The problem, in other words, is not that the US is imperialist, but that it is not imperialist enough:

> It is an empire lite, hegemony without colonies, a global sphere of influence without the burden of direct administration and the risks of daily policing. ... key question is whether the empire lite is heavy enough to get the job done.[42]

So what the world needs is not less empire but more – indeed, according to Ignatieff, the world requires a sort of imperial makeover: 'The imperial problem is much larger than Afghanistan, Bosnia or Kosovo. Nothing less than the reconstruction of a global order of stable nation states is required.'[43] While Ignatieff concedes that this is beyond the task of any imperial power, this shortcoming is something to be lamented.

Ferguson is even more forthright in his defence of American empire, suggesting that it should take over the glorious mantle of the British Empire. Ironically invoking Kipling's poem, 'The White Man's Burden,' Ferguson believes that the US today has a similar civilizing mission to spread liberal institutions, free markets and bring stability, order and good governance to the rest of the world. Like Ignatieff, he laments that the US is not committed enough to the task, that it lacks the staying power and political will to properly fulfil its imperial destiny. Indeed, he chastises the US for being coy about its imperial status, and for not being imperial enough. Ferguson declares:

> Unlike the majority of European writers who have written on this subject, I am fundamentally in favour of empire. Indeed, I believe that empire is more necessary in the twenty-first century than ever before ... There are those who would insist that an empire is by definition incapable of playing such a role; in their eyes all empires are exploitative in character. Yet there can be – and have been – such a thing as a liberal empire, one that enhances its own security and prosperity precisely by providing the rest of the world with generally

beneficial public goods: not only economic freedom but also the institutions necessary for markets to flourish.[44]

At the risk of sounding like those recalcitrant 'Europeans' (perhaps a veiled reference to Rumsfeld's dismissal of those who refused to go along with the imperial invasion of Iraq as 'old Europe'?) we continue to see empire, even if it is dressed up in liberal democratic colours, as exploitative and destructive. Indeed, there are a number of serious problems with Ignatieff's and Ferguson's argument for liberal empire.

Firstly, there is an assumption that because the US is ostensibly a liberal democracy, that these institutions and ideals will be reflected in the imperial form taken; that because America is liberal and democratic and respects human rights at home, it will be liberal and democratic and respectful of human rights abroad. In the words of Ignatieff: 'As an empire run by Western liberal democracies, chiefly America, its moral grace notes are all liberal and democratic. Its purpose is to extend free elections, rule of law, democratic government to peoples who have only known fratricide.'[45] However, as we have shown, the US and other Western powers that claim to be liberal democratic are openly violating their own liberal and democratic principles and practices in the name of 'national security'. Secondly, there is no guarantee that even if the US and other Western powers are liberal democratic, that they will apply these principles and institutions elsewhere. Indeed, the current course of US imperialism seems to be suggesting something very different. Ferguson says that 'when the Americans say they come as liberators, not conquerors, they seem to mean it.'[46] The torture and degradation of detainees and the massacre of civilians and the bombing of civilian targets might seem a peculiar form of liberation to the Iraqi and Afghan people, as might the continual support of the US for the Israeli occupation of Palestine. The possibility that liberal democracies – so-called – can be illiberal beyond their own borders seems not to have occurred to Ferguson and Ignatieff.

The second theme in Ignatieff's and Ferguson's defence of empire is that hypocrisy doesn't matter – in other words, that even though the US might be acting from self-interested motives, its imperialism can still have positive consequences.[47] This can be responded to in a number of ways. Firstly, and most obviously, there is little to suggest that the current course of US imperialism is having consequences that are anything other than destructive and destabilizing. The bloodbath in Iraq – created as a direct result of this 'benign' US imperialism – looks likely to continue, regardless of whether US troops stay or leave; as well as threatening to destabilize the whole region, dragging in surrounding countries like Iran and Turkey. Currently, the situation in that country, as well as in Afghanistan, serves as a most effective recruiting ground for Islamic terrorists around the world.[48] Furthermore, if any kind of order can be achieved in that country, it will most likely be one that is heavily influenced by Shia fundamentalism and which will hardly be conducive to the development of human rights and liberal institutions. Ferguson makes the dubious claim that,

> ordinary Iraqis seemed to have the same view [that they were better off without Saddam Hussein]. The first rigorously conducted poll of Baghdad, published in September last year, revealed that 62 per cent of Baghdad residents believed that 'the ousting of Saddam Hussein was worth any hardships they might personally have suffered since the ... invasion'.[49]

It would be interesting to see the results of the same survey conducted now.

Let's take the case of Afghanistan. Proponents of the liberal empire like to see this as the sort of jewel in the crown of post-9/11 humanitarian intervention: *despite what you think about Iraq and American foreign policy, surely you would have to concede that the removal of the Taliban and the establishment of a democracy in Afghanistan was a good thing*, goes the refrain. Indeed, the invasion of Afghanistan was even turned into a feminist issue, not only by Lynne Cheney and Laura Bush, but also by pro-American celebrity TV philosophers in France like Bernard-Henri Levy who claimed that if you were against the invasion of Afghanistan, then you were against the liberation of the Afghan women. And yet, nearly six years on and women are still oppressed and denied rights, Sharia law is still in place, the Burka is ubiquitous and the Taliban is making a comeback in many parts of the country. Nor should we forget, of course, that for a number of years before 9/11 the US and Western powers actually supported the Taliban, or at least turned a blind eye to its atrocities.

This brings us to the second dimension of our argument – that hypocrisy in imperial politics *does* matter. It matters, for instance, when the US claims that it is invading countries in the name of democracy and human rights, when in actual fact it is for the narrowest of self-interested motives; just as it matters when the US singles out certain countries for 'humanitarian' and 'democratic' invasions when it is perfectly prepared to tolerate, and even actively support, other authoritarian regimes which violate human rights when it suits their strategic interests. This inconsistency matters – or should matter – for two reasons, aside from the basic ethical and philosophical problems with hypocrisy: firstly, because such blatant hypocrisy turns more and more people around the world against the US – the majority of people around the world do not see the Americans as liberators but as self-interested militarists; and secondly, because the shifting attention and priorities of US imperialism – such as supporting the mujahideen against the Soviets in Afghanistan during the Cold War – has lead directly to the terrorist 'blowback' that can be seen today.[50] It is not possible, then, to separate the motives from the consequences of US imperialism, as Ignatieff, Ferguson and others do – the former obviously shapes the latter.

We can also point to an implicit racism that lingers beneath this notion of the liberal empire. Ferguson's continual ironic references to 'The White Man's Burden', Kipling's racist justification of British imperialism, seems to symbolize the basic assumption that he, along with Ignatieff, make – that Western liberal institutions and values are culturally superior to those of the 'darker' regions of the world. American imperialism has a new 'White Man's Burden,' which is to foster the spread of Western civilization against what Ignatieff calls, in a reference to the enemies of the Roman empire, the 'barbarians':

> Just beyond the zone of stable democratic states, which took the World Trade Centre and the Pentagon as its headquarters, there are border zones, like Afghanistan, where barbarians rule and from where, thanks to modern technology, they are able to inflict devastating damage on centres of power far away.[51]

There is no mention here of the way that for many years the US supported these 'barbarians'; nor is there any consideration of the barbarism of imperialism itself, or of a society which, while claiming to be civilized, spends, amidst massive poverty and inequality – where 30 million of its own citizens, let alone the countless millions around the world, live below the poverty line – more on weapons than the rest of the world combined. Furthermore, the problem with such an account, its barely veiled racism aside, is that it naively sees fundamentalist terrorism in simplistic terms as that which threatens our civilized societies, and for which the best defence is empire. It does not consider the very obvious ways in which empire might itself have produced terrorism as a reaction against it.

The future of American empire

In opposition to these apologists for imperialism, we would maintain that imperialism has never been a good thing – that it has always been driven by narrow self-interests and that it has always entailed violent domination and economic plundering; and, moreover, that the current form of US neo-imperialism is not any different. It does not bring democracy, freedom and respect for human rights; nor does it provide peace and stability. Rather, the US reigns over an empire of disorder. Indeed, recent developments suggest that the current phase of US imperialism may itself already be in a state of crisis – the situation in Iraq and Afghanistan speaks both to the reach of American imperial power and to its limits.

However, predictions about the decline of the American empire[52] might be somewhat premature. The US still has by far the world's biggest economy and the strongest military – and, despite domestic political pressure, Bush's foreign policy has lost little of its arrogance and aggressiveness in the latter stages of his second term, although this increasingly looks like a sign of desperation. The economic sanctions on Iran and the recent tough talk about its nuclear programme – echoed now by both John McCain and Hillary Clinton – and covert involvement in Iraq, may be a sign of future action against that country, as might the State Department's attempt to have the Iranian Revolutionary Guard classified as a terrorist organization. Recent arms sales to Israel and Saudi Arabia gives little ground for hope for a more moderate and enlightened policy in the Middle East. Moreover, the public disapproval with Bush should not necessarily be taken as a sign of a broader opposition to the 'war on terror' or to America's imperial role in the world; rather it is prompted by the mishandling of the war effort. Bush has taken to comparing the Iraq war with the Vietnam war – turning what would be an otherwise unfavourable comparison into an argument for keeping the troops in Iraq, thus entirely twisting and perverting the meaning and significance of that other disastrous war.

Moreover, we should not have high hopes that a change of administration will produce a fundamentally different and less aggressive and imperialistic foreign policy: Hillary Clinton has restyled herself just as hawkish as the Republicans, while Barack Obama, the supposedly more progressive candidate, has said that as President he would be prepared to order pre-emptive strikes against Al Qaeda in Pakistan, without the permission of the Pakistani government. Whether under the Democrats or Republicans, some form or other of imperialist politics looks set to continue.

Conclusion

In this chapter we have considered the question of American empire and its impact on the international system. We have suggested that while imperialism has been a constant in US politics and foreign policy, under the Bush Administration the project of empire has become explicit – something that can be seen in its overt militarism, its doctrine of pre-emptive strikes and regime change and in the ideological and political discourse of neoconservatism. We have also attempted to present a critique of imperialist politics on both ethical and pragmatic grounds, taking issue with those who justify US empire in terms of either liberal humanitarianism or of promoting a stable world order. US imperialism, as we have shown, does neither – these effects are nullified by its blind pursuit of self-interest. The next chapter will consider more specific ethical questions relating to the response of states – both domestically and internationally – to perceived terrorist threats.

Notes

1. Kaplan, 'Where is Guantanamo?', p. 832. Indeed, Guantanamo Bay has always been a symbol of US imperialism: it is the location of the oldest US naval base, the territory having been ceded to the US in 1903 at the end of the Spanish–American war – a US war of expansion to seize control of Spanish territories such as Puerto Rico, Guam and the Philippines – and leased on a permanent basis (for a nominal rent), a permanent occupation on foreign soil which is in violation of a number of international conventions.
2. This point has also been made by John Milbank (2003) 'Sovereignty, Empire, Capital, and Terror', in S. Hauerwas and F. Lentricchia (eds) *Dissent from the Homeland: Essays after September 11* (Durham: Duke University Press).
3. See B. Barber (2003) *Jihad vs. McWorld* (London: Corgi). For an excellent critical commentary on Barber's thesis, see also B. S. Turner (2002) 'Sovereignty and Emergency: Political Theology, Islam and American Conservatism', *Theory, Culture & Society*, vol. 19: 4, pp. 103–19.
4. See M. Hardt and A. Negri (2000) *Empire* (Cambridge, MA: Harvard University Press).
5. In their sequel to *Empire*, Hardt and Negri have attempted to incorporate some of these developments into their analysis – although not terribly convincingly. See (2004) *Multitude: War and Democracy in the Age of Empire* (New York: Penguin).
6. See D. Harvey (2003) *The New Imperialism* (Oxford: Oxford University Press), pp. 26–7.
7. See Report on Military Spending – MIT Center for International Studies. http://web.mit.edu/CIS/fpi_military_spending.html (accessed 24 August 2007). Moreover, Bacevic documents examples of the profligacy and wastefulness of US military spending – billions are spent on weapons programmes

and systems that are unmitigated failures, without this causing any degree of concern among the American people. See A. J. Bacevic (2005) *The New American Militarism: How Americans are Seduced by War* (Oxford: Oxford University Press), p. 216.
8. See W. L. Huntley (2005) 'The Weaponization of Space: U.S. Strategy in a Global Context', Simons Center for Disarmament and Non-Proliferation Research – Liu Institute for Global Issues, University of British Columbia (July). http://www.ligi.ubc.ca/admin/Centres/527/WH%20-%20The%20Weaponization%20of%20Space%20July%2025%2005.pdf (accessed 24 August 2007).
9. *The National Security Strategy of the United States of America* (September 2002), p. 30.
10. See M. Bromley, D. Grahame and C. Kucia (2002) 'Bunker Busters: Washington's Drive for New Nuclear Weapons', *Research Report* (July) British American Security Information Council. http://www.basicint.org/pubs/Research/2002BB.pdf.
11. As Bacevic explains, 'By the end of the twentieth century, with Americans consuming one out of every four barrels of oil produced worldwide, remaining US reserves accounted for less than 2 per cent of the world's total. The United Arab Emirates and tiny Kuwait alone each had reserves four times larger than the United States', Iraq almost six times greater and Saudi Arabia twelve times greater. Projections showed the leverage of Persian Gulf producers mushrooming in the years to come, with oil exports from the region expected to account for between 54 per cent and 67 per cent of world totals by 2020.' *The New American Militarism*, p. 184.
12. See Harvey, *The New Imperialism*, p. 19.
13. Bacevic, *The New American Militarism*, p. 191.
14. The covert involvement of the US government in these coups was officially confirmed in recently declassified CIA documents, known as the 'Family Jewels'.
15. G. Steinmetz (2003) 'The State of Emergency and the Revival of American Imperialism: Toward an Authoritarian Post-Fordism', *Public Culture*, vol. 15: 2, pp. 323–45. However, now, after the failure of the Iraq policy, we are perhaps seeing a crisis of this neoimperial form.
16. Rumsfeld's comment prior to the invasion of Iraq that the US did not need the UK's help was no doubt severely embarrassing for Blair, who had risked his political neck to justify the UK's involvement.
17. H. A. Giroux (2006) 'The Emerging Authoritarianism in the United States: Political Culture Under the Bush Administration', *Symplokè*, vol. 14: pp. 1–2, pp. 98–151, p. 124.
18. See Bacevic, *The New American Militarism*, p. 2.
19. See Harvey, *The New Imperialism*, p. 184.
20. For a thorough discussion of the origins and rise of the neoconservative movement in the US, see Bacevic, *The New American Militarism*, Chapter 3: pp. 69–96.
21. See S. Halper and J. Clarke (2004) *America Alone: The Neoconservatives and the Global Order* (Cambridge: Cambridge University Press).
22. Quoted in Bacevic, *The New American Militarism*, p. 85.
23. See Project for the New American Century. http://www.newamericancentury.org/ (accessed 28 August 2007).
24. Quoted in Bacevic, *The New American Militarism*, p. 88.

25. Recently, the US announced arms deals worth $20 billion to Saudi Arabia and five other oil-rich Gulf States – not one of them democracies.
26. See A. Dawson and M. J. Schueller (2007) *Exceptional State: Contemporary U.S. Culture and the New Imperialism* (Durham: Duke University Press), p. 2.
27. See A. Kaplan (2004) 'Violent Belonging and the Question of Empire Today: Presidential Address to the American Studies Association, October 17, 2003', *American Quarterly*, vol. 56: 1 (March), pp. 1–17.
28. Quoted in Kaplan, 'Violent Belonging and the Question of Empire Today', p. 3.
29. Robertson said, using perverse logic, 'If he thinks we're trying to assassinate him, we really ought to go ahead and do it', thus retroactively confirming Chavez's paranoia. http://www.cnn.com/2005/U.S./08/24/robertson.chavez/ (accessed 25 August 2007).
30. See A. Joxe (2002) *Empire of Disorder*, trans., A. Hodges (New York: Semiotexte), p. 104.
31. A. Badiou (2006) 'Fragments of a Public Journal on the American War against Iraq', *Polemics*, trans., S. Corcoran (London: Verso), p. 45.
32. Global Policy Forum. http://www.globalpolicy.org/empire/intervention/2003/0710imperialmap.htm (accessed 26 August 2007).
33. Kaplan, 'Violent Belonging and the Question of Empire Today', p. 8.
34. Kaplan, 'Violent Belonging and the Question of Empire Today', p. 10.
35. George W Bush's State of the Union Address 2004. http://www.whitehouse.gov/news/releases/2004/01/20040120-7.html (accessed 27 August 2007).
36. Tony Blair speech 21 March 2006. http://www.number-10.gov.uk/output/Page9222.asp (accessed 27 August 2007).
37. While US forces were evicted from an airbase in Uzbekistan, following US criticisms of the Karimov's government's bloody repression of protests in 2005, they have, since early 2008, been returning after a thaw in relations – without there having been any obvious political reforms in Uzbekistan.
38. See A. Cowell (2005) 'U.S. "Thumbs its Nose" at Rights, Amnesty Says', *New York Times* (26 May). http://www.mindfully.org/Reform/2005/U.S.-Thumbs-Nose26may05.htm (accessed 27 August 2007).
39. L. Freedman (2005) 'The Age of Liberal Wars', *Review of International Studies*, vol. 31, pp. 93–107, p. 95.
40. See N. Klein, 'Baghdad Year Zero'. This is further expounded in Klein's *The Shock Doctrine*.
41. Ignatieff has subsequently changed his position on Iraq, saying that it was a mistake to support the invasion – although this is perhaps more to do with his political ambitions in Ottawa, than with any principled ethical and political position.
42. M. Ignatieff (2003) *Empire Lite: Nation-building in Bosnia, Kosovo and Afghanistan* (London: Vintage Books), pp. 2–3.
43. Ignatieff, *Empire Lite*, p. 125.
44. N. Ferguson (2004) *Colossus: The Price of America's Empire* (London: Allen Lane), pp. 24–5.
45. Ignatieff, *Empire Lite*, pp. 112–13.
46. Ferguson, *Colossus*, p. 203.
47. A similar argument is made by Daryl Glaser in (2006) 'Does Hypocrisy Matter? The Case of U.S. Foreign Policy', *Review of International Studies*, vol. 32, pp. 251–68.

48. A CIA report released in 2005 said that Iraq had replaced Afghanistan as the major training and recruitment ground for terrorists around the world. See Washington Post, 14 January 2005. http://www.washingtonpost.com/wp-dyn/articles/A7460-2005Jan13.html (accessed 7 March 2008).
49. Ferguson, *Colossus*, p. 164.
50. See C. Johnson (2004) *Blowback: The Costs and Consequences of American Empire* (New York: Holt). See also Johnson, *The Sorrows of Empire*.
51. Ignatieff, *Empire Lite*, p. 3.
52. See E. Todd (2004) *After the Empire: The Breakdown of the American Order*, trans., C. J. Delogu (Constable: London).

6
The Lesser of Two Terrors: Ethical Questions

Political responses to terror have to be understood in context of the kinds of prejudice and irrationality that underlie and mar relations between Western and non-Western cultures. But do orthodox liberal democratic conceptions of political justice and good political practice have the resources to combat these prejudices and their role in the formation of political judgement? Reflection on political responses to terror must also acknowledge the remarkable failures and moral obscenities that have issued from the response to terror. Do orthodox liberal democratic conceptions of political justice and good political practice have the resources to understand and respond to these failures? Is the moral failure of the 'war on terror' the result of the unlucky fact that administrations in the US and Britain just happened to have been mendacious in their accounts of the reasons for war and overconfident in their prosecution of it? Or does the moral failure of the 'war on terror' uncover deep inadequacies in the way politics is normally done in liberal democracies? More central to our concerns: is the moral failure of the 'war on terror' a sign of some deep failure in liberal democratic conceptions of politics?

There are two kinds of deflationary response to the moral failure of contemporary counterterrorism, and they ought to be kept apart. In the first kind of response, the system of protections and checks and balances already in place in well-functioning liberal democracies is not at fault. This is a defence of the institutions, conventions and modes of practice of liberal democracy as they currently stand – most prominently in the US, but also in countries such as Britain and Australia. The defence takes a familiar form. The US judicial system has managed to put a number of breaks on the Bush administration's mistreatment of suspected enemy combatants. Since late 2005, parts of the US press and Congress have put the Bush administration under sustained pressure for its strategic failures in Iraq and this has helped undermine popular support for that war. The self-corrections of liberal democracies are painfully slow and alarmingly patchy, but eventually they work to correct many flagrant violations of rights and to ameliorate, or in some way deal with, the violent excesses of counterterrorist effort directed at international targets, most importantly, the waging of war against Afghanistan and Iraq. Moral failure may be inevitable, but its inevitability does not represent any flaw in the system *per se*. It arises from fallible human engagement in the system and this fallibility is not something that can be eliminated at an institutional or systemic level. The checks and balances of a liberal democracy – both formal and informal, both constitutionally mandated legislative and judicial review of executive decision and the practical requirement to defend controversial political decisions in a public forum, in the face of a critical and independent press – are the best available means of ensuring the minimization of moral error. The war on terror, according to this line of argument, has not exposed the institutions and modes of practice of liberal democracies; it has, perhaps, exposed their vulnerability to individual mendacity and foolishness and demonstrated the robustness of their capacity to eventually respond to this mendacity and foolishness. This is a hard line defence of liberal democratic practice in the face of a seemingly devastating indictment.

A second deflationary response to the failures of counterterrorism focuses on the principles underpinning liberal democracies. Perhaps the moral disaster of contemporary counterterrorism does indeed unveil an inherent failure of liberal democratic institutions and modes of practice, at least in some jurisdictions. Institutions, conventions, traditions and so on, are legitimated by the liberal democratic values they advance or protect. Roughly, the idea of a liberal democracy is the idea of a society that effectively balances the representation of majority interests with protection for minorities, where these protections are primarily conceptualized in terms of rights. Recent adventures in counterterrorism betray these founding ideas in a number of ways. However, while they may demonstrate failures in the institutional realization of liberal democratic values, they do not demonstrate failure of the ideas themselves. A view like this represents a defence of liberal democratic conceptions of politics, rather than the practices of liberal democratic regimes, and is *prima facie* much more plausible than the hard line defence.

Michael Ignatieff provides a defence of the deflationary responses to the challenge of counterterrorism's moral failure.[1] He tends to equivocate between the two kinds we have just outlined, but his primary allegiance is to the latter response. He offers a way of conceiving the task of counterterrorism which does not, he thinks, betray the fundamental values of liberal democracy and appears to leave open the question of the extent to which reform of institutions and practices might be needed to secure effective liberal democratic practice in the face of the ongoing threat of terrorism. Ignatieff's work, then, is a kind of apologetic for the status quo, framed either at the level of extant practice and current institutional arrangement or at the level of ideas and values. But he promises more than this. He promises a political ethics: an approach to the challenge of terrorism that offers the best available outcome for liberal democracies combating terrorism, one that manages to reconcile the fundamental ideals of a liberal democracy with demands for the physical security of its citizens. He calls such reconciliation, the lesser of two evils.

Ignatieff's twin perils

Ignatieff starts with a question which, in the context of his inquiry, is remarkably fatuous: 'What lesser evils may a society commit when it believes it faces the greater evil of its own destruction?'[2] (LE p. 1). Even the most alarmist predictions of terrorist success envisage no threat to the actual existence of states such as the US and Britain. The destruction of states are not at issue, as Ignatieff eventually acknowledges (LE p. 54). But this way of setting up the problem is chosen for a reason. By starting with a challenge to the very existence of a state, a dichotomy between necessity and rights is eased onto the page. Ignatieff dramatizes the predicament by quoting Gibbon's account of a massacre of Gothic youth in 378 AD. This massacre was an attempt on the part of the Romans to prevent a European war against the Goths from spreading to Asia. At the time, the war in Europe was going badly for the Romans and they feared that an outbreak of war against the Goths in Asia would threaten the empire. Goths had immigrated to many Asian towns and cities of the Roman Empire and were becoming numerous there. According to Gibbon, they signalled their hostile intent by refusing to learn the language of the empire, and it was impossible to hide from them the great progress Goth's were making in their struggle against the Romans in Europe. Gibbon sets the Goths up as unintegrated, capable and energetic, and motivated for rebellion.[3] This is a paradigm instance of 'the enemy within'. And the Roman response was to organize the Gothic youth of

Asia to assemble in local town squares on a designated day, lured by the promise of land and money, only to be massacred by waiting Roman troops. In just war theory, following on from Michael Walzer's work, a situation in which the existence of the state is threatened, along with a realistic expectation that the end of the state will bring with it wide-scale deprivation or enslavement, is labelled a 'supreme emergency'.[4] It is doubtful that the massacre of Gothic youth was a response to a supreme emergency, but it raises the question well enough. What are we morally permitted to do in a supreme emergency? Gibbon passes over the question. Ignatieff insists that it must be answered.

Perhaps it must, but why start out an inquiry into political ethics in an 'age of terror' with this question? Terrorist threats within Western nations do not constitute a supreme emergency for them or anything remotely like it. The reason Ignatieff starts off his inquiry by raising the spectre of a supreme emergency is rhetorical. It sets up a handy false dichotomy, one that drives his thesis from beginning to end. Thinking of challenges to the very existence of a state, we are made to confront a choice between doing whatever it takes to defend the state from its enemies and the desirability of promoting the rights, liberties and privileges of its citizens. Must we choose between war without restraint and the reckless and self-indulgent pursuit of liberty? This is an obvious false dichotomy, and Ignatieff's tactic is to present a middle path between the two extremes. The mean between two contrary errors is bound to look rational and sensible. Of course, it is one thing to call up a middle path – it is quite another to have the conceptual resources to ground any particular choice of middle path. Our claim is that Ignatieff does not have these resources; that, indeed, he has no clear idea at all about how to negotiate a path between the twin perils he sets up for us.

The lesser evil

What is Ignatieff's account of this middle path? It involves finding a balance 'between the commitments to individual dignity incarnated in rights and the commitments to majority interest incarnated in popular sovereignty' (LE p. 18). He continues:

> In times of danger, this conflict of values becomes intense. The suppression of civil liberties, surveillance of individuals, targeted assassination, torture, and preemptive war put liberal commitments to dignity under such obvious strain, and the harms they entail are so

serious, that, even if mandated by peremptory majority interest, they should be spoken of only in the language of evil.

(LE p. 18)

The language of evil has a cloudy and unwieldy background; but it functions here to distinguish what are highly significant moral wrongs from mere harms. Evils, on this view, are wrongs done to persons, not merely harms suffered by them. A choice of the lesser evil is ordinarily taken to be a choice of the least evil action in tragic choice situations. If this is what Ignatieff has in mind, then he must have in mind a tragic choice situation faced by liberal democracies as they respond to the challenge of international terrorism. This can't be a choice between acting wrongly and suffering harms; it must be a choice between acting wrongly in one way and acting wrongly in a worse way. What is this choice? What is this other evil? It must be a failure to do everything one might do to protect citizens from possible attack. Failing to detain potential terrorists indefinitely, for example, might constitute an evil if a government had a moral obligation to do *everything* it could to protect its citizens, including breaking its own commitments to due process. This is quite implausible, of course, and Ignatieff makes clear that he isn't really thinking of the situation like this.[5] The choice of the lesser evil, as Ignatieff thinks of it, is not a matter of confronting a tragic choice situation; it is better thought of as an encounter with dirty-hands choice situations. In dirty-hands situations, agents are confronted with the choice of either betraying deep moral commitments or allowing others to cause great harm. Thus, Ignatieff's choice of language is misleading. With this caveat in mind, however, we will continue to write of Ignatieff's political ethics as a search for the lesser evil. It is worth quoting Ignatieff's account of the lesser evil at length:

> In a war on terror, I would argue, the issue is not whether we can avoid evil acts altogether, but whether we can succeed in choosing the lesser evils and keep them from becoming greater ones. We should do so, I would argue, by making some starting commitments – to the conservative principle (maintaining the free institutions we have), to the dignity principle (preserving individuals from gross harms) – and then reasoning out the consequences of various courses of action, anticipating harms and coming to a rational judgment of which course of action is likely to inflict the least damage on the two principles. When we are satisfied that a coercive measure is a genuine last resort, justified by the facts as we understand them, we

have chosen the lesser evil, and we are entitled to stick to it even if the price proves higher than we anticipated. But not indefinitely so. At some point – when we 'have to destroy the village in order to save it' – we may conclude that we have slipped from the lesser to the greater. Then we have no choice but to admit our error and reverse course. In a situation of factual uncertainty in which most decisions about terrorism have to be taken, error is probably unavoidable.

(LE pp. 18–19)

As Ignatieff presents it, the lesser evil is that course of action which is most likely to optimally satisfy the conservative principle and the dignity principle. Ignatieff's account of the dignity principle in this passage is misleading. From the liberal perspective Ignatieff is defending, dignity is not a matter of protection from gross harms, it is a matter of protection from a particular kind of wrong – violation of the basic conditions of human dignity. Ignatieff's only explicit statement of the dignity principle is this,

> a democratic war on terror needs to subject all coercive measures to *the dignity test* – do they violate individual dignity? Foundational commitments to human rights should always preclude cruel and unusual punishment, torture, penal servitude, extrajudicial execution, as well as rendition of suspects to rights-abusing countries.
>
> (LE pp. 24–5)

We'll look at how seriously Ignatieff takes these foundational prohibitions later. For the moment, let us use this quotation to give a little content to Ignatieff's idea of dignity. Respecting the dignity of another is a matter of protecting the conditions of human dignity, and Ignatieff signals here that he would give these conditions a human rights interpretation. Rights constitutive of conditions of dignity are considerably broader than those mentioned by Ignatieff. What he furnishes in spelling out the principle of dignity, then, is a number of the most obvious and significant violations of conditions of dignity. There is no reason to think that Ignatieff's list is meant to be exhaustive.

Ignatieff presents the search for the lesser evil as a matter of optimizing satisfaction of two principles: one aimed at preservation of institutions (a free press, an independent judiciary, constitutional protection of rights, etc.); the other aimed at protection of individual rights that are necessary conditions of human dignity. However, optimization is a relation between contrary forces, and the conservative and dignity principles do not conflict, at least not as a result of putative responses to terrorism. What is in fact being optimized is a relation between the two principles and a public good, namely protection from physical threat. How is the balance to be achieved? How are we to determine when the lesser evil tips over into the greater evil? According to Ignatieff, we have only slipped from the lesser to the greater evil when 'we have to destroy the village in order to save it'. It is hard to take this move seriously, but doing so generates the following kind of principle: the greater evil occurs when actions threaten the liberal democratic basis of society. This is the village destroyed: not literally, but morally. Exceptions to normal liberal democratic processes, bounded and curtailed, do not destroy the village; they embarrass the village, perhaps, and wrong a small minority of village dwellers (as well, perhaps, as a vast number outside the village). But so long as such violations of principle remain exceptions, they do not threaten the foundational commitments of society as such, so they do not slip from the lesser to the greater evil.[6] However, as we have suggested in the chapter on the state of exception, exceptions to liberal democratic rule *do* precisely undermine the liberal democratic framework in serious ways, even as they are to some extent accommodated within it.

Is this, then, Ignatieff's definitive account of the middle path between a ruthless and pragmatic 'war on terror' and uncompromising civil libertarianism? In fact, Ignatieff equivocates between precluding violations of the principle of dignity and advocating a balancing act between satisfying the principle and maximizing public safety. The idea that a greater evil constitutes a threat to the liberal democratic character of institutions is only a part of his account. It is one kind of greater evil, but not the only, or even the most pressing, kind of greater evil. Thus, Ignatieff's one attempt to specify the point at which a lesser evil becomes a greater one is extraordinarily wide of mark. Apart from an appeal to the idea of a balance – an entirely indeterminate solution without a principled basis for preferring one balance over another – and apart from an appeal to process – something we examine later – Ignatieff has nothing to say about the point at which lesser evils become greater evils. Thus, when Ignatieff comes to describe the transition from lesser to greater evils, he alights upon the only trope ready to hand that appears even superficially as if it might do the job: a lesser evil becomes greater when 'we have to destroy the village in order to save it'.

Ignatieff provides one more attempt to articulate the point of balance between principle and public safety (LE pp. 23–4). The account consists of five propositions.

1. Responses to terror must pass the dignity test, which precludes significant violations of conditions of individual dignity.
2. Responses to terror must pass the conservative test, which precludes any departures from existing due process standards that 'damage our institutional inheritance', that is, which involve a long-term diminution of due process standards and other rights protections.
3. Responses to terror must pass an effectiveness test. Will the response enhance security in the short and long term?
4. Responses to terror must pass a last resort test. Are there feasible non-coercive alternatives?
5. Finally, responses to terror must pass the test of adversarial review. Have they been subjected to adversarial review in either legislative or judicial settings or in the press? (In emergency cases, will they be subject to review in a timely fashion?)

The first two elements of Ignatieff's scheme register the significance of the dignity principle and the conservative principle respectively. They are the most elusive part of the scheme. The conservative test, however, is very weak. Its value lies in, for example, preventing the long-term erosion of liberal democratic standards of due process, but it allows for all kinds of states of exception provided they are bound by sunset clauses, in the case of legislative responses, or by other means of curtailing long-term effects.

It is the dignity test which concerns us primarily. How seriously are we to take the test? As Ignatieff articulates the test, it sets up absolute prohibitions. Torture is precluded in any response to terror, as is rendition of suspected terrorists to rights abusing countries. Extrajudicial killings are also precluded. Indefinite detention and suspension of habeas corpus rights are not explicitly precluded by him and nor is preventative war. If Ignatieff means what he says here, we are to consider individual actions such as the torture of a terrorist leader in a 'ticking bomb' scenario as a greater evil. However, given Ignatieff's unsatisfactory account of the greater evil and his professed concern to find a *balance* between preserving dignity and ensuring public safety, his list of absolute prohibitions is hard to justify and seems ad hoc. Balance requires compromise, but in what ways and to what extent are the conditions of dignity to be compromised in the interests of public safety? Ignatieff defends the idea of absolute prohibitions in only the vaguest of terms. He writes: 'It is the nature of democracy that it not only does, but should, fight with one hand tied behind its back. It is also in the nature of democracy that it prevails against its enemies precisely because it does' (LE p. 24). This is political speech-making (a search for a nicely rounded sound bite), not philosophical argument. So we are left with three key questions.

Does Ignatieff really advance absolute prohibition of offences against human dignity or is he committed to the possibility of compromising satisfaction of the principle of dignity for the sake of public safety? Does he choose between permissible and impermissible offences against human dignity in a principled, reasoned way? Is he able to coherently describe certain violations of the principle of dignity as greater evils or does the greater evil rhetoric drop out of the picture at the point at which potential responses to terrorism are actually debated? Let us pursue these questions by examining Ignatieff's views on assassination, preventative detention and torture.

Assassination, Detention, Torture and the Principle of Dignity

Ignatieff claims that torture, illegal detention, unlawful assassination are 'beyond the pale' (LE p. ix), but the devil is in the detail. Although, he clearly stipulates that extrajudicial killings violate the principle of dignity, Ignatieff defends the practice of targeted assassination. He sets out the following constraints on the practice:

> Assassination can be a justified lesser evil, but only against bona fide terrorist targets actively engaged in hostilities against a democratic state and even then only under certain conditions: (a) where less violent alternatives, like arrest and capture, endanger U.S. personnel or civilians; (b) where information exists that the targets in question are planning imminent attacks that cannot be stopped in any other way; and (c) where all reasonable precautions are taken to minimize collateral damage and civilian harms.
>
> (LE p. 133)

Notice how weak these constraints on assassination appear to be. The idea is that assassinations are morally permissible as long as they are aimed at terrorists engaged in hostilities towards a state like ours (i.e. a democratic one); alternative courses of action would be somewhat risky (for us); there is appropriate intelligence (which likely falls a long way short of a compelling case against the suspects); and only a manageable number of innocents will likely be blown to pieces (whatever this number happens to be). An example of the kind of justifiable assassination Ignatieff appears to have in mind is the assassination of al-Harethi and five other Al Qaeda operatives in Yemen in 2002. In that case, the targets were travelling by car about 160 kilometres east of Yemen's capital San'a, clearly not in the middle of a terrorist assignment. Nonetheless, it was clearly not feasible to capture the men, and there was credible intelligence about the Al Qaeda connections of the occupants of the car, and it was a reasonable supposition that they were involved in planning terror strikes in the very near future.

Is targeted killing of this kind compatible with the principle of dignity? As we have seen, Ignatieff precludes extrajudicial killings when introducing the principle of dignity, but the kinds of killing he advocates are only 'extrajudicial' because they occur outside the jurisdiction of US courts. This juridical happenstance cannot make the difference between something that satisfies the principle of dignity and something that violates it. So is Ignatieff recommending that the principle be set-aside in some situations or has he revised his account of the principle? Ignatieff does not say, but he might hold that targeted assassinations undertaken by the US military or the CIA, outside of the jurisdiction of US courts, are somehow compatible with the principle of dignity. Perhaps he is seduced by the rhetoric of war. War is a cover for the killing of enemy combatants, and the conception of terrorists as combatants in a war – a 'war on terror' – rather than, say, criminals plotting murder, encourages the idea that pre-emptive assassination might after all be compatible with the principle of dignity. In an openly declared war, killing those actively engaged in battle against oneself is not a violation of their basic dignity, but an acceptance of their status as soldiers engaged in battle. Part of the point of declaring a war on terror is to make ourselves comfortable with the extrajudicial killing of suspected enemies. Nonetheless, the moral comfort of a declaration of war is stretched beyond recognition when suspected enemies are not really in open battle against us, but are thought to be plotting or perpetrating acts of gross criminality. The standards of war do not apply to terrorists planning or perpetrating terrorist operations, just as suspected terrorist captives are excluded from 'privileged combatant' provisions of the Geneva Convention relative to the Treatment of Prisoners of War.[7] The pre-emptive killing of suspected, potential murderers has to be seen as a violation of the principle of dignity, as must the pre-emptive killing of suspected terrorists.

It turns out, then, that Ignatieff does not in fact advance a plausible version of the principle of dignity as a set of minimal standards of behaviour. He either artificially restricts the principle or he allows violations of it to count as lesser evils. The most charitable interpretation has Ignatieff advancing a lesser evil interpretation of violations of the principle of dignity. Consider the case of preventative detention. Attorney General John Ashcroft's campaign of preventative detention in the months following 9/11 used mostly (or minimally) legal means to imprison and deport thousands of innocent men of Arab or Muslim background. The technique was to use immigration law, criminal law and a material witness law (allowing detention of persons deemed material witnesses in a grand jury inquiry) as pretexts to detain any person considered possibly suspicious. In the racially charged and paranoid weeks following 9/11, this amounted to the unjust imprisonment of perhaps as many as 5,000 men; men imprisoned or deported simply because they fell under a particular racial profile or because they raised the hostile attention of a public informer by, say, praying in public or just looking too Muslim.[8] Ignatieff acknowledges that the whole exercise 'seems to have been as unnecessary as it was unjust' (LE p. 10). It was unjust because it violated a principle of the individuality of guilt: 'any detention policy must be targeted at individuals against whom probable cause can eventually be demonstrated' (LE p. 10). Surely, however, this is a misstatement. Detention policies cannot guarantee that probable cause for a detention *will* be demonstrated unless it already has been demonstrated, that is, unless the discovery of probable cause is a precondition of detention. So Ignatieff must mean that detention policies should be targeted at individuals against whom probable cause is likely to be demonstrated. But who is to judge this likelihood? Not a judicial officer, who would be looking for actual probable cause rather than the expectation of probable cause. The idea must be to leave this judgment up to appropriate non-judicial US authorities such as the FBI or the US Citizenship and Immigration Service. Thus, Ignatieff's account of legitimate preventative detention seems to allow for the arrest and detention of people who, in the judgment of officials, will probably yield probable cause for their detention, perhaps under intense interrogation. Such a flexible approach to civil liberties certainly makes sense in a lesser evil ethics, where a balance of some kind is sought between public safety and civil liberties. Ignatieff turns his attention to Ashcroft's round-up because it offers him an easy case; but it is the hard cases which test his account of the lesser evil.[9]

Torture represents the hardest case of all, or so Ignatieff would have us believe (LE p. 140). Ignatieff develops a case for an absolute prohibition on physical torture, and part of his case is set out in terms of the principle of dignity. Ignatieff claims that the physical torture of individuals amounts to an ultimate violation (LE p. 136) and that 'torture, when committed by a state, expresses the state's ultimate view that human beings are expendable' (LE p. 143). This is a view, he claims, which is antithetical to any society committed to human dignity and freedom (LE p. 143). Although, the dignity principle appears to be playing an essential role here, there are in fact two distinct arguments at work in Ignatieff's case for a prohibition on physical torture: an argument from dignity and a moral hazard argument. We discuss them in turn.

Of course, Ignatieff is right to insist that there is no plausible way of reconciling physical torture with the principle of dignity, but as we have seen, he is prepared to compromise the principle of dignity in the case of pre-emptive killing and probably in the case of preventative detention as well. The mere fact that an action violates the principle of dignity does not make it a greater evil on Ignatieff's account. So why are some violations of dignity permitted and others not? Ignatieff addresses the question by focussing on the distinction between killing one's enemies and torturing them:

> How can one object to the torture of persons to secure valuable information for reasons of state, and not object to killing them? Both could simply be regarded as acceptable lesser evils, forced on unwilling liberal democracies by the exigencies of their own survival. But the cases are not the same. A liberal society that would not defend itself by force of arms might perish, while a liberal society that refused to torture is less likely to jeopardize its collective survival. Besides, there is a moral difference between killing a fellow combatant, in conformity to the laws of war, and torturing a person. The first takes a life; the second abuses one. It seems more legitimate to ask a citizen to defend a state by force of arms and, if necessary, to kill in self-defense or to secure a military objective, than it does to ask him to inflict degrading pain face-to-face. On this reading of a democratic moral identity, it may be legitimate to kill in self-defense, but not to engage in cruelty.
>
> (LE p. 137)

The argument here is based on a misleading contrast: torturing terrorist suspects is compared to killing soldiers in active combat. Yet the more relevant contrast is between torture and pre-emptive killing. Setting up the contrast between torture and combative self-defence allows Ignatieff to play the survival card once more. A preparedness to kill in self-defence is a prerequisite for security; absolute pacifism might conceivably endanger a state's very existence. No state would be threatened by a prohibition on pre-emptive killing. Yet pre-emptive killing is the appropriate contrast case. Pre-emptive killing – say, killing a person because we have information that they actively plan a terrorist outrage and there is no really safe way for us to apprehend them – is a violation of the principle of dignity. The question now is why pre-emptive killing may be regarded as a lesser evil while physical torture constitutes the greater evil? Why is blowing a person into a thousand pieces sometimes a permissible violation of duties of dignity towards them, but submitting a person to painful interrogation is not? Killing a person violates their right to life, whereas torturing a person violates their right to physical security and their right not to be made to suffer and be humiliated and degraded. Are the latter rights deeper or more fundamental than a right to life? Perhaps a right to life is something that can be forfeited in certain circumstances, whereas rights of physical security and dignity are always with us. It is possible to argue for a moral distinction between killing and torturing in these terms, but the argument is difficult and Ignatieff shies away from it. Instead he turns to a different kind of argument: an argument from moral hazard.

The argument from moral hazard focuses upon the moral condition of torturers. As Ignatieff presents the case, it is part of the moral identity of liberal democratic nations that they eschew cruelty towards their enemies. What finally decides the case against torture, he claims, is not the fact that torture violates the rights of the tortured. It is, rather, the harm the practice of torture does to torturers and those in whose interest torture is done. He writes:

> The most plausible case for an absolute ban on physical torture (as opposed to coercion) in every circumstance is related precisely to this issue of moral hazard. No one should have to decide when torture is or is not justified, and no one should be ordered to carry it out. An absolute prohibition is legitimate because in practice such a prohibition relieves a state's public servants from the burden of making intolerable choices.
>
> (LE p. 142)

Why should a state be willing to pre-emptively kill its enemies, engage in preventative detention of suspected enemy aliens, not to mention a state willing to wage preventative war, experience torture as an intolerable choice? If a state is willing to wage a war, knowing full well that it will lead to the deaths of tens or hundreds of thousands and the displacement of perhaps millions, the intolerability of the choice of torture looks like mere squeamishness. Moreover, why should we think that the order to torture someone would necessarily psychologically or morally damage the torturer or would be experienced as an intolerable choice by the public servant? Could this be said, for instance, about the private military contractors whose excessive zeal in inflicting pain and humiliation during interrogation has been widely reported; could this be said about the torturers in Abu Ghraib who seemed to take such a perverse delight in their sadistic activities?[10] There are two main avenues of development for the moral hazard argument Ignatieff is making. One is to emphasize the moral damage done to those in charge of ordering or carrying out a 'torture warrant'. The other is to emphasize the long-term damage done to the moral character of a society that has normalized the practice of torture. Ignatieff tries on both strategies, but emphasizes the second. Nominating Chile and Argentina in the 1970's as two societies deeply damaged by the normalization of practices of torture and concomitant rights violations (disappearances, illegal executions), Ignatieff points to the severe hazards awaiting any state that takes the route of torture.

The point is not that Ignatieff has reached the wrong conclusions about torture: he is obviously, blindingly correct to insist upon the absolute prohibition of physical torture. Our point is that he does not have the resources to clearly demonstrate the need for this prohibition. Once the principle of dignity ceases to function as a genuine test of the moral adequacy of a response to terrorism, it cannot be used to rule out the possibility of torture.

Another way to demonstrate the shortcoming of Ignatieff's approach is to examine his definition of torture. By 'torture' he means, 'the deliberate infliction of physical cruelty and pain in order to extract information' (LE p. 136). Psychological torture is relegated to extreme practices of 'coercion' and does not fall under Ignatieff's prohibition on torture. Ignatieff writes that '[t]he interrogation methods of which the Americans have been accused since 9/11 are held to include nothing worse than sleep deprivation, permanent light or permanent darkness, disorientating noise, and isolation' (LE p. 138).

Of course, he writes this before the offences of Abu Ghraib became known. Even so, Ignatieff's report of US interrogation techniques ignores the widespread use of stress positioning, waterboarding, verbal abuse, humiliation, threats, religious desecration and sacrilegious insult, which appears to have become normalized behaviour in high intensity counterterrorist interrogations. These are counted as largely inconsequential by Ignatieff. Nonetheless, the techniques of psychological torture recently perfected by the US military and the CIA also violate the principle of dignity. To be imprisoned in a wire-cage, disorientated, shackled, prevented from moving or lying down; to be kept without sleep until distressed, interrogated for long hours, threatened, insulted, humiliated, deprived of exercise, deprived of conversation, deprived of information about your family and information about where you are and what charges you face: this eventually becomes a kind of torture.[11] Or consider incarceration in a permanently lit and freezing cold cell; isolated, with unbearable music played loudly and continuously: this is also a form of torture and a transparent violation of the principle of dignity. Mock execution, sleep deprivation and the practice of waterboarding – initiating a gag-reflex to simulate the experience of drowning – are all examples of coercive interrogation techniques that readily become psychological torture. On what basis does Ignatieff decide that psychological torture is a permissible violation of the principle of dignity – mere coercion – whereas the physical techniques of torture violate the principle in a wholly unacceptable way?[12] Perhaps the elision hides discomfort at the wholesale assault on detainees' dignity and rights which appears to have become a standard practice in high-intensity counter-terrorist interrogation.

A lesser evil approach does not just make it hard to draw a line between legitimate pursuit of public safety and the illegitimate violation of human rights and derogation of civil liberties. In Ignatieff's hands, it furnishes no principled grounds for drawing the line in any one place rather than another. As political ethics, the result is radically indeterminate. Although the principle of dignity is presented as a test for any response to terrorism, in fact it functions as one factor in the mix along with others. So how are we to specify legitimate compromise of the principle of dignity?

Preventative war

The biggest, if not the hardest, question of all is the question of war. Ignatieff, an early advocate of the invasion and occupation of Iraq, appears to have altered his position by the time *The Lesser Evil* was published in 2004. He blames the US and Britain misinformation:

> Instead of claiming in the run-up to the Iraq war, as they had good reason to do, that the Iraqi regime possessed both the intentions and the resources to *eventually* acquire weapons of mass destruction, the president and the British prime minister asserted that the regime

had actually developed and deployed these weapons. In stretching the evidence, they sought to manipulate democratic consent for war, and even those who supported them cannot feel that a desirable end justified such means. As it happened, the war does not appear to have had a preemptive justification at all.

(LE p. 163)

So what are the conditions of justified war on Ignatieff's account? He nominates four (LE p. 166). Any war waged in response to a threat of terrorism must: (1) be authorized in conditions of genuinely democratic disclosure (i.e. must not be undertaken for secret reasons or knowingly promoted on false grounds); (2) be undertaken only after genuine efforts to obtain multilateral support have been made (but can be undertaken unilaterally if multilateral support is not forthcoming); (3) be a last resort; and (4) must not leave conditions in the invaded country worse off. As Ignatieff acknowledges, this characterization of a military war on terror evades many hard questions. On what basis is a judgement made that one has reached the last resort? (There are almost always further peaceful courses of action available.) On what basis are we to judge that an invaded and subjugated nation is not worse off? In answer to this last question, Ignatieff nominates only structural features of a nation's condition (replacement of a tyrannical regime with a democratic one) and the self-interest of the invaders (prevention of a wider war) (LE p. 166). He does not mention the million people fleeing and the tens or hundreds of thousands dead. Leaving an invaded country at least as well off as it was before the invasion cannot stand as a criterion of decision making. That criterion might be something like this: it is *likely* that the population of the invaded country will be at least as well off as they were before the invasion (e.g. we will replace a tyrant with a parliament and invest in the country's economic recovery). These judgments are impossible to make reliably; so a precautionary principle ought to be applied here. The criterion ought to be something like: there is a wide, expert, independent consensus that it is overwhelmingly likely that the people of the invaded country will be at least as well off as they were before invasion on all key indicators of welfare. Of course, no such criterion has ever been satisfied and none is ever likely to be. Ignatieff himself was clearly not applying such a strict criterion when he supported the invasion and occupation of Iraq.

One of the most troubling aspects of Ignatieff's support for military wars on terror is his slide from pre-emption to preventative war. According to just war theory, a pre-emptive war is *only* ever justified in cases where the signs of imminent invasion are unmistakable.[13] However, Ignatieff licences war on the grounds that a country is quite probably developing weapons of mass destruction and will perhaps allow these to fall into the hands of terrorist activists planning attacks on Western targets. It turns out that Iraq had abandoned its weapons programme well before its invasion and occupation (as it said it had, and as international teams of weapons of inspectors were in the process of discovering). But if it turned out that Iraq was, say, developing a range of chemical weapons, then the invasion and occupation of Iraq would seem to have been justified in Ignatieff's eyes (*ex ante*, without the wisdom of hindsight). But this kind of war is no pre-emption. It is preventative war: war aimed at preventing either a worse war some time in the future or a terror campaign aimed at Western targets some time in the future. One of the cornerstones of modern just war theory is a determination to preclude resort to preventative war, so Ignatieff can find no support in this tradition for his account of resort to war in response to threats of terror.

Ignatieff's conditions of justified preventative war set out necessary, but not sufficient, conditions for a war's justification. The most difficult and intractable part of the question is left to a consequentialist calculation, i.e. a risk analysis: do the potential benefits of successful military action outweigh the risks? Who is to bear the risks and on what basis? Who is to share in the benefit? Does a risk of the development of weapons of mass destruction – the risk that international efforts of curtailment and containment of weapons programmes fail – justify the invasion of a country and the consequent risks borne by the population of that country?

Furthermore, who is to make the risk analysis on which preventative war is waged? Democratic processes of decision making – at popular, legislative and executive levels – are unlikely to arrive at decent and just risk analyses, except in rare circumstances. We almost inevitably judge the risks to ourselves in one way and the risks to others in quite another. This reflects deeply entrenched, perhaps ineliminable, bias. Consider the case of memorialization. Every night the US dead from the Iraq war are given a tribute on US television. In PBS's Lehrer's News Hour, for example, a sombre and moving tribute is run every weeknight, with the names and portraits of the US dead parading slowly and silently on the screen, one after the other. There is not enough television time to memorialize the Iraqi dead in similar fashion – even if it would remotely occur to a US television executive to do so. This is no accident. It is an inevitable feature of our assessments of harms that they are made with deep partiality. Our moral imagination is simply not up to the job of analysing the risks of harm to others and the benefits to ourselves in a perfectly just and impartial fashion, and because of this the idea that a nation might legitimately and unilaterally decide to embark on a preventative war makes little sense.

Entertaining the possibility of a preventative war entails wholesale compromise of the principle of dignity. War unleashes a series of predictable and unavoidable assaults on the basic conditions of dignity of an invaded people, and dressing up a military campaign as a liberation movement does nothing to ameliorate this. The war on Iraq has proved the dismal truth of this once more (if further proof were necessary). In advocating the legitimacy of a preventative war on terror, Ignatieff demonstrates just how dispensable he takes the principle of dignity to be. And this makes all the more urgent the need to articulate rational and principled grounds upon which the dignity and rights of a people can be set aside in the interests of maximizing security of Westerners. Ignatieff does not provide these grounds, but he has one more card up his sleeve. This is what we shall call the retreat to process.

The retreat to process

If political ethics offers no account of the point at which lesser evils become greater evils – that is, the point at which an optimal balance is reached between respect for rights and liberties on the one hand and public security on the other – then it fails the principle requirement on ethical theories: to guide action by furnishing an account of the right-making features of action, that is, those features of an action which account for its being morally right or morally wrong. Since Ignatieff's political ethics is conspicuously silent on these right-making features in all but the easiest cases, the specification of the lesser evil is left radically indeterminate. Ignatieff folds a procedural requirement into his account of the lesser evil and this may be intended to deal with this indeterminacy. He writes,

> it would be wrong to trust [our leaders] to decide the larger question of how to balance liberty and security over the long term. For these larger questions, we ought to trust to democratic deliberation through our institutions. Adversarial justification is an institutional response, developed over centuries, to the inherent difficulty of making appropriate public judgments about just these types of conflicts of values.
>
> (LE pp. 2–3)

The point, then, is to trust in the checks and balances of adversarial review to settle on the right point of balance between liberty and security. There are three basic ways of thinking about this retreat to process: one is a teleological perspective; another is a justice perspective; and the third a practical perspective. From a teleological perspective, the value of adversarial review is that it is a generally reliable process of discovering the truth, or of discovering the most justified conclusion that can be drawn from available reasons and available evidence. This makes sense of the ordinary practice of adversarial review, in which people take themselves to be aiming at the most justified available conclusion by advancing and testing arguments. From a justice perspective, by contrast, adversarial review is valuable in that it embodies just or fair standards of deliberation. Just deliberation eschews the kinds of deceptive and conniving behaviour that flourishes in secret. Just deliberation also allows conflicting value judgments their 'day in court'. From this perspective, the point of adversarial review is not to discover the truth, or failing that, the most justified opinion. The point is to deliberate and decide fairly. Given reasonable disagreement about significant issues – ones that, for practical reasons, must be decided – deliberative justice requires that the main sides of the debate have a legitimated voice. Adversarial review in liberal democracies is a very imperfect tool in this respect. Institutions from the legislature through to the judiciary exclude and silence unwelcome views as a matter of course. In formally liberal democratic countries such as the US, Britain and Australia, the press is a shallow and manifestly inadequate forum for fair discussion. Still, Ignatieff may insist that our traditions of adversarial review are still our best tools for achieving a fair representation of views in public debate. If it is, after all, a very bad system, it might be less bad than other practical alternatives.

The third perspective on the value of adversarial review is not aimed at deliberation over policy settings. It values adversarial review as a means by which liberal democratic institutions avoid culpable error. A well-known recent example is the judicial review of Yaser Esam Hamdi's indefinite detention as an unlawful combatant. Hamdi, who held dual citizenship of Saudi Arabia and the US, was captured by the Northern Alliance during the US invasion of Afghanistan in 2001. He was handed over to US military and determined – on hearsay evidence from members of the Northern Alliance – to be an unlawful combatant engaged in hostilities against the US and its allies. After stints in Camp X-Ray and a naval brig in Norfolk, Virginia, Hamdi was eventually imprisoned in Charleston, South Carolina; to be held indefinitely without access to legal advice or court review of his imprisonment. Hamdi's father, Esam Fouad Hamdi, filed a habeas corpus petition on behalf of his son in June 2002. After a number of rounds at District Court level and Fourth Circuit Court level, the matter was considered by the US Supreme Court. In this case – Hamdi vs Rumsfeld – a majority of Supreme Court justices (eight out of nine; Justice Clarence Thomas dissented) found that the US executive did not have the authority to detain US citizens indefinitely without due process protections enforceable through judicial review. Although, the court reached majority agreement on this issue, no full opinion achieved majority. The US Supreme Court remains divided on a host of issues surrounding the 'war on terror' and on the due process owed non-citizen detainees.[14]

Hamdi vs Rumsfield demonstrates both the strength and the weakness of judicial review as a means of correcting culpable error committed by executive powers. It demonstrates how such review can sometimes work to correct gross and obvious injustices, but also demonstrates the severe limitations of this process and its fragility. Hamdi's father faced an extraordinary battle in taking on the Bush Administration. Without a great deal of sponsorship, the case would never have left the Fourth Circuit Court. Had Hamdi not been a US citizen, the case would have been almost impossible. Justice Clarence Thomas found for the government and a different Supreme Court, one stacked with conservative and security-obsessed justices, may well have compounded the moral error of Bush's imprisonment of Hamdi. With the ascendancy of a conservative majority on the court in 2007, civil liberties protections afforded by the court are likely to decline.

Many conceptions of good deliberative practice attempt to combine all three perspectives. However, each account draws a very different picture of the significance of adversarial review. It is not clear which interpretation of the significance of adversarial review Ignatieff has in mind. He writes that,

> [c]itizens are bound to disagree about how far the government is entitled to go in any given emergency. Because we disagree deeply about these matters, democracy's institutions provide a resolution, through a system of checks and balances, to ensure that no government's answer has the power to lead us either straight to anarchy or to tyranny.
> (LE p. 3)

This is no help. There is a great deal we may expect from a government over and above avoidance of anarchy and tyranny. It is worth pointing out that Ignatieff's commitment to the moral value of adversarial review appears to collapse when it comes to decisions of war. He requires only that declarations of war be made under conditions of appropriate disclosure, that is, that a war not be promoted on grounds that are known to be false, and that hidden agendas not drive decisions to wage war. This falls well short of adequate adversarial review. He also requires that sincere efforts be made to secure wide multilateral support for a war. The international community may be consulted, and its help sought, but it is not to be trusted to decide upon a war's merits. In Ignatieff's vision of preventative war, multilateral support is a bonus, not a requirement. Yet the most valuable adversarial review of decisions to wage war lies at an international level, where the spectres of undigested self-interest, self-obsession, self-righteousness and prejudice loom less large.

Ignatieff does not make his interpretation of the significance of adversarial review clear, so let us consider all three possibilities. Clearly, the practical character of adversarial review – its ability to sometimes put a check on abuses of power – is of great significance. But it does not adequately address the fundamental issues of political ethics 'in a time of terror'. What about the teleological interpretation of adversarial review? If a lesser evil political ethics is as deeply indeterminate as Ignatieff's account of it suggests, then appeals to the teleological value of adversarial review are wrong-headed. Adversarial search for the truth requires some truth to be found; adversarial search for the most reasonable opinion requires there to be a most reasonable opinion to be found. If there really is a best opinion to be found, it is the business of a political ethics to specify it, or at least furnish conceptual resources on whose basis it can be specified. Thus, a teleological take on the principle of adversarial review cannot compensate for the aporia in Ignatieff's account of the lesser evil.

What about the process of adversarial review understood from the justice perspective? Does this redress the aporia in Ignatieff's political ethics? The very idea of just deliberation might seem to be a perfectly valid and unexceptional one, even though its instantiation in actual political decision making would require a profound deepening of contemporary practices of democracy. But what does it mean for political ethics if the hard questions are delegated to a process of deliberation which, though just and fair, is unlikely to settle on an objective standard of best opinion? A retreat to process, understood in this way, is an acknowledgement that rational progress is unlikely to be made in the development of political ethics. To offer a retreat to process in these circumstances is to claim that the best we can do is to somehow give differing opinions an appropriate weight in political deliberation, where appropriate weight is a function of authenticity and depth of considered opinion and, crucially, the number of people of like opinion. Of course, extant deliberative practices fall so far short of ideals of fairness that there is precious little comfort to be taken for defenders of extant liberal democratic institutions from appeal to ideally fair deliberation over basic policy options.

The sketch of just deliberative practice given earlier – in which differing opinions are weighed in terms of authenticity of considered opinion and the number of people who hold them – does not have the resources to resist imposition of majoritarian will. If moral issues cannot be determined rationally, then fair deliberation, understood in the way we outline here, will almost inevitably support the majority view. And in turn this will likely express the majority interest where the majority has a recognized common interest, or majority prejudice where the majority has a common, recalcitrant prejudice. One response to this potential shortcoming is to beef up our account of just deliberation by thinking of it, not as a fair negotiation between different interests and perspectives, but as a species of ideal deliberation: well informed, non-prejudicial and disinterested. The hope is that ideal deliberation – or some accessible approximation of it – will come up with a better outcome than appeal to vote-centric versions of deliberation. In philosophical versions, this is taken to be an idealized process that literally constitutes moral facts. The moral truth, or the best available moral opinion, *just is* what would be agreed to in an ideal deliberation. The idea is to combine justice and teleological perspectives into an attractive package. Moral truth, or best moral opinion, is one that would emerge from a disinterested, informed and non-prejudicial consensus.[15]

What are the chances for such deliberation? What practical outcomes might we expect from an appeal to ideal deliberation? Can any actual deliberation transcend the exercise of prejudice and self-interest? In contractualist versions of this idea, morally right principles are those that would be agreed to in a process of open, properly informed and disinterested deliberation, one in which all parties are equally committed to the project of living together on the basis of mutual and equal respect.[16] Thinking about what it would be to apply such a contractualist account of morally correct principles to the kinds of thorny issues we are discussing demonstrates just how difficult it is to make the model work. One problem is the specification of the position from which deliberation is supposed to start. The concept of equal mutual respect is both ambiguous and contested. It might mean no more than that we hold each other accountable for our actions; that is, we treat each other fundamentally as reasonable beings. And this might mean no more than that we demand that others appeal to reasons for their choices, where such reasons can be seen as emerging from coherent value positions.[17] If equal mutual respect means something more substantial than this, then commitment to it reflects a basic value choice which is properly the subject of the moral deliberation we have in mind. Folding contested value choices into the specification of just deliberation, where just deliberation sets itself the task of settling contests of value, is a cheat.

The upshot of this critique of the appeal to process is that ideals of deliberative process cannot be used to support the liberal project. In particular, they cannot be used to address the obvious stress that liberal democratic perspectives and institutions find themselves are under when people regard themselves (albeit mostly falsely) as severely threatened by terrorism. The liberal ideal involves a balance between majoritarian control of general public policy and protection of individual rights. But shunting the problem of articulating the fundamental balance between public security and respect for individual rights onto majoritarian deliberation puts the fate of one half of the liberal equation in the hands of the other half. If majorities get to decide the fate of minorities, then the fundamental project of liberalism has been betrayed.

This, then, is Ignatieff's predicament. He has failed to articulate a rational basis on which the balance between public security and individual liberty can be decided. Instead, he has simply refined the choice situation, by nominating a series of tests that rule out the easy cases – gross violations of the principle of conservatism, say, or hasty and unnecessary actions – but leave open the basic question of how the principle of dignity and (to a lesser extent, because it is a much weaker principle) the principle of conservatism are to be balanced against the primary interest that the majority has in maximizing their physical security and punishing their projected enemies.

The retreat to process exacerbates the problem. Processes of adversarial review play a vital role in putting some checks on an executive's abuse of power, but this is beside the point. Appeals to the outcome of adversarial review do not substitute for a well-reasoned political ethics. If the idea is that fair deliberation must decide the balance between maximizing physical security and protecting individual liberties in the absence of any determinative rational warrant, then the issue of protecting individual liberties has, in the balance, been delegated to the majority, whose voice will inevitably dominate in any properly structured version of such fair deliberative practice. Ignatieff nominates adversarial review of executive decision as a test that any legitimate response to terrorism must pass. We agree on the importance of this test. Our claim is simply that the retreat to process cannot prevent Ignatieff's political ethics from being evasive on all the hard questions.[18]

Conclusion: Liberalism and the response to terror

Something very fundamental is going wrong in Ignatieff's account of the lesser evil, and this is not an accidental feature of his handling of the discussion. Ignatieff is responding to tensions within the liberal democratic tradition – mercilessly exposed by the pressures of international terrorism – and it is no accident that he discovers no clear way to resolve them. Two fundamental flaws are exposed. The liberal democratic tradition Ignatieff is working within is a form of nationalist liberalism, one in which cosmopolitan commitments are secondary and the focus of appraisal falls primarily on the state and its protection of those within its borders. This generates two kinds of flaw: the failure to adequately conceptualize the protection of individual and minority interests within a state; and the failure to adequately conceptualize the demands of international justice and its effects on the pursuit of state interests.

We briefly highlighted the second of these failures in our discussion of Ignatieff on war. Let us now concentrate our discussion of the first of the failures. The liberal democratic tradition has always represented an uneasy balance between individual rights and liberties and majority rule. Both are seen as essential aspects of the legitimation of coercive political arrangements. In Rawls, for example, individual protections are enshrined in the liberty principle and the priority accorded to it.[19] Rawls also takes the basis of democratic justice to be a special application of the liberty principle; he calls it the principle of equal participation. According to the principle of equal participation: 'all citizens are to have an equal right to take part in, and to determine the outcome of, the constitutional process that establishes the laws with which they are to comply'.[20] Because Rawls derives both aspects of liberal doctrine from the liberty principle (adding an egalitarian focus by way of the lesser equal opportunity principle and difference principle) it is easy to overlook the ease with which the principle of equal participation comes into conflict with the remainder of the liberty principle.[21] This is the fault-line that extreme threats of terrorism expose in liberal democracies.[22] When it comes to laws protecting public security, the equal participation of all in framing those laws will quickly lead to the derogation of minority and visitor rights when members of minorities and visitors are viewed as the source of extreme threat. This seems inevitable unless the process of establishing rights-derogating security laws is checked by robust constitutional obstacles. The traditional liberal balancing act works so long as dangers to public safety aren't too high, or aren't perceived as too high. But the nightmare scenario of an unhindered international conspiracy of terrorists, unaccountable to anyone and bent on mass murder, appears to raise the perceived stakes too high for the liberal balancing act to work any longer. What would occupants of the original position come up with if they believed that their society is to face a long and terrible insurgency or an ongoing campaign of mass terror? Ignatieff does a robust job highlighting this basic tension within liberalism. What he can't do, coming from within the tradition itself, is resolve the tension.

Of course, current threats of terrorism are wildly exaggerated; and so the most promising liberal response may simply be a deflationary one. If we can only get clear about our real risk situation, the tension between rights and security may largely evaporate. The trouble with this solution is that it wholly underestimates the force and incorrigibility of the prejudice and self-deception that underlies perceptions of risk from 'the other'. We neither fully appreciate, nor have the resources to expunge, the prejudice with which we regard our 'threatened' place in the world. Islamic terrorism is constructed as a wholly alien phenomenon: it is perpetrated by fanatics who hate us for no good reason and who act from motives it is impossible to understand, except in utterly pathologizing ways. We do not see Islamic terrorists as responding to the injustices, cruelties, humiliations and stupidities of US foreign policy, but as warriors for a cause we can neither understand nor appreciate and which makes only theological sense. They are the radical other, whose alterity marks them as inexplicable, unpredictable and supremely dangerous. The forces that drive this picture are not simple cognitive errors. This dismal, partial understanding of terrorist threats has a firm grip on the ordinary imagination of Westerners. It is not a straightforward mistake we are making, but an expression of deep and incorrigible prejudice. If we are right about this, then the liberal balancing act will not be easily restored. We need another way to think about the grounds of respect for individuals and minority voices, and another way to think about the legitimacy of the public's interest in its safety and security. Ignatieff's work demonstrates just how hard it is to do this within the liberal democratic tradition.

In using Ignatieff to highlight some of the tensions within liberal democracy, and the difficulties it faces in reconciling conflicting principles of liberty and security, individual rights and majority rule, we approach a central political problem – one that haunts contemporary debates on the war on terror: what does liberal democracy mean today? Does it continue to exist in any intelligible form, what with the continual exceptions to, and violations of, its basic principles and practices? What aspects of liberal democratic politics are worth salvaging and fighting for; and how might liberal democracy be rethought and reinvigorated today? In other words, what are the ways forward – if any – for liberal democratic politics today? We will attempt an answer to this in the next, and final, chapter.

Notes

1. Ignatieff, *The Lesser Evil*.
2. Ignatieff, *The Lesser Evil*. Henceforth, in this chapter, all references to this work will appear in the text as [LE].
3. E. Gibbon (1960) *History of the Decline and Fall of the Roman Empire* (London: Chatto & Windus) Chapter 26.
4. M. Walzer (1977) *Just and Unjust Wars* (New York: Basic Books), pp. 251–68.
5. For example, Ignatieff's illustration of 'tragic choice' is Euripides' account of Medea's choice to kill her children rather than have them murdered by strangers. If we take Medea's word for this, she faced a choice between doing something evil and allowing others to do something worse (murder another's children) (LE pp. 13–14).
6. A useful point of reference for this kind of claim is Locke's account of conditions of legitimate revolution. At a certain point, exceptions to good liberal democratic functioning threaten the liberal democratic basis of society. As neatly summarized by the framers of the American Declaration of Independence: 'when a long train of abuses and usurpations, pursuing invariably the same Object evinces a design to reduce [the citizenry] under absolute Despotism, it is their right, it is their duty, to throw off such Government and to provide new Guards for their future security' Declaration of Independence (1776).
7. http://www.unhchr.ch/html/menu3/b/91.htm, Article 4.
8. See D. Cole (2003) *Enemy Aliens* (New York: The New Press), pp. 17–39.
9. Interestingly, Ignatieff criticizes Ashcroft's roundup in terms of the conservative principle, not the dignity principle. His primary concern, it seems, is with the institutional inheritance of the US justice system rather than the gross assault on individual rights that the round-up produced.
10. See Maj. Gen. A. M. Tabuga (2004) 'The Tabuga Report' – Article 15–6 of 800th Military Police Brigade: U.S. Army Report on the Abuse of Iraqi Prisoners (5 May 2004) *Counterpunch*. http://www.counterpunch.org/taguba05052004.html (accessed 26 February 2008).
11. This roughly describes many of the conditions of Camp X-ray detention, instituted early in the Bush Administration's 'war on terror' and shut down in 2002.
12. According to a recent study, the long-term effects of physical and psychological torture are indistinguishable. M. Basoglu, M. Livanou and C. Crnobaric (2007)

'Torture versus other cruel, inhuman & degrading treatment: Is the distinction real or apparent?' *Archives of General Psychiatry*, vol. 64, pp. 277–85.
13. See Walzer, *Just and Unjust Wars*.
14. US Supreme Court Media. http://www.oyez.org/cases/2000-2009/2003/2003_03_6696/ (accessed 28 June 2007).
15. There are many possible refinements to this basic idea, explored both in the literature on deliberative democracy and in the philosophical literature on constructivist and moral realist theories in metaethics.
16. See T. M. Scanlon (1999) *What We Owe to Each Other* (Cambridge: Belknap Press) for an example of this kind of approach.
17. Kant, the source of contractualist thought, held that practical reason could issue in only one coherent set of moral maxims, but we assume he was overconfident in thinking this.
18. It is not that Ignatieff refuses to answer all the hard questions; as we have seen he answers a number of them. The point is that his answers are not meaningfully derived from his ethics.
19. Rawls's liberty principle requires that the basic structure of a society reflect the fact that every citizen has an equal claim to a fully adequate scheme of rights and liberties, compatible with the same scheme for all. J. Rawls (1999) *A Theory of Justice* (Cambridge, MA: Harvard University Press), p. 53.
20. Rawls, *A Theory of Justice*, p. 194.
21. The priority rules determining the order of Rawl's principles of justice are designed to settle tensions between the principles in a rationally defensible way. However, Rawls has no scheme, and appears not to have seen the need for a scheme, to adjudicate tensions *within* his principles of justice.
22. It is worth noting that Rawls does not even list physical security as a primary social good. See *A Theory of Justice*, p. 79.

7
On Ways Forward

> Where there is no vision, the people perish.
> Proverbs 29:18 (and Al Gore)

The previous chapter explored some of the ethical and political tensions central to liberal democracy – tensions highlighted in Ignatieff's ultimately unsuccessful attempt to reconcile liberal democratic principles and institutions with various forms of state violence and coercion in response to the threat of terrorism. Unlike Ignatieff, we have argued that enhanced security measures and military responses to terrorism, right up to extra-judicial detention, targeted assassination and preventive wars – all of which Ignatieff allows under his ethics of the 'lesser evil' – cannot be enacted without doing major damage to the very liberal democratic principles in defence of which these measures are supposedly taken. Neither the slippery logic of the 'lesser evil', nor blind faith in judicial scrutiny and adversarial review, gets around this problem. We are left in a quandary: what would be an ethically and politically legitimate response to terrorism?

Part of the problem here is the notion that there must be a certain 'trade-off' – between liberty and security, between human rights and counterterrorism, between democracy and the 'safety of our societies'. In this book, we have been questioning this received wisdom, showing that, on the contrary, the restrictions on liberty, the delimitation of democracy and extra-judicial state violence and militarism are not only too high a price to pay for the vague illusion of security, but they are also dangerous and, in a very real sense, increase our insecurity. Therefore, the question of how to respond to terrorism must be part of a much larger question – which is how to respond, ethically and effectively, to the current post-9/11 political paradigm. Throughout this book, we have been exploring different aspects of post-9/11 politics: from the politics of security, to the violent state of exception, to the culture of mendacity and the imperialist and militarist drives of US foreign policy. We have also explored deeper, underlying factors – psychological states of prejudice, racism and religious fundamentalism – which feed into, and in turn are fed into by, the 'war on terror'. It is our contention that any critical response to the 'war on terror' must, firstly, examine it in its broader social, political, cultural and psychological context, and understand its complex interactions with prejudice, fundamentalism, group dynamics, national identifications and modes of violence.

However, developing an effective critical response to the 'war on terror' must involve more than building a coherent picture of the problems we encounter. It must actually propose alternative responses and political strategies aimed at addressing these problems. On our analysis, problems inherent in post-9/11 politics run deep. What role can a critical response to this politics play beyond critique and explanation? How can the critic help move politics out of its current, disastrous formation? What basic kinds of positive response are available to us, given the nature of the problems we have exposed?

The task is a very difficult one given the critical stance we have adopted throughout this book. Rather than assuming existing liberal democratic systems to be largely intact and self-correcting, a critical response sees current abuses in the 'war on terror' to be symptomatic of much deeper structural problems in this system, and therefore calls for a certain transformation of this system. Any comprehensive response will have to involve measures which not only limit the damage done to liberal democratic institutions by the 'war on terror', but also entail broader political, social and economic changes, including a rethinking of democracy.

Halting the security paradigm

One obvious place to start would be a political challenge to the security paradigm that has become so ubiquitous and dominant today – a challenge aimed not simply at limiting its dangers, but at overturning it completely through a rigorous reassertion democratic rights and civil liberties. In the first chapter, we highlighted the dangers of the current obsession with security: the threat it poses to democratic life and basic freedoms. Any effective resistance to the security paradigm would involve both legal and constitutional reforms, as well as an attempt to change public perceptions about the efficacy of security measures and the everyday importance of basic rights and liberties. What is needed, then, is a new form of politics which directly confronts the drive to securitization.

At a minimum, much, if not all, of the counterterrorism legislation that has been implemented since 9/11, as well as before, must be repealed. The scrapping of the Patriot Act, the UK and Australian anti-terrorist bills and other pieces of draconian legislation would be a basic first step in countering the authoritarian tendencies of contemporary democracies. This would mean ending preventative detention and limiting the power of police and security services to arrest, arbitrarily search and spy on citizens and non-citizens. Guantanamo Bay and other more secretive places of detention must be closed down and the activities of security and intelligence services subject to much greater judicial oversight and democratic scrutiny. The civil liberties and democratic rights that have been taken away by this recent legislation must be fully restored: the right to trial by jury and due process, the right to freely assemble and protest, the right to free political speech (even if this might involve statements in support of terrorism), the right to silence, the right to greater privacy, the right to move and associate freely and so on. In effect, what is needed is a wholesale dismantling of the legal infrastructure that supports the security paradigm as well as the development in its place of a system of laws that enhance individual and democratic rights and freedoms, and check and constrain the power of the executive. The fact that these rights and liberties sound almost quaint today shows how far removed we are from what was once considered the norm in liberal democracies.

While these legal and political reforms sound radical, almost utopian, in the present climate, they are also in some senses 'conservative': they are about restoring what has been taken away; reintroducing, in a formal legal sense, a situation that previously existed and which was seen as a fundamental part of liberal democratic polity. Of course, one should not romanticize pre-9/11 liberal democracies – in the past they have been characterized by all sorts of rights violations and abuses of power. However, the problem today is that transgressions of liberal democratic rules have become normalized and institutionalized. We have suggested that 'actually existing' liberal democracies are a long way removed from their 'ideal type'; and that they are in the process of transforming themselves into post/non-liberal regimes that have more in common with the authoritarian police states that they claim to distinguish themselves from.

Most standard definitions of liberal democracy list a number of key features, in the absence of which a particular political system can no longer be defined as such. David Beetham lists five main characteristics: (1) Freedoms of expression, movement and association, and legal and constitutional protections of individual rights, particularly the individual rights which also foster democratic participation, such as the right to meet collectively, to have access to information, to persuade others; in other words, 'individual rights which are necessary to secure popular control over the process of collective decision-making on an ongoing basis'. (2) The institutional separation of powers, without which the rule of law – which may guarantee the protection of individual rights, the right to fair trial and due process, the accountability to law of public officials, and the means of legal redress against abuses of office – would be meaningless. (3) A popularly elected representative assembly with powers to scrutinize the executive. (4) The principle of the limited state and the separation of the public and private – that is, an autonomous civil society. (5) An epistemological pluralism – the premise that there is no one single truth that defines society, and that the notion of the public good is contingent and defined by the people, not by a particular agent who claims access to a superior knowledge.[1]

If one looks at Western democracies today one sees that most of these institutional features have been seriously undermined in one way or another. (1) Freedoms of expression, movement, association and people's free access to information have been severely curtailed by various pieces of counterterrorist legislation, increased surveillance, restrictions on protests, as well as by continual invocations by governments of official secrecy and executive privilege on the grounds of 'national security'. (2 & 3) Even in the country with the most formalized system of the separation of powers in the world, the US Congress and the Supreme Court have recently either failed, or have been unwilling, to exercise sufficient constraint and scrutiny over the Bush administration and to protect citizens' rights and legal protections. This is to say nothing, of course, about the more endemic lack of representation, corruption and big money influence that characterizes the representative institutions of the US and other countries.[2] (4) In their post-9/11 security mode, states in Western societies have become anything but limited: they have expanded exponentially in size, cost, power and intrusiveness, creating new agencies and bureaucracies – such as the Department of Homeland Security – with unprecedented powers to spy on citizens and detain them without charge. Indeed, intrusions into private life and personal communication and associations have become so extensive and widespread as to place in jeopardy the very distinction between public and private. Michael Hardt speaks here of a 'post-civil' condition characterized by a blurring or folding of the public and private spheres. The public sphere has become increasingly privatized, with the private ownership and management of what were once public institutions and services; and on the other hand, the private sphere has become subjected to a kind of continual public surveillance. The spaces for personal privacy and autonomy have become fewer, with most transactions and communications coming under various forms of surveillance.[3] The folding of the public and private sphere would eventually produce a new social space in which one is no longer a citizen with rights and liberties (this liberal paradigm applied only when there was an autonomous civil society) but rather a citizen whose movements must be continually controlled and monitored, and whose identity must be continuously verified. Moreover, the paradox of the modern *neoliberal* Leviathan is that while the state downsizes itself – privatizing social services, cutting social welfare spending, deregulating markets and giving tax cuts to the wealthy – it expands ever more in the area of security and war making. We shall return to this question of neoliberalism later in the chapter, but it is clear that the idea of the limited state and an autonomous civil society are no longer clearly identifiable characteristics of contemporary post-liberal regimes. (5) Lastly, even the principle of epistemological pluralism has been to some extent eroded: the influence of the religious Right over the Bush Administration, the continual invoking by leaders like Bush and Blair of God's will to justify failed policies in Iraq, and their quasi-religious, Manichean good and evil world view which led to such disasters, all suggest that a new kind of political theology has to some extent displaced the formal secularism and pluralism of liberal societies. If religious authority supplements political authority, if certain political leaders claim moral authority and legitimacy for their actions from God rather than from the people, then arbitrary power and unchecked sovereignty become the new 'truth' of liberal democracies.

So to claw back fundamental rights and liberties that have been lost, to insist once again on previously accepted checks and limitations on government power, to defend the principle of the separation of Church and State, is simply to demand – no more, no less – that liberal democracies in some measure live up to their name, that they do not openly violate their own principles, that they conform, in an institutional, legal sense, to a reasonably coherent picture of what a liberal democracy is supposed to look like.

Moreover, there is already some pressure – albeit narrow in scope and nowhere near extensive enough – to limit some of the security measures that have recently been implemented: for instance, recent rulings by the US Supreme Court against the Bush Administration's military tribunals and against its exemption of Guantanamo detainees from US law;[4] or the parliamentary defeat of the Blair government's proposal in 2005 to extend the period of detention for terrorist suspects; or lawsuits brought by the ACLU against the Department of Homeland Security over its use of telephone wiretaps on US citizens without court approval. While these are limited moves, they are nevertheless signs of an increasing scepticism about the security paradigm; an attempt – half-hearted, piecemeal and perhaps ultimately futile – but nevertheless an *attempt* to curb some of its excesses. The fact that such moves are vigorously opposed by governments and security agencies highlights the political stakes involved in even the most limited questioning of the security paradigm.[5]

However, while there are moves from certain legal and political sectors to limit the security machine, one also needs to acknowledge that there may not be the same impetus from democratic majorities. It would seem that many people in Western societies are either unconcerned about intensified security measures and the loss of civil liberties (or if they are concerned, are not concerned enough to do anything about it) or even support these measures. Most opinion polls conducted in recent years appear to suggest that a majority of people are sufficiently worried about terrorism (along with illegal immigration, crime etc) to regard these measures as justified in the current climate. Whether or not this is due to government and media manipulation of public opinion, it still leaves us with the problem of largely complacent democratic majorities who may be resistant to the reforms proposed earlier, or who may be hostile to the rights of minorities. To simply propose a set of reforms – as limited as they are – is not enough; there must be some explanation of how a new kind of political culture can be created which values freedom, minority rights and a plurality of forms of life. To simply point out the ineffectiveness of counterterrorism measures, the threat they pose to individual freedom and the injustice they do to ethnic minorities who are commonly their targets (although they ultimately affect everyone) does not necessarily get around this problem. To assume, for instance, that perceptions can be changed and popular prejudices dislodged through rational debate, neglects the power of fear and insecurity in shaping those perceptions, as well as the psychological attachment to modes of prejudice and intolerance and the desire for authority.

One part – only a part, but a vital part – of resistance to the rising tide of authoritarianism is a reconceptualization of democratic practice as something involving sustained political participation, inclusiveness and equality. In this sense, the practical reforms proposed earlier would be part of a much broader project of re-establishing democracy. We shall return to this question later. Yet it is clear at this point that without basic rights to protest, to associate freely, to communicate and speak without restriction, to circulate information freely, there exists only the shadow of democracy. In this sense, to demand the restoration of democratic and liberal rights is not *simply* to demand narrow institutional and legal reforms but to engage in an ongoing process of democratization.

Hand in hand with this rethinking of democracy is a radical critique of the very concept of security, and perhaps the development of a new 'politics of anti-security'. Central to the politics of anti-security is a rejection of even the goal of striking a balance between security on the one hand and freedom and democracy on the other. In any such balance, it must be democracy and freedom which gives way to security. As we have suggested, behind the very idea of achieving such a balance lies a growing authoritarianism. A political discourse of anti-security would seek not only to highlight the ineffectiveness, immanent violence and danger of securitization, but also question the very language of security. The goal is to invent a form of politics which is no longer attached to the signifier of 'security' – which no longer takes security as its central prerogative and motif. The central imperative of governance, on such a view, is not to discover a compromise between ensuring the security of citizens and the normal operations of an open democracy (as if these are commensurable values subject to a process of optimization), but to protect democratic spaces by *protecting democratic spaces*. The signifier of 'security' may be replaced to a large extent by that of 'risk'. Risk is intrinsic to democracy, and the risks of living in a democracy are not countered by negating the democratic part of the equation. (Risks *in* a democracy must be sharply distinguished from risks *to* a democracy: a conflation which is at the core of most authoritarian responses to terrorism.) To reject the language of security is at the same time to affirm the element of risk, vulnerability and contingency that is central to any coherent concept of democracy. It is to engage in a kind of political wager, to *risk* democracy – and indeed, to risk *more* democracy and *more* freedom in the face of the spectre of terrorism. In other words, if – as Ignatieff himself recognizes – the aim of the terrorists is to destroy democracy in the West, or, more precisely, to make us destroy our own democracy through increased securitization, then one important way to confront the challenge posed by terrorism is not to work for more security, but for more democracy, more individual freedom and greater levels of political and economic equality.

As Mark Neocleous says, 'The genuinely radical position now requires us to be *against* security ... '.[6] While mainstream politics is increasingly obsessed with questions of national and internal security, a more radical position would be to develop a form of politics which is articulated around alternative questions – such as equality and autonomy. This kind of political intervention seems audacious in the current climate; yet it is precisely this sort of political audacity that is needed right now, something that breaks the formal ideological consensus around 'security' that has gripped both sides of the political spectrum. Indeed, there are already signs of resistance at the grass roots level to the security paradigm: perhaps as they are coming to realize that they are the true targets of 'security', activists, ethnic minorities, civil liberties groups and anti-globalization protesters have mobilized, in different contexts, to challenge the excesses of the security state. Indeed, it is only through the vigorous reassertion and expansion of democratic accountability, fundamental rights and freedoms and the rule of law domestically and internationally, that the principle of politics can prevail over that of violence.

Reining in empire

In the book, we have pointed to a link between the internal restriction of freedom and democracy and external violence and aggression. In particular, as commentators like Kaplan and Giroux have shown, the growing authoritarianism in the US is simply the other side of its outward aggression and its unfolding imperial project.[7] Indeed, there have been numerous critiques of US imperialism and militarism in recent times – most notably from public intellectuals like Noam Chomsky, as well as Chalmers Johnson, Andrew Bacevic, Arundhati Roy and Tariq Ali and many others. For instance, Chomsky for many years has been describing the hypocrisy, inconsistency, brutality and naked self-interest that has driven US foreign policy, arguing that the US increasingly resembles a failed state whose activities place its own citizens at greater risk of terrorism.[8] Indeed, he suggests that if the US was actually serious about guaranteeing the security of its citizens it would dramatically reverse the current course of its foreign policy and implement a series of what he sees as relatively 'conservative' measures aimed at fostering a more just international order:

> In addition to the proposals that should be familiar about dealing with the crises that reach to the level of survival, a few simple suggestions for the United States have already been mentioned: (1) accept the

jurisdiction of the International Criminal Court and World Court; (2) sign and carry forward the Kyoto protocols; (3) let the UN take the lead in international crises....(4) rely on diplomatic and economic measures rather than military ones in confronting terror; (5) keep to the traditional interpretation of the U.N charter; (6) give up the Security Council veto and have a 'decent respect for the opinion of mankind,'...(7) cut back sharply on military spending and sharply increase social spending.[9]

It is at least questionable to say, as Chomsky does, that 'these are very conservative suggestions; they appear to be the opinions of the majority of the US population, in most cases, the overwhelming majority.'[10] Chomsky seems to think that the majority of US citizens are with him, share his views and have been with him all along. If so, Chomsky is almost certainly mistaken. By assuming that the majority are in agreement with his views, he has avoided the need to confront the deeply conservative and prejudicial reflexes of this majority as it is constituted in the current political environment. As Chomsky himself says, such reforms are linked to the question of 'democracy promotion at home'. In other words, as we have suggested, reigning in the aggressive and imperialist drives of US foreign policy – drives which do indeed place US citizens and citizens of other countries, at great danger – depends upon a radical reconfiguration of domestic democratic politics.

Furthermore, these imperialist drives must be checked not only domestically but also internationally. To address the problem of imperialism today requires fundamental changes to the international system, with the goal of making the international system more just and democratic. Of course, this would depend on 'the sort of "Copernican transformation" on the part of US leaders that Georges Bataille called for in 1949, when the world was trading in a World War for the Cold War'.[11] That of course never came about. The end of the Cold War presented another opportunity for a radical change in political outlook. Arguably, the current state of intolerable US domination, along with curtailment of civil liberties, lack of political representation and the like, presents yet another chance for the kind of radical shift in institution, practice and discourse required to prevent the slide into a new kind of global political despotism and violence.

International human rights

Because the problem of terrorism is so closely interlinked with that of US imperial hegemony, as well as to more fundamental failings in the international system and the inequalities generated by capitalist globalization, a crucial aspect of any response to both terrorism and the 'war on terror' must involve significant institutional changes to the international order. Among these would be the development of a more robust and enforceable infrastructure of international law and human rights norms, based on – but not limited to – already existing legal and human rights conventions. For instance, the Universal Declaration of Human Rights (1948) provides a comprehensive framework of individual and collective political, social, cultural and economic rights, which could serve as a basis for major institutional reforms – the sorts of reforms that for a long time have been called for by numerous NGOs and international human rights groups.

There are, of course, a myriad of problems with the idea of an international human rights regime, not least of which are objections, on the grounds of cultural difference, to the presumed universality of human rights. Many around the world see human rights as a Western conception and mode of politics that is being imposed upon them and yet which is alien to them. They have a point. However, perhaps the objection here is more to do with the inconsistency and hypocrisy of Western governments than it is about universal validity of certain rights. That is to say, the major obstacle to the legitimacy of human rights around the world is that the Western governments who preach human rights to the rest of world – say to Iraq (prior to the invasion), Zimbabwe and China – themselves transgress and violate these rights in all sorts of ways, perversely in the very name of applying them. Robert Mugabe (Zimbabwe) is absolutely right that the governments of the US, the UK and Australia are incapable of lecturing him on issues of human rights. In operating offshore detention camps, torturing detainees, showing a reckless disregard for civilian lives (and rights), by launching illegal and illegitimate wars, as well as by supporting certain strategically important, yet repressive, regimes, certain Western governments, led by the US, demonstrate to the rest of the world that their claims to uphold human rights cannot be taken seriously, that they are merely ideological mystifications barely concealing the self-interest, aggression and obsequious servility which in reality drives their foreign policy. It is little wonder, then, that the human rights language propounded by Western leaders is met with cynicism and incredulity around the world:[12] in using the supposed introduction of human rights to the Iraqi people as a fallback justification for bringing devastation to that country (after the falsity of the WMD justification was exposed), while sadistically humiliating detainees in one of Saddam's former prisons and bombing Fallujah with massive civilian casualties, the US has twisted and perverted the discourse of human rights beyond all recognition. As Nietzsche believed, behind claims to universal moral values there is often concealed a particular will to power and domination, as well as a desire for revenge.[13] In the case of the US, claims to uphold human rights and to spread democracy concealed an imperial drive to domination, supplemented by a desire for revenge for the psychic humiliation of 9/11.

Yet perhaps the response to this should not be to abandon the whole idea of universal human rights but, precisely, to *universalize* it – to take its universality seriously. In other words, human rights norms and sanctions should be concretely and consistently applied to everyone, not just to non-Western countries. The discourse of human rights should be no longer monopolized by Western governments, who define the terms of these rights for the rest of the world while at the same time violating and transgressing them. A move to genuinely universalize human rights would involve giving more support – political, institutional and financial – to international legal bodies such as the International Criminal Court (ICC) and the International Court of Justice, as well as to transnational human rights organizations. The current situation where the US backs international war crimes tribunals in their prosecution of Serbian war criminals, while at the same time exempting its own personnel from their jurisdiction, is intolerable: while it continues, the idea of an international human rights regime will have no credibility. The very idea of American exceptionalism, which ideologically underpins its imperialistic foreign policy, must be challenged at all levels by international legal institutions, governments and activist networks. There are many examples of this: international anti-war protests and protests against Guantanamo Bay; the activities of numerous human rights and civil liberties organizations, both within and outside the US and UK; as well as moves to bring criminal cases against high profile members of the Bush administration (including Bush himself) for war crimes and crimes against humanity – cases which have been filed by prosecutors in various courts around the world, for instance Germany and the Netherlands.[14] Such cases have perhaps more symbolic importance than anything else at the moment, but they are nevertheless concrete attempts to demonstrate the universal jurisdiction of human rights and the rule of law. Even the idea that those in power can be held legally accountable for their actions, anywhere and by any court, and that national borders do not mean legal immunity, is a powerful symbolic challenge (and may one day prove a *real* challenge) to the sovereignty of governments and their propensity to ignore human rights norms and international law. While the current international order is still based on the hegemony of nation states, there is an emerging conception of international justice which transcends national borders and which increasingly constitutes a kind of counter-sovereignty. Indeed, these legal cases are effective in exposing the inconsistency and hypocrisy of the US and other Western governments by highlighting the gap that exists between their formal pronouncements about the universality of human rights and the exceptionalism and national interests which determine their policies. The argument here, then, is simply to take the promise of universal human rights and international justice at face value in an almost naive way, beyond any consideration of realpolitik: in other words, to apply these laws and rights consistently, *everywhere* – in Palestine, in Iran, in Saudi Arabia, in the US and UK; to apply the same standards of impartial justice, for instance, to both non-state terrorist organizations and to national governments; and to campaign for legal, economic and political sanctions against actors who violate these principles. This sort of rigorous application of international law and human rights norms would not only act as a check on imperialist foreign policy (as well as domestic security policy), but may even deprive terrorism of some of the oxygen of resentment and humiliation upon which it thrives.

Aside from these questions relating to the consistency of the application of human rights, other questions emerge around their ontological foundations as well as their actual content. Here Wendy Brown, in a critique of Ignatieff's defence of human rights, provides a useful deconstruction of their proclaimed minimalism.[15] In other words, many liberal advocates of human rights – including Ignatieff – claim that rights are in a sense non-political, that they simply have the virtue of protecting human life from suffering and state oppression. Of course, if they do this, they are worth fighting for. But Brown detects behind this supposed neutrality and minimalism, a broader political and moral project to promote hegemony of liberal capitalism and to impose it on other parts of the world. This underlying ideological perspective – once again a false universality behind which lies the assertion of a particular position of power – can be found in various slippages, blind spots and hidden assumptions that Brown exposes in Ignatieff's argument. For instance, his claim that human rights are a form of individual empowerment, firstly, obscures the question of the precisely disempowering effects of Western military-style human rights interventions, which are often a guise for the imposition of US imperial power; and, secondly, neglects and, indeed, wards off questions of *collective* empowerment and autonomy. In other words, because most articulations of human rights are based on the individual as the bearer of those rights, they privilege a liberal individualism which is suspicious of any idea of collective politics. Moreover, Ignatieff's belief that basic human rights can serve as a foundation on which people can improve their social and economic conditions chimes in with a liberal claim about the efficacy of the free market based on these rights – especially property rights – in promoting the economic well-being of people. In this conceptualization, economic and social rights are seen as secondary in importance to liberal political rights – and indeed, as Brown shows, Ignatieff warns against the expansion or 'inflation' of the language of rights into other (social and economic areas) as something that undermines the legitimacy of 'core rights'.[16] Recall from our argument in the previous chapter that Ignatieff defends even the narrow core only when it suits.

In opposition to this circumscription of human rights to narrow, negative political and legal rights (although as we have said, these are in themselves extremely important and should be defended) we would argue for a much broader conceptualization of rights. To seek to universalize human rights means not only to apply them consistently, but also to see the concept of right as a broad conceptual tool at work in political discourse. The 'inflation' of rights must always be a possible achievement of political struggle. There is no reason why human rights cannot also mean economic rights; for instance, the rights to the collective ownership of land and resources which can be claimed by indigenous people around the world.[17] It is precisely this radical reassertion of rights – in which rights claims exceed and transform the narrow terms of conventional liberal discourse – that highlights the limited and disingenuous nature of Ignatieff's liberal humanitarianism. Human rights mean little unless they can also be understood as economic and social rights; human rights mean little unless they can be asserted against US imperial domination which uses them as its ideological mantle; human rights mean little unless they genuinely empower both individuals and collectives, rather than constructing them as depoliticized subjects in need of humanitarian–military intervention by Western powers. It is here, perhaps, that Brown is correct to suggest that in its current articulation, the international human rights project – certainly in the form proposed by those such as Ignatieff – is insufficient, and that such a project should be transformed into a much broader struggle for emancipation and global justice:

> If the global problem today is defined as terrible human suffering consequent to limited individual rights against abusive state powers, then human rights might be the best tactic against this problem. But if it is diagnosed as the relatively unchecked globalization of capital, postcolonial political deformations, and superpower imperialism combining

to disenfranchise peoples in many parts of the first, second and third worlds from the prospects of self-governance to a degree historically unparalleled in modernity, other kinds of political projects, including international justice projects, may offer a more appropriate and far-reaching remedy for injustice defined as suffering and as systematic disenfranchisement from collaborative self-governance.[18]

Global justice and public legitimacy: Counteracting violence

Of course, even the most limited proposals for a universal human rights regime depend upon the development of an international legal structure which to a certain extent supersedes national governments and which has real powers of enforcement.[19] This cosmopolitan vision of a just global order goes back to Kant's idea of a federation of republics, and yet it has historically foundered on the rock of national sovereignty. We should therefore not be too sanguine about the possibilities of such an order emerging now, especially at a time when US unilateralism and exceptionalism seem to have overridden even limited attempts to apply international law. Yet this sort of cosmopolitan order, while not in itself sufficient, would certainly be more normatively desirable than the current situation, as well as being a much more effective antidote to terrorism. In challenging the state-based response to the 9/11 attacks, Daniele Archibugi and Iris Marion Young call for an alternative strategy to combat terrorism, based on the international rule of law, one that would have involved criminal prosecutions and police actions against individuals, rather than state-based military aggression against other states like Afghanistan and Iraq. In doing so, they outline a certain vision of a 'just and democratic global governance' based on the following proposals: (1) legitimizing and strengthening international institutions, such as the UN, which should also be reformed to make it more democratic and effective; (2) coordinating law enforcement and intelligence gathering institutions across the world; (3) increasing financial regulation, in order to cut off the cash flow to terrorist organizations; (4) using international courts to prosecute terrorists; and (5) narrowing global inequalities.[20]

In the present climate such proposals might seem unlikely to succeed; however, many have highlighted deeper tendencies inherent within globalization which point to the future possibility of a more cosmopolitan order and new kinds of global institutions.[21] One of these tendencies is the emergence of the idea of a global civil society.

The proliferation and activities of transnational organizations, social movements and activist networks suggest a new form of politics which is no longer limited to the nation state model and which questions the sovereignty of national governments in the name of a more universal conception of justice and human rights.[22] Such movements and organizations work both with and against national governments and institutions, applying pressure, campaigning, protesting and drawing international attention to their abuses. Cosmopolitan politics must not be based only on global institutions and legal structures, but on a certain interaction – and even an antagonism – between these institutions and transnational social movements, in particular movements that campaign for greater global democracy, inclusiveness and economic and social justice. Indeed, a neoliberal cosmopolitan global order, based on borderless free market exchanges, in which global institutions exist primarily to enforce contracts and guarantee property rights, would likely be more unjust, viciously unequal, violent and unstable than the current one.[23] Debates over what form globalization should take will become more pronounced in years to come and therefore the role of activists in proposing and fighting for more democratic and egalitarian conceptions of globalization will become increasingly important.[24]

One of the central questions here is whether any form of global governance can be legitimized – whether it can appear legitimate in the eyes of the people, whose understanding of political participation and democratic acceptability is based on the nation state model. In other words, can a cosmopolitan political order foster notions of democratic citizenship, acceptability and even loyalty that are just as compelling as those fostered by the nation state? Given people's attachment to a national identity – an attachment which can promote nationalist forms of politics, driven by prejudice, racism and hatred of the Other – such a cosmopolitan identification often seems difficult to imagine. Here, though, Jürgen Habermas has argued that the pressures of economic globalization are leading to what he calls a post-national condition, in which the nation state is no longer the primary arena of economic decision making, and in which new international and transnational institutions are displacing many of its traditional functions. The problem for Habermas is therefore one of political legitimation and identification:

(a) How can we envision the democratic legitimation of decisions beyond the nation-state? And (b), what are the conditions for a transformed self-understanding of global actors in which states and supranational regimes begin to see themselves as members of a community, who have no choice but to consider one another's interests mutually, and to perceive general interests?[25]

Here Habermas proposes the idea of 'constitutional patriotism' as an answer to these questions: people would increasingly affiliate themselves no longer with a national identity or particular ethnicity, but rather with a set of rules, norms and procedures that derive from a shared liberal culture of rights. Indeed, this form of identification – from which would derive a new form of democratic legitimacy – will become inevitable in societies that are increasingly multi-ethnic and plural, and in a global order which is increasingly fragmented: 'To the degree that this decoupling of political culture from majority culture succeeds, the solidarity of citizens is shifted onto the more abstract foundation of a "constitutional patriotism"'.[26]

There are a number of problems, however, with this attempt to found a post-national order on this new model of legitimacy.[27] Firstly, it assumes the existence of a shared liberal culture, including agreement about the discursive rules of deliberation aimed at reaching a rational consensus. Here Habermas invokes the Kantian idea of the public use of reason:

> Accordingly, the democratic procedure no longer draws its legitimizing force only, indeed not even predominantly, from political participation and the expression of political will, but rather from the general accessibility of a deliberative process whose structure grounds an expectation of rationally acceptable results.[28]

Without wanting to discount the importance of rational public debate and deliberation (which are indeed essential in developing critical responses to the politics of authoritarianism and imperialism, and to promoting more democratic forms of globalization) Habermas' model of rational communication seriously underestimates the pervasive effects of the unconscious psychological dimensions that we have been emphasizing in this book. It is not that Habermas denies the existence of sources of irrationalism, but that he sees them merely as empirical conditions interfering with processes of otherwise rational debate; they are a kind of noise or distortion overlaying an intact signal. We see them as constitutive of the terms of much of political debate, and a commitment to deliberation under constraints of rational deliberative norms is no kind of adequate response to this fact. Rational norms of discourse can't operate as *regulative* ideals' of political debate because, by themselves, they lack the capacity to *regulate*. People's visceral attachments to 'irrational' prejudices, nationalism, racism and religious fundamentalism are often intractable and cannot be dislodged simply through rational debate. To claim that they can is to succumb, as we have suggested, to a liberal illusion. Consider the task of ameliorating racist prejudice and its destructive, often hidden, influence on the political violence. We need to recognize that prejudice has work to do, work in defence of the ego. Prejudices are not removed through enlightened, rational debate; rather, we find our way out of them – to the extent that we do – by undoing the need for this work, by ameliorating the social triggers of ego threat and by furnishing less destructive and less prejudicial (if also, perhaps, less pleasure-driven) avenues of ego defence. As we suggested in our discussion of prejudice in Chapter 2, the basic – all but universal – response to 9/11 in the US was one of affront: a deeply defensive reaction to the accusation and contempt signified by the 9/11 attacks. The US was always going to do something to defend its narcissistic ego construction in the face of this affront. Understanding this means that positive responses from critics of US unilateralism – such as Habermas himself – ought not to consist merely in rational argument about the rights and wrongs of war. It is remarkable how easily the arguments were won by the critics of the war in the lead-up to the 2003 invasion and subjugation of Iraq. And it is remarkable how little this mattered in the US political environment of 2002–3. In addition to the refutation of a march to war, what was needed were compelling suggestions for alternative strategies of ego defence: how the construction of US innocence and good will could be reasserted in the face of the anger and hostility of the vast preponderance of people in the Islamic world. It is difficult for leftist critics to perform this task because we see all too clearly that the narcissistic construction of the US self image is a self-serving delusion, a cover for the terrible work of empire. Still, we have a greater responsibility than speaking the truth to power (though of course we have that responsibility too).

This is why it is not sufficient to see, as Habermas does, terrorism and other forms of political violence, as simply instances of a breakdown or failure of rational communication. For Habermas,

> conflicts arise from a distortion in communication, from misunderstanding and incomprehension, from insincerity and deception.... The spiral of violence begins as a spiral of distorted communication that leads through the spiral of uncontrolled reciprocal mistrust, to the breakdown of communication. If violence thus begins with

a distortion in communication, after it has erupted it is possible to know what has gone wrong and what needs to be repaired.[29]

The problem with this view is that it assumes that a situation of rational, undistorted communication is the norm, and that modes of violence – such as those driven by fundamentalist terrorism, racism and nationalism – can be simply resolved by returning to the accepted rules of discourse. While conflicts may ensue from miscommunication and distortion, what this view ignores is the nature and source of such distortions – which derive from modes of ego defence and other psychological mechanisms – and the passions which make these miscommunications intractable and often insurmountable. They cannot necessarily be explained through a lack of access to truth; nor can they be overcome by making the facts available. Habermas is right, of course, to point out other background factors behind terrorism – such as poverty, economic dislocation caused by globalization and the humiliation of other people – but he is wrong to suggest that the problem of political violence, including terrorism, can be solved entirely through rational communication and the assertion of intersubjectively shared ethical norms.

The question of democracy

So far in this chapter we have set up a series of ameliorative responses to the 'war on terror' and criticized certain overly sanguine and naive interpretations of them. We have not suggested, even in outline, the means by which even modest goals might be brought about. This is no accident. The main thrust of this book has been to uncover the depth of the problems confronting contemporary politics: the robustness of the logic of securitization (Chapter 1); the profound incorrigibility of sources of violence (Chapter 2); the inevitable fragility of democratic discourse, its vulnerability to mendacity, lies and manipulative spin, its vulnerability to prejudicial distortion and discursive violence (Chapters 2 and 3); the resourcefulness of sovereignty, its capacity to respond to challenges and to invent challenges for purposes of its own, its constitutive power to declare a state of exception (Chapter 4); the sturdy and multiply reinforced nature of American Empire (Chapter 5). To suggest an easy exit route from this constellation of challenges would be intellectually dishonest. Just this kind of dishonesty is on display in Ignatieff's attempt at a liberal political ethics (Chapter 6). Nonetheless, any account of change for the better must reckon with the democratic potential of contemporary politics. There is no bringing about change for the better without widespread political will to change; and there is no bringing about widespread political will to change without reinvigorating, or indeed re-establishing, the potential of democracy to bring about a better world. (The re-establishment of democracy is, of course, also a central feature *of* such a world.)

Dismantling the security paradigm, for instance, depends upon the political will of democratic majorities and yet undoing the politics of securitization is necessary for the re-establishment of democracy. Constraining the imperial drives of the US is crucial, and this is also something which in part depends on the will of the electorate in that country. Despite the unpopularity of the war and the unpopularity experienced by the Bush administration generally in the final stages of its tenure, there is little evidence to suggest the political impetus for a dramatic change in direction of US foreign policy. Moreover, checking and limiting the power of the US also depends upon a restructuring of the international system, whether through a more robust and consistent human rights regime or by some other cosmopolitan form of governance. Yet as we have suggested, for human rights to have full significance today they must not only be applied consistently, but collective political projects of equality, power sharing and economic justice must be represented as human rights issues. Global governance, on the other hand, must work hand in hand with mechanisms of democratic accountability and legitimacy, which poses the question of political community, whether it is constituted trans-nationally or remains within the framework of the nation state. Here questions arise about how such a community is sustained, how its limits are constituted and how cosmopolitanism is to be reconciled with the nationalist orientation of domestic political constituencies. We have argued that the idea of liberal constitutionality based on intersubjectively shared rational norms of communication does not adequately answer these questions.

All these questions and problems require us to take stock of contemporary democratic politics: its limitations, its fragility and its potential. Addressing the democratic deficit implicit in a politics most unusual does not automatically address all the failures and injustices of this politics – the US's treatment of non-citizen temporary residents, for example, is not simply an issue *of* democracy, though it is clearly an issue *for* democracy. Any sort of fundamental change to existing political practices and policies must take place to some extent or another at the level of domestic democratic politics. Yet the current state of politics in the West – its growing authoritarianism, its imperial excesses, its internal and external violence, its endemic political alienation – amounts to a debilitation of democratic politics. The savage irony of this, of course, is that the 'war on terror' is being fought in the name of democracy: the logic of security is legitimized through the claim that it protects our 'democratic way of life'; and the hegemony and violence of the US imperial project takes the spreading of democracy as its principal ideological justification.

We are witnessing a certain crisis of legitimacy for Western democracies. This democratic malaise can be seen in growing voter disinterest and apathy in many Western societies, where political space is constructed through the media and where 'the people' exists in an increasingly virtualized form – as an entity whose 'preferences' are determined, and also constructed, through the simulacra of opinion polls, spin doctoring and media representation.[30] The re-election in 2008 of media tycoon Silvio Berlusconi as Italian prime minister, amidst ongoing allegations of corruption, symbolizes this profound blurring of the line between the media and politics – in this case a politician gets around the problem of media representation by simply *becoming* the media. Democratic politics has for the most part been reduced to the banal level of a reality TV show.

Voter disillusionment and the mediatization of contemporary politics can be seen as symptomatic of a much broader deterioration of democratic political culture: endemic structural problems such as inadequate representation have combined with an ideological convergence (apparent for some time now) between the two sides of politics; massive social and economic inequalities, which in a very real sense translate into political inequalities; the influence of lobbyists and big money special interests on political campaigns and agendas; right up to corruption and vote rigging, as was seen in the notorious US elections in 2000.[31] Indeed, the fact that such a clear case of electoral fraud was met with a sense of complacency on the part of the electorate shows the extent to which democracy and accountability have become undermined. Here, Colin Crouch speaks of 'post-democracy':

> Under this model, while elections certainly exist and can change governments, public electoral debate is a tightly controlled spectacle, managed by rival teams of professionals expert in the techniques of persuasion, and considering a small range of issues selected by those teams. The mass of citizens plays a passive, quiescent, even apathetic part, responding only to the signals given them. Behind this spectacle of the electoral game, politics is really shaped in private by the

interaction between elected governments and elites that overwhelmingly represent business interests.³²

In a sense, citizens are given only the illusion of voting, the illusion of choice. Post-democracy corresponds, according to Crouch, with the decline in political significance of the working class in Western societies, the erosion of the welfare state and the retreat from the idea of social democracy – in other words, with a general crisis of egalitarian politics. Moreover, it harkens back to a pre-democracy – a situation characterized by the domination of certain elites and enormous and growing inequalities in power and wealth. From our perspective, Western liberal democracy is starting to resemble a kind of feudalism in which hierarchies of power and wealth go unchallenged, in which powerful commercial interests dominate the political agenda, in which the workings of the executive become more and more inscrutable and secretive, and in which the gap between political elites and the people perpetually widens. The only role ordinary people have appears to be the symbolic and illusory one of legitimizing – through an increasingly limited franchise and often highly flawed voting systems – the rule of a political elite that has largely converged around a neoliberal consensus.

Neoliberalism

This deracinated democracy should be understood within the context of neoliberalism – an economic orthodoxy and political ideology which has become pervasive in most Western societies, and which has over the past decade become a dominant feature of global capitalism. Neoliberalism ought not to be understood simply as the ideology of the free market, something which advocates privatization of public utilities and services, the deregulation of financial markets and the rolling back of the welfare state. Neoliberalism, according to Brown, can also be understood in a Foucauldian sense as a political rationality and a mode of governmentality, in which are produced new conceptions of politics and subjectivity that are profoundly hostile to democracy. Importantly, neoliberalism is to be distinguished utterly from liberalism – both in terms of its rejection of modern liberalism's inclusion of social democratic and egalitarian policies, as well as its authoritarian tendencies and its very narrow understanding of individual freedom as primarily market freedom. For Brown, neoliberalism is more than simply a withdrawal of the state and the institution of unregulated – or barely regulated – markets; it is something that projects a certain vision of the social and permeates all aspects of society and government policy: 'neoliberalism carries a social analysis which, when deployed as a form of governmentality, reaches from the soul of the citizen-subject to education policy to practices of empire'.[33] In this sense, neoliberalism can be seen as the broad social, political and economic logic which encompasses many of the aspects of post-9/11 politics that we have been analysing in this book. The problems of post-9/11 politics cannot of course be entirely reduced to those generated by neoliberal conceptions of governance, but the pervasiveness and largely uncontested authority of neoliberalism is an important part of the problem: part cause, part symptom, part effect of other symptoms. For this reason, neoliberalism and its relation to democracy deserve specific attention.

According to Brown, neoliberalism's main effects are: (1) a reorganization of political spheres according to a market rationality, in which individual actions, social practices and government policies and decisions are appraised in terms of economic utility and submitted to a cost-benefit analysis; (2) the project of reconstructing institutions according to the dictates, mechanisms and priorities of the market – so that the state becomes an instrument of the market, not simply in the sense that its policies are determined by market prerogatives and interests, but also that its structures and practices now take on the characteristics of the market; (3) a certain moral vision of the individual as a responsible, utility-maximizing citizen-consumer. This is a model of political engagement which is extremely limited and ultimately hostile to the idea of a democratic public space. As Brown says:

> A fully realized neoliberal citizenry would be the opposite of public-minded, indeed it would barely exist as a public. The body-politic ceases to be a body but is, rather, a group of individual entrepreneurs and consumers ... which is, of course, exactly the way voters are addressed in most American campaign discourse.[34]

An examination of the Democratic primary race in the US in the run-up to the 2008 presidential election confirms this view of contemporary politics. With countless millions poured into campaign coffers and with the emphasis on spin and carefully constructed media profiles, both candidates sought to appeal to voters on the basis of image rather than content. They appeared as commodities in the political market, advertising their wares through the media, appealing to the tastes of consumers and hypersensitive to anything that may detract from their image.[35] The 'excitement' generated over the race – deemed by certain people to represent a new 'politics of hope' – was belied by the absence of any real alternative, progressive vision for politics, with the same mantras of 'national security' and 'protecting America's overseas interests', and with the same protestations of religious faith ('God bless America') being trotted out time and time again. From the technocratic perspective of neoliberalism, elections just *are* a kind of market process; one in which votes are a form of consumer purchasing power and political competition is competition for control, preferably monopolistic control, of the market. From a neoliberal perspective, there is no *essential* difference between a race for the White House and commercial competition between rival consumer technologies. Both represent competition for market share in an environment where there can only be one major winner.

The permeation of neoliberal governmentality throughout modern societies generates yet another kind of democratic deficit. It translates much official and authoritative discussion of public policy into the economic and instrumental rationality of cost-benefit analysis and thus erodes the distinction between ethical and political imperatives and economic ones. In this way, the political is either reduced to a kind of consumer behaviour – something to be manipulated, predicted, polled, focus grouped, assuaged, pandered to, competed over – or it is written out of public discourse altogether. The hegemony of neoliberalism has thus played a crucial role in diminishing the democratic capacities of liberal democratic polities. As Brown puts it,

> neoliberal rationality has not caused but rather has facilitated the dismantling of democracy during the current national security crisis. Democratic values and institutions are trumped by a cost-benefit and efficiency rationale for practices ranging from government secrecy, even government lying, to the curtailment of civil liberties.[36]

In other words, what should be seen as moral and political outrages – governments lying to their own people about reasons for going to war, undermining their civil liberties, denying access to information and so on – tend to be judged, not according to their morality or the extent to which they violate accepted notions of democratic accountability and political freedom, but according to their alleged efficacy and efficiency, to their success in achieving certain quantifiable outcomes. A tendency to efface the political and moral dimensions of public discussion in favour of perceptions of costs and benefits can be seen in domestic US debate over the US occupation of Iraq. What undid the reputation of the Bush Administration in its last term of office was not the political/moral obscenity of its military adventures, but the fact that, in the end, the invasion and occupation of Iraq proved to be bad business (not for Haliburton, perhaps, but as a general enterprise). The war was originally sold to the US population on the basis of a nebulous cost-benefit analysis. The winning argument had this form: we cannot *afford* the risk to security that a rogue-state in possession of weapons of mass destruction represents. This is, at heart, an appeal to technocratic notions of risk management and cost-benefit analysis. Of course, this is not to say that the argument originally *won* in the US because of its appeal to a particular cost-benefit analysis. The cost-benefit analysis – or rather the vague gesturing towards such an analysis – worked as legitimating cover for the real motivators: resentment and a longing for a violent reassertion of power. The neoliberal/technocratic form of debate worked to hide this fact and deprive critics of the discursive framework in which to effectively point it out.

Despite its pervasiveness, neoliberalism is a passionless discourse of technocratic management – on its own it fails to mobilize the overt political support of the masses, relying on much more subtle techniques of microconstitution and management of subjects. This is why the neoliberal project has at times to rely on more visceral forces, such as nationalism, social conservatism and religious fundamentalism. While these are important and dangerous discourses in their own right, they tend to operate today, at least in the West, as a kind of ideological supplement to neoliberalism, as mobilizing populist ideas which shore up support at the political level for the neoliberal project. Neoconservatives invoke a certain fantasy image of a unified community – a national community or a community of religious faith or conservative 'family values' – which is under attack from immigrants, Muslim terrorists, Godless atheists and secularists, 'liberals', the sexually permissive and so on. In doing so they play upon and incite racist and religious prejudices as modes of ego defence against the perceived Other which threatens them. In post-9/11 US politics we therefore see a convergence between neoconservatism and neoliberalism – discourses which are in themselves quite different, but which resonate together and which formed the ideological and political impetus for the policies of the Bush administration.[37]

Contesting neoliberalism: Which way forward for liberal democracy?

It is clear, then, that if democratic politics is to extricate itself from its current authoritarian and militaristic formation, it must find a way of overcoming the discursive hegemony of neoliberalism. This will not be easy; as we have said, neoliberalism not only pervades the political space but draws upon reactionary tendencies and prejudices among the electorate. Neoliberalism also relies on a more general sense of political apathy, generated by what Galbraith saw as a 'culture of contentment'.[38] While it is difficult to dislodge, it is nevertheless possible to resist and indeed reverse many aspects of the neoliberal project. Indeed, there are important signs of resistance to neoliberal hegemony in many parts of the world – particularly in Latin America, where at the level of social movements as well as at the state level, there are numerous and ongoing experiments with collective ownership, land redistribution, renationalization of oil and gas resources and forms of decentralized democratic decision making in which corporate power is challenged through the reinvention of a public, collective space. And it is precisely this notion of the public, democratic space which needs to be reasserted and reinvented in the global North.

To see democracy in this way – that is, in terms of the potency of an egalitarian public democratic space – is to go beyond current narrow understandings of political participation usually associated with liberal democracy. Yet there is no reason why the liberal democratic political model cannot be made to work in more egalitarian ways – indeed this is something that most relatively mainstream democratic theorists have urged both before and after Shumpeter. It is a matter of historical contingency that liberal democracy came to be associated with capitalism. And there is clearly a tension between liberal democratic principles and ideals and the prerogatives of neoliberal capitalism, a tension highlighted by the post-9/11 authoritarian political configuration. Also, many of the rights and liberties associated with liberal democracy – free speech, freedom of assembly – emerged from democratic and socialist struggles during the nineteenth century, which had nothing to do with the interests of industrial capitalism and which in many ways worked against these interests. It should not be forgotten that such far-reaching political change goes hand in hand with considerable social change. Liberal democratic rights and freedoms, as well as the idea of popular sovereignty, can be mobilized in forms of political action against neoliberalism, including political action at the level of formal representative and legislative institutions, as well as at the level of social movements and groups within civil society. This sort of democratic action invokes the idea of a public space which is not determined by economic imperatives, which embodies an autonomous political dimension from which it is possible for new and more egalitarian visions of society to emerge. Moreover, as Chantal Mouffe and others have observed, liberal democracy relies on a creative and constitutive tension between two fundamental principles – the democratic principle of political equality and popular sovereignty, the liberal principle of individual rights and freedoms, the rule of law and checks on the power of government.[39]

While this tension is never fully reconcilable, it opens up the possibility of new forms of politics based on new articulations of freedom and equality. For instance, in challenging the logic of securitization, a radical liberal democratic response might take several forms: to assert fundamental individual rights and liberties as pre-eminent in the face of securitization, even if increased security measures have the support of the majority; or to show also how securitization limits and conflicts with free political participation and therefore with the interests of the majority or how it violates the principle of political equality by unjustly targeting ethnic and religious minorities. The broader point here is that there is something in liberal democracy which exceeds its current articulations and which can work against neoliberalism, neoconservatism, imperialism and political authoritarianism.

The question that remains, however, and which to some extent has haunted this whole discussion, is how to legitimize this liberal democratic vision of a new public space in the eyes of the people, and how to do so in the face of often deep-set prejudices, conservative reflexes, authoritarian tendencies and fundamentalist world views; how to construct an egalitarian and democratic public space in the face of opinions, convictions and beliefs which might be hostile to such a notion. This is really the biggest challenge that we face, and there can be no credible critique of the 'war on terror' unless one engages with this problem. The challenge is therefore not simply to construct a new political space in an institutional sense, but to seek to foster a new kind of political culture or cultures in which authoritarianism, militarism and imperialism (as well as terrorism) are no longer desirable. As we have suggested elsewhere, the solution here cannot be to repress prejudicial and intolerant impulses, but rather to redirect them into alternative, less destructive avenues of expression. We know from psychoanalysis that repression never works perfectly – what is repressed will likely return, often in more violent guises. This is why, for instance, hate speech legislation is ultimately ineffective: not only does it entail restrictions on the freedom of speech, but it also intensifies and heightens the prejudices that motivate it. Moreover, as Butler points out, hate speech legislation gives the state the power over speech itself, the power to determine the impact of certain words – to determine which words and statements are hateful and which are not, thus fixing an injury to a particular speech act.⁴⁰ Hate speech legislation also, we would argue, serves as a guise or veil for state racism: the state restricts certain utterances that are deemed racist or intolerant, while at the same time practicing racial profiling and other forms of discrimination against minorities.⁴¹ Butler's solution to the problem of hate speech is to leave it to civil society to 're-signify' hate speech in less harmful and injurious ways, indeed in ways that produce new meanings and which allow people – who are often the targets of hate speech – to resist their subordination and exclusion: for instance, the way that 'queer' is openly affirmed by gays as an act of resistance, thus inverting the hitherto injurious and discriminatory power of this term. As Butler says, '[t]he word that wounds becomes an instrument of resistance in the redeployment that destroys the prior territory of its operation'.⁴² In the same way, we would argue that a political community should not try to repress prejudicial beliefs, but rather to allow them to be aired, and to work to transform them or at least redirect them in less destructive and violent directions. The deeper problem is not racist utterances or statements justifying terrorism from certain individuals in society, but rather the articulation through state discourses and practices – particularly those directed towards its own minorities, as well as towards many people around the world – of the much more real and devastating racism and terrorism of the state.

Rather than seeking to repress and censor prejudices, one of the aims of the project of creating a new form of democratic politics would be, firstly, to understand prejudices as modes of psychic defence against certain threats and to try to remove or ameliorate some of these threats – for instance, to address threats such as economic insecurity, unemployment and marginalization, and to try to reduce the sense of vulnerability and deracination that these create. It is no accident that it is the dislocated remnants of the working class in our societies, whose livelihoods are threatened by the economic impacts of globalization, who at times turn to racist, nationalist, conservative populist and anti-immigrant forms of politics. Indeed, in the US, Bush has drawn upon this sort of working-class populism – the populism of the 'NASCAR dads' – which often finds expression in patriarchal, conservative and Christian evangelical values, values which are manipulated, incited and channeled into political support for the Republicans. The irony is that it is this conservative political and ideological formation – that which Connolly has referred to as the 'evangelical-capitalist resonance machine'⁴³ – which promotes a big-business agenda at the expense of American workers. However, what is going on here, according to Slavoj Žižek, is an economic class struggle that is distorted and recoded into a cultural war: so that what should be an antagonism between a wealthy business elite and the oppressed and economically marginalized working and underclass, becomes an antagonism between a 'politically correct' liberal elite and a working class which represents conservative, 'family values' (recruited on the side of big business). Žižek describes this paradoxical situation characterizing contemporary American politics,

> the economic class opposition (poor farmers, blue-collar workers versus lawyers, bankers, large companies) is transposed/coded into the opposition of honest hard-working Christian true Americans versus the decadent liberals who drink latte and drive foreign cars, advocate abortion and homosexuality, mock patriotic sacrifice and 'provincial' simple way of life, etc. The enemy is thus perceived as the 'liberal' who, through federal state interventions (from school-busing to ordering the Darwinian evolution and perverse sexual practices to be taught), wants to undermine the authentic American way of life. The main economic interest is therefore to get rid of the strong state which taxes the hard-working population in order to finance its regulatory interventions – the minimal economic program is thus 'less taxes, less regulations'.... From the standard perspective of enlightened rational pursuit of self-interests, the inconsistency of this ideological stance is obvious: the populist conservatives are literally voting themselves into economic ruin. Less taxation and deregulation means more freedom for the big companies that are driving the impoverished farmers out of business; less state intervention means less federal help to small farmers; etc. In the eyes of the U.S. evangelical populists, the state stands for an alien power and, together with UN, is an agent of the Antichrist: it takes away the liberty of the Christian believer, relieving him of the moral responsibility of stewardship, and thus undermines the individualistic morality that makes each of us the architect of our own salvation – how to combine this with the unheard-of explosion of the state apparatuses under Bush? No wonder large corporations are delighted to accept such evangelical attacks on the state, when the state tries to regulate media mergers, to put strictures on energy companies, to strengthen air pollution regulations, to protect wildlife and limit logging in the national parks, etc.[44]

The way to approach this problem is not to retreat further into the bastion of political correctness, so that the gap between progressive values and the working class/underclass widens even further – but rather to try develop a progressive populism: in other words, to recode and change the terms of this 'cultural' opposition in such a way as to reveal the economic antagonism at its heart. Progressives should recognize that populist passions can be mobilized in different directions and in support of different causes, even egalitarian causes; there is no essential link between these passions and political conservatism. Rather than allowing populist passions to be hegemonized by the Republican right, the progressive left can articulate an egalitarian and radical democratic agenda on a more visceral register – and in doing so, show the working and underclass that their true enemy is wealthy business elite who supposedly represents their 'values'. This does not mean, of course, that progressives should simply adopt or pay lip-service to the socially conservative values and symbols that certain sectors of the working class currently rally around – the spectacle of Hillary Clinton attending church groups, trumpeting her conservative credentials, talking tough on national security, examining the Israeli 'security' wall with obvious approval and claiming to defend the interests of 'working people' simply reinforces this conservative position. Rather, the progressive left must try to resignify these populist passions in more egalitarian directions by developing a new political vocabulary and new symbols, in which one equality, freedom and anti-imperialism are located on a more visceral level. Richard Rorty makes a similar claim about the need for the American Left to drop their politically correct elitism and once again try to appeal to and mobilize the working class – yet the solution he proposes amounts to a vapid, empty liberal reformism that centres around a resurrection of American national pride, and which explicitly rules out more radical propositions such as economic egalitarianism and power sharing.[45]

Conditions for the return of democracy

We have been arguing for a new way of representing moral and political imperatives in democratic discourse; we have suggested that such a thing is possible and also necessary if we are to effectively resist the most alarming features of post-9/11 politics. We do not pretend that it is a sufficient response to the challenge of 9/11 politics. First, the causes of this political formation are highly complex. They include historical, political, economic, geographical, demographic, cultural, psychological and institutional factors, as well as brute contingency. The challenges facing contemporary liberal democratic politics are formidable. There is, as we have said, no easy exit route; and the re-establishment of robustly democratic modes of public discourse is no easy exit route. Second, a reinvigoration of democratic discourse is no guarantee that the moral calamities of the 'war on terror' will come to an end. The constitutive risk of democracy is that the popular will may come to be profoundly *undemocratic*. The constitutive risk of *liberal* democracy is that, under even the mildest pressure, the popular will may become profoundly *illiberal*. Opening up spaces of democratic discourse, reinvigorating the discourse of the egalitarian politics, challenging the hegemony of technocratic/neoliberal discourse, promoting the politics of anti-security: none of this eliminates the risk of democracy. Democracy *is* a kind of risk.

And yet the most accessible form of resistance to a politics most unusual lies in this project of reinvigorating democracy by establishing the conditions for open and creative democratic discussion and breaking down the stifling effects of the hegemony of neoliberal discourse.[46] What we can offer at the end of this book on a politics most unusual is a philosophical sketch of the conditions for such an opening of democratic discursive spaces. This ought to be framed, not just as a matter of media reform or of reform of means of public deliberation, but as the re-establishment of democracy itself. Democracy worthy of the name does not consist merely in a system of constitutional arrangements, but in the democratic life of people. We highlight four conditions for the return of democracy.

First, a certain degree of social and economic equality is necessary, not only on grounds of justice, but also as a *precondition* for democracy. Massive inequalities in wealth not only limit democratic participation and translate into political inequalities, but they also generate resentments and prejudices against those who are different. Therefore, as a minimum condition for democracy, there must be mechanisms to redistribute wealth and to guarantee access to vital social goods like housing, healthcare, decent employment, education and a social wage.[47]

Second, democracy cannot be limited to the nation state. Indeed, democracy suggests a form of politics which not only generates diverse practices and institutions within a national space, but outside it as well. To see democratic politics as limited to the nation state constrains it in a number of ways. It imposes certain restrictive prerogatives on democratic debate, such as 'national security' or 'national interest'; as well as tying democracy to a territorial location and to a narrowly defined concept of national citizenship. However, globalization makes the idea of a national democratic space increasingly untenable, and it is now possible to conceive of a reconfiguration of the democratic beyond the territorial limits of the nation state. A nonterritorial democratic space would involve transnational activists and networks of regional actors organizing their activities across national borders. Instead of calling for simply a global adoption of democracy – a call which could, in a perverse way, come from the lips of George W. Bush himself, and which might serve merely as the ideological guise for a ruthless pursuit of imperial interests – what is being invoked here is something far more radical, something which to some extent calls into question the very idea of national sovereignty itself: the non-territorial democratization of global issues.[48]

Third, democracy requires the permanent possibility of dissent. Democracy is a method of taming political conflict: a way of turning enemies into adversaries.[49] (An adversary remains broadly cooperative in the face of political defeat; an enemy does not.) The possibility of dissent – expression of deep disagreement that is not merely indulged or tolerated, but is fully engaged with – is needed to accomplish this transformation of enemies into adversaries. It is also necessary to prevent democratic discourse sliding into stultifying consensus. An easy and unthinking consensus deprives political discourse of the means of reinvention. The permanent possibility of radical dissent is also necessary for maintaining the self-critical capacities of democracy. Without a ready engagement with radical disagreement, and the unhindered flow of information required for informed dissent, profoundly undemocratic and illiberal policies pass all but unobserved. Without the oppositional thoughts of a dissident, vast injustices can come to seem ordinary, no more than the unremarkable consequence of living in a difficult world.

A fourth condition on the successful return of democracy is a culture of pluralism and respect for difference. This is in many ways the deepest philosophical challenge to the possibility of genuine democracy. Democracy, as we have observed, is inherently risky. Democratic *discourse* is inherently risky. It is easily dominated by the loudest, most articulate, most sophistic, most unscrupulous, most bullying members of a discursive community – those *least* interested in the merits of opposing views, those *most* likely to be driven by a prejudicial economy of desire or self-interest. (One thinks of third world participants confronting a literal phalanx of US representatives at trade talks; or the conservative student shouted down and derided in a class dominated by conventionally liberal students.) The usual liberal response to this problem is to propose rule-based, norm-guided procedural principles of discourse. (Habermas's discursive model of procedural democracy is the most prominent example of this.) As we have argued at length in this book, such an approach is naive and unrealistic. There are no procedural rules – no set of action-determining norms – immune to manipulation and exploitation for dishonest purposes. All systems of rules conceal aporia. There is no way of setting up a system of rules, for example, that mandate the adequate coverage of a disputed topic: things are easily left unsaid; people and groups are easily left unrepresented.[50] No practical set of procedural rules for democratic discourse can mandate the participation of all interested parties, let alone guarantee that they won't be deceived, bullied and ignored. In short, no set of rules works in the absence of the good will and judgment required to make them work. Moreover, any set of mandatory procedural rules will exclude those who are in dissent of the rules themselves.

One response to these difficulties is to call for the virtuous transformation of the citizenry. For example, writing about how pluralist or agonistic accounts of democracy deal with the reality of religious conflict, Conolly writes:

> We think that in a world marked by the coexistence of multiple faiths on most politically organized territories, the horizontal relations between faiths require as much attention as the vertical dimension of each. *Expansive pluralism supports the dissemination of general virtues across diverse faiths.* The key, again, is the relational sensibility with which individuals and communities express their faiths and the general ethos through which relations between alternative faiths are negotiated.[51]

The problem is that this call for the dissemination of virtue among the religious is a call for the ethical transformation of the citizenry as a condition of genuine democracy. But what realistic hopes can we have of this? The place to start is with the most problematic and intractable attitude of the democratic spirit: respect for difference. An attitude of respect for difference is fundamental to the success of any democratic discourse that acknowledges and deals with the ineliminability of political conflict. It is the crucial attitude enabling adversaries to remain adversaries.[52] But what are the prospects of such an attitude becoming a pervasive aspect of democratic discourse? Is an ethos of respect for difference even possible? To answer these questions, we need to understand the attitude a little better.

The liberal tradition of political philosophy generally deals with difference by making it a matter of *indifference*. Irreconcilable differences are banished to a private realm of the Good where they remain a matter of public indifference. The trick, however, works neither philosophically nor practically. Political differences run too deep and involve inevitably contested philosophical assumptions. There is no uncontested philosophical ground from which to divide the Good from the Right or to answer the residue of questions left over once the Good is set aside as a matter of political indifference. Under a liberal conception of political life, respect for difference is grounded in respect for privacy. But what options are available for an alternative conception of respect for difference? There are two principal options: grounding respect for difference in an unmediated respect for the Other (i.e. in a basic ethical response to the person of another) or grounding respect for difference in shared values. To set store in the former option is entirely unrealistic. This is to call for the radical ethical transformation of people as a condition of genuine democracy and no such radical transformation is even a remote possibility. This is a naive and psychologically unrealistic hope. We are left, therefore, with an appeal to shared values as a ground for the possibility of an ethics of respect for difference.

On the shared-values conception of respect for difference, the possibility of genuine democratic discourse depends upon a shared background of values: not a shared background of constitutional arrangements, rules of discourse, conceptions of justice, religious commitments, national affiliations and the like, but a shared background of the overarching values of democracy as such. The fundamental values constitutive of democracy divide into those associated with the *legitimacy* of the democratic project and those associated with *justice*. As we mentioned earlier in this chapter, democracy exists in a constitutive tension between the realization of these two values: between, on the one hand, ideas of popular sovereignty, consent, deliberative inclusion and equality of citizenship; and, on the other hand, ideas of the rule of law, the transparency of law, protection of minorities and individuals from the tyranny of government, protection of minorities and individuals from the tyranny of the majority, as well as concerns for the just distribution of social goods. Both aspects of the project of liberal democracy demand our allegiance; both must be realized in a liberal democracy in one way or another. To sacrifice individual freedoms in the service of popular sovereignty, for example, is to already move beyond the bounds of the democratic. However, since each basic value of the democratic project is in perpetual tension with the other, there are many ways of realizing basic democratic values in political practice. Respect for those who differ profoundly in their politics – respect for their opinions, respect for their voice – is based on the realization of this fact. Adversaries remain adversaries because they share, at a very basic level, a conception of the value of the democratic project.

The major enemy of democracy today is not terrorist extremism, but the complacency which comes from a false and shallow consensus about the realization of democratic values. The hard edge of this false consensus is the neoliberal elimination of the political; but it is easy to show how deeply anti-democratic this consensus is, and how little it deserves our respect.

Conclusion: Democracy most unusual

At the current moment, the world suffers both from an excess of 'democracy' as well as from a severe democratic deficit – indeed, these are two sides of the same coin. 'Democracy' is now the only globally acceptable form of government; and, moreover, democracy (along with security) forms the ideological symbol of the West's 'war on terror', even if this is only inconsistently, limitedly and hypocritically applied. However, the 'war on terror' is also a profoundly *undemocratic* war – a war generated by the ailing post-democracies of the West and foisted on a world steeped in violence, poverty and inequality. In this book, we have explored a series of problems and dangers associated with the current post-9/11 political paradigm we find ourselves in: a creeping authoritarianism that goes by the name of 'security'; an infusion into the political space of all sorts of racial and religious prejudices, which fuel the West's contempt for the rest of the world; a political obscurantism and a culture of mendacity, in which people believe the lies of their leaders and where political accountability has been seriously diminished; a violent state of exception, in which sovereign power acts outside the boundaries of domestic and international law; and a ruthless imperialist politics, in which US exceptionalism, aided and abetted by its obsequious allies, rides roughshod over international law, world opinion and human rights norms. Added to this is a world order which is increasingly disordered, and characterized by economic dislocation, inequality, dwindling resources and both state and non-state terrorism.

It should not be imagined that democracy is the answer to all these problems. However, we should nevertheless insist on a certain intrinsic relationship between democracy and the openness of politics. Democracy is the only 'regime' which presupposes a certain openness of the political space, a certain contingency of borders, identities, institutions, structures and practices. Democracy, in this sense, is both a political regime as well as a certain principle of indeterminacy generated around endless articulations of equality and liberty. Here one can invoke Derrida's notion of the 'democracy to come' (democracy *avenir*). Democracy to come can be seen as an unforseen event – an event which comes from the outside, from the future, but at the same time emerges from within the radical potential of democracy itself, urging democracy to live up to its own promise, its own *perfectibility*.[53] Democracy is what cannot be represented, what cannot be satisfied by a number of minimum conditions or embodied in a certain regime – democracy always points to a horizon beyond, to the future; it is always 'to come'. However, this does not mean that we should give up on democracy – on its promise of perfect liberty with perfect equality. On the contrary, it means we should never be satisfied with existing forms taken by democracy and should always be working towards its perfectibility.

As we have shown, while the 'war on terror' seriously endangers democratic politics today, in all sorts of ways it also creates the conditions and opportunities for its rethinking and revitalization.

Notes

1. Beetham, *Democracy and Human Rights*, pp. 34–5.
2. See, for example, S. Overton (2004) 'The Donor Class: Campaign Finance, Democracy and Participation', *Pennsylvania Law Review*, vol. 153, pp. 73–178.
3. M. Hardt (1998) 'The Withering of Civil Society', in (eds) E. Kaufman and K. J. Heller, *Deleuze and Guattari: New Mappings in Politics, Philosophy and Culture* (Minneapolis: University of Minnesota Press), pp. 23–39, p. 37.
4. This has to be balanced by the US Justice department's opinions presented to the US Congress that redefines torture and recommends the Geneva Convention that prohibits torture be overridden in some circumstances.
5. Due to sustained pressure from Republicans, and Bush's threat to veto any bill which did not grant retroactive immunity to telecommunications companies who assisted the administration in its illegal phone taps, the Senate passed the FAA (FISA Amendment Act) which granted the sought – after immunity.
6. See M. Neocleous, 'Against Security', *Radical Philosophy*, vol. 100, pp. 7–15. Cited in Neocleous (2007) 'Security, Liberty and the Myth of Balance: Towards a Critique of Security Politics', *Contemporary Political Theory*, vol. 6, pp. 131–49.
7. See Kaplan, *Violent Belonging and the Question of Empire Today*.
8. See N. Chomsky (2006) *Failed States: The Abuse of Power and the Assault on Democracy* (London and New York: Penguin).
9. Chomsky, *Failed States*, p. 262.
10. Chomsky, *Failed States*, p. 263.
11. G. Achcar (2006) *The Clash of Barbarisms*, trans., P. Drucker (London: SAQI Books), p. 154.

12. This was visibly demonstrated when the Cuban government, in response to the US embassy's attempt to highlight the cause of political prisoners in Cuba, erected large billboards outside the embassy depicting the orange clad, shackled inmates of Guantanamo Bay.
13. F. Nietzsche (1989) *On the Genealogy of Morality*, trans., W. Kaufmann and R. J. Hollingdale (New York: Vintage Books).
14. One such case has been filed by prosecutors in a German court, has been brought by former inmates of Guantanamo against Donald Rumsfeld over their torture and mistreatment. See *Time*, 10 November 2006.http://www.time.com/time/nation/article/0,8599,1557842,00.html (accessed 27 April 2008).
15. W. Brown (2004) '"The Most We Can Hope For...": Human Rights and the Politics of Fatalism', *The South Atlantic Quarterly*, vol. 103: 2/3 (Spring/Summer), pp. 451–63.
16. Ignatieff, quoted in Brown, 'The Most We Can Hope For...', p. 457. See M. Ignatieff (2001) *Human Rights as Politics and Idolatory* (ed.) A. Gutmann (Princeton: Princeton University Press), p. 89.
17. Groups such as MOSOP (Movement for the Survival of the Ogoni People) claimed such rights against foreign oil companies such as Shell, whose predatory commercial activities in the Niger Delta, in collusion with the Nigerian government, led not only to the dispossession of local indigenous people, but also to their political oppression. Indeed, MOSOP used the very language of human rights and the rights against genocide to make their claims for control of the oil resources of that region as well as the right to be protected against cultural, environmental and social and economic degradation. See the Ogoni Bill of Rights (1990), a document which was presented to the Nigerian government, but more importantly, addressed to the international community. http://www.mosop.net/MosopOBR.htm (accessed 2 May 2008).
18. Brown, *The Most We Can Hope For...*, p. 462.
19. Although here it is curious that Ignatieff sees the most effective mechanism of human rights enforcement to be not the international community but the US empire. See *Empire Lite*.
20. D. Archibugi and I. M. Young (2002) 'Envisioning a Global Rule of Law', *Eurozine*, vol. 14: 6. www.eurozine.com (accessed 27 April 2008) (originally published as 'Towards a Global Rule of Law' in *Dissent* 2002, pp. 27–32).
21. See D. Held and A. McGrew (ed.) (2002) *Governing Globalization* (Cambridge: Polity Press).
22. There is an extensive literature on the concept of global civil society and its implications for international relations. See, for instance, M. Kaldor (2003) *Global Civil Society: An Answer to War* (Cambridge: Polity Press); and M. Frost (2002) *Constituting Human Rights: Global Civil Society and the Society of Democratic States* (New York: Routledge). See also Simon Caney, who argues for a cosmopolitan notion of distributive justice in (2006) *Justice Beyond Borders* (Oxford: Oxford University Press).
23. See P. Gowan (2001) 'Neoliberal Cosmopolitanism', *New Left Review*, vol. 11 (Sept–Oct). http://www.newleftreview.org/?view=2347.
24. Proposals, for instance, for a global tax on international financial circulations and currency exchanges (otherwise known as the Tobin Tax) has been one of several concrete measures suggested by transnational activist groups seeking greater global equality and corporate accountability.

25. J. Habermas (2001) *The Postnational Constellation*, trans., and ed. M. Pensky (Cambridge: Polity Press), p. 110.
26. Habermas, *The Postnational Constellation*, p. 74.
27. It is important to clarify that Habermas does not propose a world government as such, but rather a form of transnational and international governance based on a structure like the EU.
28. Habermas, *The Postnational Constellation*, p. 110.
29. Habermas in Borradori, *Philosophy in a Time of Terror*, p. 35.
30. The crucial role that right wing media outlets like Fox news played in Bush's 2000 and 2004 election victories, as well as in selling the Iraq war to the American people, has been well documented. See L. Artz and Y. Kamalipour (eds) (2004) *Bring `em On: Media and Politics in the Iraq War* (Maryland: Rowman & Littlefield).
31. See D. Kellner (2001) *Grand Theft 2000: Media Spectacle and a Stolen Election* (Maryland: Rowman & Littlefield). See also, Kellner (2003) *Media Spectacle and the Crisis of Democracy: Terrorism, War and Election Battles* (New York: Routledge).
32. C. Crouch (2004) *Post-Democracy* (Cambridge: Polity Press).
33. Brown, *Neoliberalism and the End of Liberal Democracy*, p. 7.
34. Brown, *Neoliberalism and the End of Liberal Democracy*, p. 15.
35. One thinks of the fury generated in the Obama camp over images of him appearing in 'ethnic dress', or of the controversial and 'unpatriotic' sermons from his former pastor.
36. Brown, *Neoliberalism and the End of Liberal Democracy*, p. 24.
37. See Brown, *American Nightmare*.
38. See Galbraith, *The Culture of Contentment*.
39. See C. Mouffe (2000) *The Democratic Paradox* (London: Verso), p. 5.
40. See J. Butler (1996) *Excitable Speech: A Politics of the Performative* (New York: Routledge), p. 101.
41. See Wendy Brown's critique of tolerance discourse in *Regulating Aversion*.
42. Butler, *Excitable Speech*, p. 163.
43. See W. E. Connolly (2005) 'The Evangelical-Capitalist Resonance Machine', *Political Theory*, vol. 33, pp. 869–86.
44. S. Žižek (2005) 'Over the Rainbow Coalition!', Lacan.com website. http://www.lacan.com/coalition.htm.
45. See R. Rorty (1998) *Achieving Our Country: Leftist Thought in Twentieth-Century America* (Cambridge, MA: Harvard University Press), p. 104.
46. Our emphasis on democratic *discourse* here ought not to be interpreted as a denial of the need to rethink the institutional and decision-making structures of democracy. The retheorization of democracy must involve rethinking the translation of discourse into action; but we concentrate on the most immediate and pervasive problem of contemporary democracy: the need to establish a genuine and open democratic culture.
47. Thomas Christiano outlines an egalitarian understanding of democracy, founded on an 'equal consideration of each interests' or an equality of well-being – something that would involve a more equal distribution of resources, both political and socio-economic. See Christiano 'Democracy and Equality'.
48. See W. E. Connolly (1991) *Identity/Difference: Democratic Negotiations of the Political Paradox* (Ithaca: Cornell University Press), p. 218.
49. See Mouffe, *The Democratic Paradox*, pp. 101–2.

50. If we think of the problem of democratic reform in terms of the reform of modes of democratic representation, then a corresponding problem emerges. There is no system of representation that represents all that is relevant to democratic discourse and democratic decision making. Representation by individual identity, professional identity, national identity, ethnic identity, sexual identity, class identity and so on: all are relevant features of representational success in one context or another, but clearly they cannot be combined into a single system of representation.
51. W. E. Connolly (2005) *Pluralism* (Durham: Duke University Press), p. 48.
52. On our account, the principal of secular reason, which we advocated in Chapter 2, is best thought of as a consequence of an ethos of respect for difference rather than an imposed rule of public discourse, such as a procedural rule based on regulative norms of communication.
53. Derrida, *Rogues*, p. 9.

Bibliography

Abele, R. (2004) *A User's Guide to the Patriot Act* (University Press of America).
Achcar, G. (2006) *The Clash of Barbarisms*, trans., P. Drucker (London: SAQI Books).
Agamben, G. (1998) *Homo Sacer: Sovereign Power and Bare Life*, trans., D. Heller-Roazen (California: Stanford University Press).
——. (2002) 'Security and Terror', *Theory & Event*, 5: 4. http://muse.jhu.edu/journals/theory_and_event/v005/5.4agamben.html.
——. (2005) *State of Exception*, trans., K. Attell (Chicago: The University of Chicago Press).
Ali, T. (2003) *Clash of Fundamentalisms: Crusades, Jihads and Modernity* (London: Verso).
Archibugi, D. and I. M. Young (2002) 'Envisioning a Global Rule of Law', *Eurozine*, 14: 6. www.eurozine.com.
Arendt, H. (1969) *Crises of the Republic* (New York: Harcourt Brace).
——. (1983) *Men in Dark Times* (New York: Harcourt Brace).
Armitage, J. (2002) 'State of Emergency: An Introduction', *Theory, Culture & Society*, 19: 4, 27–38.
Artz, L. and Y. Kamalipour (eds) (2004) *Bring 'em On: Media and Politics in the Iraq War* (Maryland: Rowman & Littlefield).
Auden, W. H. (1977) *The English Auden: Poems, Essays and Dramatic Writings, 1927–39*, ed., E. Mendelson (New York: Random House).
Audi, R. (2000) *Religious Commitment and Secular Reason* (Cambridge: Cambridge University Press).
Bacevic, A. J. (2005) *The New American Militarism: How Americans are Seduced by War* (Oxford: Oxford University Press).
Badiou, A. (2006) 'Fragments of a Public Journal on the American War against Iraq', *Polemics*, trans., S. Corcoran (London: Verso).
Barber, B. (2003) *Jihad vs. McWorld* (London: Corgi).
Basoglu, M., M. Livanou and C. Crnobaric (2007) 'Torture Versus Other Cruel, Inhuman & Degrading Treatment: Is the Distinction Real or Apparent?' *Archives of General Psychiatry*, 64, 277–85.
Baudrillard, J. (2005) 'War Porn' ('*Pornographie de la guerre*') *International Journal of Baudrillard Studies*, 2: 5. http://www.ubishops.ca/baudrillardstudies/vol2_1/taylor.htm#_edn1.
Beck, U. (2000) 'The Terrorist Threat: World Risk Society Revisited', *Theory, Culture & Society*, 19: 4, 39–55.
——. (2003) 'The Silence of Words: On Terror and War', *Security Dialogue*, 34: 3, 255–67.
Beetham, D. (1999) *Democracy and Human Rights* (Cambridge: Polity Press).
Benjamin, W. (1982) *Illuminations*, ed. H. Arendt and trans., H. Zohn (London: Fontana).
——. (1985) 'Critique of Violence', *One Way Street and Other Writings*, trans., E. Jephcott and K. Shorter (London: Verso).

Blum, L. (2002) *I'm Not a Racist, But... The Moral Quandary of Race* (Ithaca: Cornell University Press).
——. (2004) 'What Do Accounts of "Racism" Do?' in M. Levine and T. Pataki (eds), *Racism in Mind* (Ithaca: Cornell University Press).
Bobbio, N. (1989) *Democracy and Dictatorship: The Nature and Limits of State Power*, trans., P. Kennealy (Cambridge: Polity Press).
Borradori, G. (2004) *Philosophy in a Time of Terror: Dialogues with Jürgen Habermas and Jacques Derrida* (Chicago: University of Chicago Press).
Bovard, J. (2003) *Terrorism and Tyranny: Trampling Freedom, Justice and Peace to Rid the World of Evil* (New York: Palgrave Macmillan).
——. (2005) *Attention Deficit Democracy* (New York: Palgrave Macmillan).
Bromley, M., D. Grahame and C. Kucia (2002) 'Bunker Busters: Washington's Drive for New Nuclear Weapons', *Research Report* (July) British American Security Information Council. http://www.basicint.org/pubs/Research/2002BB.pdf.
Brown, W. (2003) '*Neo-liberalism and the End of Liberal Democracy*', Theory and Event 7: 1. http://muse.uq.edu.au/journals/theory_and_event/v007/7.1brown.html.
——. (2004) '"The Most We Can Hope For...": Human Rights and the Politics of Fatalism', *The South Atlantic Quarterly*, 103: 2/3 (Spring/Summer), 451–63.
——. (2006) 'American Nightmare: Neoliberalism, Neoconservatism and De-Democratization', *Political Theory*, 34: 6, 690–714.
——. (2006) *Regulating Aversion: Tolerance in the Age of Identity and Empire* (Princeton: Princeton University Press).
Bush's State of the Union Address 2004. http://www.whitehouse.gov/news/releases/2004/01/20040120-7.html.
Butler, J. (1996) *Excitable Speech: A Politics of the Performative* (New York: Routledge).
——. (1997) *The Psychic Life of Power: Theories in Subjection* (Stanford, CA: Stanford University Press).
——. (2004) *Precarious Life: The Power of Mourning and Violence* (London and New York: Verso).
Buzan, B., O. Weaver and J. de Wilde, J. (1998) *Security: A New Framework for Analysis* (Boulder, CO: Lynne Reiner).
Caney, S. (2006) *Justice Beyond Borders* (Oxford: Oxford University Press).
Caputo, J. (2003) 'Without Sovereignty, without Being: Unconditionality, the Coming God and Derrida's Democracy to Come', *Journal for Cultural and Religious Theory*, 4: 3 (August), 9–26.
Chomsky, N. (2006) *Failed States: The Abuse of Power and the Assault on Democracy* (London and New York: Penguin).
Christiano, T (2002) 'Democracy and Equality', in D. Estlund (ed.) *Democracy* (Oxford: Blackwell), 31–50.
Cliffe, L., M. Ramsay and D. Bartlett (2000) *The Politics of Lying: Implications for Democracy* (Basingstoke and London: Macmillan).
Cole, D. (2003) *Enemy Aliens* (New York: The New Press).
Colt, D. 'Terrorism in the Context of Other Threats: Assessing Risks and Solutions', *Security Policy Working Group Paper* – Proteus Fund. http://www.proteusfund.org/spwg/pdfs/Terrorism%20In%20The%20Context%20of%20Other%20Threats.pdf.
Connolly, W. E. (1991) *Identity/Difference: Democratic Negotiations of the Political Paradox* (Ithaca: Cornell University Press).

——. (2005) 'The Evangelical-Capitalist Resonance Machine', *Political Theory*, 33, 869–86.
——. (2005) *Pluralism* (Durham: Duke University Press).
Corn, D. (2004) *The Lies of George W. Bush* (New York: Three Rivers Press).
Cowell, A. (2005) 'US "Thumbs its Nose" at Rights, Amnesty Says', *New York Times* (26 May). http://www.mindfully.org/Reform/2005/US-Thumbs-Nose26may05.htm.
Crouch, C. (2004) *Post-Democracy* (Cambridge: Polity Press).
Darmer, K., R. Baird and S. Rosenbaum (eds) (2004) *Civil Liberties vs National Security in a Post-9/11 World* (Prometheus Books).
Dawson, A. and M. J. Schueller (2007) *Exceptional State: Contemporary U.S. Culture and the New Imperialism* (Durham: Duke University Press).
de Vries, H. (2002) *Religion and Violence: Philosophical Perspectives from Kant to Derrida* (Baltimore: The Johns Hopkins University Press).
Derrida, J. (1992) 'Force of Law: The Mystical Foundation of Authority', in D. Cornell (ed.) *Deconstruction & the Possibility of Justice* (New York: Routledge).
——. (1995) *The Gift of Death*, trans., D. Wills (Chicago: University of Chicago Press).
——. (2005) *Rogues: Two Essays on Reason*, trans., P-A. Brault and M. Naas (Stanford, CA: Stanford University Press).
Dershowitz, A. (2002) *Why Terrorism Works: Understanding the Threat, Responding to the Challenge* (New Haven: Yale University Press).
Dillon, M. (1996) *Politics of Security: Towards a Political Philosophy of Continental Thought* (London: Routledge).
Domke, D. (2004) *God Willing? Political Fundamentalism in the White House, the 'War on Terror', and the Echoing Press* (London: Pluto Press).
Drury, S. (1999) *Leo Strauss and the American Right* (New York: Palgrave Macmillan).
——. (1999) *The Political Ideas of Leo Strauss* (New York: Palgrave Macmillan).
Eagleton, T. (2005) *Holy Terror* (Oxford: Oxford University Press).
Elshtain, J. B. (2004) *Just War against Terror: The Burden of American Power in a Violent World* (New York: Basic Books).
Ferguson, N. (2004) *Colossus: The Price of America's Empire* (London: Allen Lane).
Foucault, M. (1978) *The History of Sexuality VI: Introduction*, trans., R. Hurley (New York: Pantheon Books).
——. (2002) *The Order of Things: An Archaeology of the Human Sciences* (London: Routledge).
——. (2007) *Security, Territory, Population: Lectures at the College de France 1977–78*, ed., Michel Senellart, trans., G. Burchell (Basingstoke, Hampshire: Palgrave Macmillan).
Freedman, L. (2005) 'The Age of Liberal Wars', *Review of International Studies*, 31, 93–107.
Freud, Sigmund (1929, 1930) *The Standard Edition of the Complete Psychological Works of Sigmund Freud*, trans., and ed., J. Strachey (London: Hogarth) 24 vols.
Frost, M. (2002) *Constituting Human Rights: Global Civil Society and the Society of Democratic States* (New York: Routledge).
Galbraith, J. K. (1992) *The Culture of Contentment* (New York: Houghton Mifflin).
Garcia, J. L. A. (1996) 'The Heart of Racism', *Journal of Social Philosophy*, 27, 5–45.
Gibbon, E. (1960) *History of the Decline and Fall of the Roman Empire* (London: Chatto & Windus).

Giroux, H. A. (2006) 'Dirty Democracy and State Terrorism: The Politics of the New Authoritarianism in the United States', *Comparative Studies of South Asia, Africa and the Middle East*, 26: 2, 163–77.

——. (2006) 'The Emerging Authoritarianism in the United States: Political Culture Under the Bush Administration', *Symplokè*, 14: 1–2, 98–151.

Glaser, D. in (2006) 'Does Hypocrisy Matter? The Case of US Foreign Policy', *Review of International Studies*, 32, 251–268.

Global Policy Forum. http://www.globalpolicy.org/empire/intervention/2003/0710imperialmap.htm.

Gordon, J. (1999) 'Economic Sanctions, Just War Doctrine, and the "Fearful Spectacle of the Civilian Dead"', *Cross Currents*, 49: 3. (http://www.crosscurrents.org/fall_1999.htm).

——. (1999) 'Sanctions as Siege Warfare', *The Nation* (22 March). http://www.thenation.com/doc.mhtml?i¼19990322&s¼gordon.

Gowan, P. (2001) 'Neoliberal Cosmopolitanism', *New Left Review* 11 (Sept–Oct). http://www.newleftreview.org/?view=2347.

Habermas, J. (2001) *The Postnational Constellation*, trans., and ed., M. Pensky (Cambridge: Polity Press).

Halper, S. and J. Clarke (2004) *America Alone: The Neo-Conservatives and the Global Order* (Cambridge: Cambridge University Press).

Hardt, M. (1998) 'The Withering of Civil Society', in (eds) E. Kaufman and K. J. Heller, *Deleuze and Guattari: New Mappings in Politics, Philosophy and Culture* (Minneapolis: University of Minnesota Press), 23–39.

Hardt, M. and A. Negri (2000) *Empire* (Cambridge, MA: Harvard University Press).

——. (2004) *Multitude: War and Democracy in the Age of Empire* (New York: Penguin).

Harvey, D. (2003) *The New Imperialism* (Oxford: Oxford University Press).

Held, D. and A. McGrew (ed.) (2002) *Governing Globalization* (Cambridge: Polity Press).

Hobbes, T. (1968) *Leviathan*, ed. C. B. Macpherson (London: Penguin, 1968).

House of Representatives Committee report prepared for Rep. Henry A. Waxman (2004) 'Secrecy in the Bush Administration' (September 14). http://oversight.house.gov/features/secrecy_report/pdf/pdf_secrecy_report.pdf.

Huntley, W. L. (2005) 'The Weaponization of Space: US Strategy in a Global Context', Simons Center for Disarmament and Non-Proliferation Research – Liu Institute for Global Issues, University of British Columbia (July). http://www.ligi.ubc.ca/admin/Centres/527/WH%20-%20The%20Weaponization%20of%20Space%20July%2025%2005.pdf.

Huysmans, J. (1998) 'Security! What Do You Mean? From Concept to Thick Signifier', *European Journal of International Relations*, 4: 2, 226–55.

Ignatieff, M. (2001) *Human Rights as Politics and Idolatory* (ed.) A. Gutmann (Princeton: Princeton University Press).

——. (2003) *Empire Lite: Nation-building in Bosnia, Kosovo and Afghanistan* (London: Vintage Books).

——. (2004) *The Lesser Evil: Political Ethics in an Age of Terror* (Edinburgh: Edinburgh University Press).

Inwagen, P. van (1995) 'The Magnitude, Duration, and Distribution of Evil: A Theodicy', *God, Knowledge and Mystery: Essays in Philosophical Theology* (Ithaca, NY: Cornell University Press).

Johnson, C. (2004) *Blowback: The Costs and Consequences of American Empire* (New York: Holt).
——. (2004) *The Sorrows of Empire: Militarism, Secrecy, and the End of the Republic* (New York: Metropolitan Books).
——. (2006) *Nemesis: The Last Days of the American Republic* (New York: Metropolitan Books).
Joxe, A. (2002) *Empire of Disorder*, trans., A. Hodges (New York: Semiotexte).
Kaldor, M. (2003) *Global Civil Society: An Answer to War* (Cambridge: Polity Press).
Kaplan, A. (2004) 'Violent Belonging and the Question of Empire Today: Presidential Address to the American Studies Association, October 17, 2003', *American Quarterly*, 56: 1 (March), 1–17.
——. (2005) 'Where is Guantanamo?' *American Quarterly*, 57: 3 (September) 831–1001.
Kellner, D. (2001) *Grand Theft 2000: Media Spectacle and a Stolen Election* (Maryland: Rowman & Littlefield).
——. (2003) *Media Spectacle and the Crisis of Democracy: Terrorism, War and Election Battles* (New York: Routledge).
Kierkegaard, S. [1843] (1983) *Fear and Trembling*, trans., and ed. H. Hong and E. Hong (Princeton: Princeton University Press).
Klein, N. (2004) 'Baghdad Year Zero: Pillaging Iraq in Pursuit of a Neocon Utopia', *Harper's Magazine* (September).
——. (2007) *The Shock Doctrine: The Rise of Disaster Capitalism* (London: Allen Lane).
Kritzinger, S. (2003) 'Public Opinion in the Iraq Crisis: Explaining Developments in Italy, the UK, France and Germany', *European Political Science* (Autumn). http://www.essex.ac.uk/ECPR/publications/eps/onlineissues/autumn2003/feature/kritzinger.htm.
Lafer, G. (2004) 'Neoliberalism by Other Means: The "War on Terror" at Home and Abroad', *New Political Science*, 26: 3 (September), 323–46.
Lane, C. (ed.) (1998) *The Psychoanalysis of Race* (New York: Columbia University Press).
Lefort, C. (1986) *The Political Forms of Modern Society: Bureaucracy, Democracy, Totalitarianism* (Cambridge: Polity Press).
Leone, R. and G. Anrig (eds) (2003) *The War on Our Freedoms: Civil Liberties in the Age of Terrorism* (Public Affairs).
Lincoln, B (2003) *Holy Terrors: Thinking about Religion after September 11* (Chicago: University of Chicago Press).
Mbembe, A. (2003) essay 'Necropolitics', *Public Culture*, 15: 1, 11–40.
McClellan, S. (2008) *What Happened: Inside the Bush White House and Washington's Culture of Deception* (Public Affairs).
Milbank, J. (2003) 'Sovereignty, Empire, Capital, and Terror', in S. Hauerwas and F. Lentricchia (eds) *Dissent from the Homeland: Essays after September 11* (Durham: Duke University Press).
MIT Center for International Studies, 'Military Budget'. http://web.mit.edu/CIS/fpi_military_spending.html.
Mouffe, C. (2000) *The Democratic Paradox* (London: Verso).
The National Security Strategy of the United States of America (September 2002).
Neocleous, M. (2007) 'Security, Liberty and the Myth of Balance: Towards a Critique of Security Politics', *Contemporary Political Theory*, 6: 131–49.

Nietzsche, F. (1989) *On the Genealogy of Morality*, trans., W. Kaufmann and R. J. Hollingdale (New York: Vintage Books).
Northouse, C. (ed.) (2006) *Protecting What Matters: Technology, Security and Liberty since 9/11* (Washington D.C.: Computer Ethics Institute, Brookings Institution Press).
Overton, S. (2004) 'The Donor Class: Campaign Finance, Democracy and Participation', *Pennsylvania Law Review*, 153, 73–178.
Owens, P. (2007) 'Beyond Strauss, Lies and the War in Iraq: Hannah Arendt's critique of Neo-conservatism', *Review of International Studies*, 33, 265–83.
Pataki, T. (2007) *Against Religion* (Melbourne: Scribe Publishers).
Paye, J. C. (2007) *Global War on Liberty: Anti-terrorism, Dictatorship, Permanent State of Exception*, trans., J. H. Membrez (Telos Press Publishing).
Plantinga, A. (2000) 'Pluralism: A Defense of Religious Exclusivism', in P. Quinn and K. Meeker (eds) *The Philosophical Challenge of Religious Diversity* (New York: Oxford University Press), 172–92.
Project for the New American Century. http://www.newamericancentury.org/.
Puar, J. K. and A. S. Rai (2002) 'Monster, Terrorist, Fag: The War on Terrorism and the Production of Docile Patriots', *Social Text*, 20: 3, 117–48.
Rawls, J. (1999) *A Theory of Justice* (Cambridge, MA: Harvard University Press).
———. (1993) *Political Liberalism* (New York: Columbia University Press).
Reid, J. (2007) *The Biopolitics of the War on Terror: Life Struggles, Liberal Modernity and the Defence of Logistical Societies* (Manchester: Manchester University Press).
Rich, F. (2006) *The Greatest Story Ever Sold: The Decline and Fall of Truth-The Real History of the Bush Administration* (New York: Viking).
Rorty, R. (1998) *Achieving Our Country: Leftist Thought in Twentieth-Century America* (Cambridge, MA: Harvard University Press).
Scanlon, T. M. (1999) *What We Owe to Each Other* (Cambridge, MA: Belknap Press).
Scheuerman, W. E. (2006) 'Survey Article: Emergency Power and the Rule of Law After 9/11', *The Journal of Political Philosophy*, 14: 1, 61–84.
Schmitt, C. (1996) *The Concept of the Political*, trans., G. Schwab (Chicago: University of Chicago Press).
———. (2005) *Political Theology: Four Chapters on the Concept of Sovereignty*, trans., G. Schwab (Chicago: University of Chicago Press).
Schneier, B. (2003) *Beyond Fear: Thinking Sensibly About Security in an Uncertain World* (New York: Copernicus Books).
Shaw, D. Z. (2006) 'The Absence of Evidence is Not the Evidence of Absence: Biopolitics and the State of Exception', *Philosophy against Empire* (ed.) T. Smith, *Radical Philosophy Today*, 4, 123–38.
Silber, M. D. and A. Bhatt (2007) 'Radicalisation in the West: The Homegrown Threat'. http://www.nyc.gov/html/nypd/downloads/pdf/public_information/NYPD_Report-Radicalization_in_the_West.pdf.
Steinmetz, G. (2003) 'The State of Emergency and the Revival of American Imperialism: Toward an Authoritarian Post-Fordism', *Public Culture*, 15: 2, 323–45.
Swinburne, R. (1983) 'A Theodicy of Heaven and Hell', in A. J. Freddoso (ed.) *The Existence and Nature of God* (Notre Dame: University of Notre Dame Press), 37–54.

Tabuga, Maj. Gen. A. M. (2004) 'The Tabuga Report' – Article 15–6 of 800th Military Police Brigade: US Army Report on the Abuse of Iraqi Prisoners (May 5) *Counterpunch*. http://www.counterpunch.org/taguba05052004.html.

Tocqueville, A. (1994) *Democracy in America*, trans., G. Lawrence. J. P. Mayer (ed.) (London: Fontana Press).

Todd, E. (2004) *After the Empire: The Breakdown of the American Order*, trans., C. J. Delogu (Constable: London).

Turner, B. S. (2002) 'Sovereignty and Emergency: Political Theology, Islam and American Conservatism', *Theory, Culture & Society*, 19: 4, 103–19.

Venn, C. (2002) 'World Dis/Order: On Some Fundamental Questions', *Theory, Culture & Society*, 19: 4, 121–36.

Waldron, J. (2003) 'Security and Liberty: The Image of Balance', *The Journal of Political Philosophy*, 11: 2, 191–210.

Walzer, M. (1977) *Just and Unjust Wars* (New York: Basic Books).

Young-Bruehl, E. (1996) *The Anatomy of Prejudices* (Cambridge, Massachusetts: Harvard University Press).

Žižek, S. (2005) 'Over the Rainbow Coalition!', Lacan.com website. http://www.lacan.com/coalition.htm.

Index

7/7, 4
9/11/post-9/11, viii–x, xii, 1, 3–5, 10, 13, 16, 19, 22, 31–32, 34, 41, 44, 53–54, 59, 62, 64, 72, 75, 77–78, 84, 88, 94, 97, 98–99, 103, 109, 126, 129, 143–146, 153, 156, 159, 164, 166–167, 171, 176
Abu Ghraib, 7, 78–79, 86–87, 129
ACLU, 148
Adversarial review, 134–136, 138–139, 143
Afghanistan, 7, 78, 80, 85–86, 97, 107–111, 115, 117, 134, 156
Agamben, Giorgio, 7, 21, 79, 87–89
Al Qaeda, 84,111, 125
Al-Harethi, 125
Ali, Tariq, 82, 89, 150
Allende, Salvador, 98
American
  culture, 99
  empire, xi, 90–115, 160
  exceptionalism, 46, 100, 153
  hegemony, 20, 98
  imperialism, 105–106, 111moral mission, 100
  politics, 170
  society, 99
  values, 76
  way of life, 102, 170
anti-Semitism, xii, 32
Arab Americans, 17, 72
Arbenz, Jacobo, 98
Archibugi, Daniele, 156, 178
Arendt, Hannah, 45, 49–53, 59, 64, 66, 8
  imagination, 51–52
  on lying, 50–51
Argentina, 129
Aristotle, 57
Ashcroft, John, 126, 141
assassination
  moral permissibility of, viii
  pre-emptive, 125
  targeted, 28, 119, 124–125, 143
  unlawful, 124
Attention Deficit Democracy, 15
Auden, W.H., 44, 64
Australia, 20, 22, 44, 48, 77, 87, 116, 134, 145, 152
Australian government, 21
authoritarian(ism), ix, 16, 18, 62, 76, 148–150, 158, 161, 166–168, 176
Axis of evil, 14, 91

Bacevic, A.J., 97, 113, 150
Badiou, Alain, 102, 114
Baghdad, 109
BAE, 49, 65
Barber, Benjamin, 93, 112
Bataille, Georges, 151
Baudrillard, Jean, 88
Beck, Ulrich, 5–6, 21
Beetham, David, 64, 146, 177
Benjamin, Walter, 87–88
Berlusconi, Silvio, 162
bio-politics, 8
Blair, Tony, 2–3, 8, 10, 19, 21–22, 45, 47–48, 68, 82, 85, 89, 94, 97, 104–105, 113–114, 146, 148
Bobbio, Norberto, 64
border control, 3–4
Bosnia, 98, 107
Bovard, James, 15–16, 21, 23
British government, 11
British High Court, 65
British imperialism, 110
Brown, Gordon, 21
Brown, Wendy, 22, 24, 41, 62, 66, 154–155, 163–164, 178–179
Bush Administration, xi, 10, 14, 20, 54, 65–66, 72, 75–77, 84, 88–89, 91, 98, 101, 112, 116, 135, 141, 146–148, 153, 165–166
Bush, George, HW, 96–97

Bush, George, W., x, xii, 2–4, 8, 9, 12, 14, 19–20, 42, 45–49, 61–62, 68, 73, 82, 84–85, 94, 97, 99, 104–105, 111, 147, 169–170, 173, 177, 179
Bush doctrine, 96, 99
Butler, Judith, 24, 41, 79, 88, 168–169, 179

Camp X-ray, 134, 141
Carter administration, 97
Catholic Church, 57–58
character type, 25, 35
Chavez, Hugo, 102
checks and balances, 17, 116–117, 134, 142
chemical weapons, 132
Cheney, Dick, 99
Cheney, Lynn, 109
Chile, 97–98, 129
China, 96, 152
Chomsky, Noam, 150, 177
Christiano, Thomas, xiii, 179
CIA, 91, 97–98, 113, 115, 130
civil society, 63, 103, 146–147, 167–168
 post-civil condition, 146–147
civil liberties, 2, 16–17, 21, 70, 73, 104, 119, 135, 144–145, 148, 151, 153, 165
civilian casualties, 152
civilization
 Christian, 104
 clash between, 104
 Western, 110
Civilization and its Discontents, 41
Clinton-Obama, xii
Clinton, Hillary, 111, 171
Clinton, William, 50, 97–98
Coalition of the willing, 99
Cold war, 94, 96, 110, 151
 post-, 93
collateral damage, 124
combatants/noncombatants, viii, 134
Communism, 84, 92, 93–94,105
Congress (U.S.), 4, 14, 77, 117, 146, 177
Congressional oversight, 65
Connolly, W.E., 169, 174, 179–180

conservative principle/test, 120–123, 138
constitutional
 authority, 64, 69, 71–72, 74, 77
 limitations, 72
 order, 71
 protection, 146
 reforms, 144
 rights, 72
constitutionalism
 liberal, 71–72
 safeguards, 70
control orders, 4
cosmopolitan order, 156
court warrants, 4
Crosby, Bing, 36
Crouch, Colin, 162–163, 179
cruel and unusual punishment, 121
Cuba, 90, 178
Cuban government, 178
'culture of contentment', 62,167
culture of pluralism, 173–174
culture wars, 169

Declaration of Independence, 141
deflationary responses, 116–118, 140
Deir Yassin, 80
deliberative process/practice, 138
de Menezes, Jean Charles, 1, 7
democracy
 agonistic, 174
 American, 12
 anti-democratic, ix
 concept of, 149
 conditions for return of, 172–176
 constitutional and institutional, ix
 contemporary, ix, 145, 17
 'democracy to come', 177
 and free market, 105–106, 155
 global adoption of, 173
 liberal, xi, 2–4, 45, 70, 76–77, 80, 108, 120, 143
 minimum condition for, 172
 most unusual, 176–180
 post-democracy, 162–163, 176
 potential of, 161, 177
 procedural, 173
 respect for, 2
 rethinking of, 144, 149

democracy (cont.)
  return of, 171–176
  risks, 149, 172
  self-critical capacities, 173
  social, 163, 172
  Western liberal, 163
democratic
  accountability, 2, 68–69, 150, 161, 165, 176
  citizenship, 157
  culture, xii
  deficit, 161, 165, 176
  despotism, 13
  discourse, 171, 173–175, 179–180
  dissent, 11, 173
  electorates, 11, 19
  governments, 13
  institutions, 43, 117, 135, 142
  legitimation, 157–158, 175
  majorities, 148
  parliaments, 72
  participation, 146, 172
  politics, 18–19, 68, 141, 151, 161, 166, 169, 172
  polity, 145
  procedure, 48, 158
  project, 175–176
  public space, 164, 167–168
  representation, 180
  rights, 2, 4, 10–11, 15–16, 106, 144–145, 147
  scrutiny, 145
  society, 45, 122
  space, 11, 15, 149, 172
  values, 117, 175–176
Democrats/Republicans, 4,111, 169–171, 177
  primary race, 164
Derrida, Jacques, 14–15, 22, 81–82, 89, 177, 180
Dershowitz, Alan, 17, 23
Detention, 4, 7, 70, 145
  extra-judicial, 143
  illegal, 124
  indefinite, 77, 79, 104, 123, 134
  offshore, 90, 152
  preventative, 17, 28, 87, 124, 126, 145
  without trial, 76

Dick, Cressida, 20
dignity principle, 120–128, 130, 133, 138, 141
Dillon, M., 15, 21, 23
dirty hands, 46, 48, 120
dissidents, 5, 173
divine right of kings, 89
Domke, David, 13–14, 22
double-effect, viii
due process, 2, 4, 72, 145–146

effectiveness test, 123
egalitarianism, 16, 170–171
ego-defence, x, 25, 28–34, 40, 52, 159–160, 166
Ego and the Id, 60
ego-ideal, 60
ego threat, 159
Egypt, 10, 104
electorate(s), 11, 15, 69
El Salvador, 97
Elshtain, Bethke, Jean, 42, 65–66
empire, 94–101,150, 159
envy and guilt, 35–36, 59
epistemological pluralism, 146–147
equal consideration of interests, ix
Essay on Liberty, xiii
ethical
  judgment, 62
  and political imperatives, 165, 171
  questions, 116–142
  responsibility, 64
  transformation, 174–175
Euripides, 141
Euthyphro, 39
Evangelical Christianity, 59, 169–170
evil
  language of, 120
exceptionalism, 70, 86, 154, 156
  logic of exception, 80
extrajudicial, 4, 69, 72
  execution, 121
  killings, xi, 123, 125
  state violence, 143
extra-legal, 70, 72, 78–79

Fallujah, 80, 152
Falwell, Jerry, 59
family values, 166, 170

Feith, Douglas, 99
Ferguson, Niall, 101, 107–110, 114–115
Fleischer, Ari, 21
Foucault, Michel, 8, 20, 22, 78, 88
Fourth Circuit Court, 135
Fox News, 66, 179
France, 109
Freedman, Lawrence, 105, 114
freedom (s)
  basic, 144
  curtailment of, ix
  enemies of, 14
  language of, 103
  of protest, 4
  and rights, 2
  of speech, xiii, 4, 5
free market, 163
free-trade, 95
Freud, Sigmund, 36, 41, 44, 49–51, 55–64, 66, 106
friend/enemy distinction, 83–84, 86, 91
fundamentalist (ism), 2, 8, 36, 39, 83
  Christian, 81
  Islamic and Christian, 83
  political paradigm, 13, 16 68
  Shia, 109
  terrorism, 93, 110, 160
  world views, 168
Fukuyama, 93
Future of an Illusion, 36

Galbraith, K. John, 62, 66, 167, 179
Garcia, J.L., 27, 41
Gaza, 80
Geneva Convention, 46, 125, 177
Germany, 54, 66, 153
Gibbon, Edward, 118–119, 141
Giroux, Henry, 45, 64, 99, 113, 150
global
  capitalism, 92–96, 155
  civil society, 156, 178
  governance, 156–157, 161
  inequalities, 156
  institutions, 156–157
  justice, 155–160
globalization, 3, 152, 157, 169
  anti-, 11, 22, 150
  democratic forms, 158
  economic, 92
  and sovereignty, 92–94
God's commands, 38–39
Gonzales, Alberto, 75
Good and Evil, 82
Gore, Al, 143
Goths, 118
government
  cover-ups, 1
  democratically elected, 98
  function of, 3
  power, 2, 168
governmentality, 8, 163, 165
Grenada, 97
group
  behavior, 56–57
  identifications, 41, 55, 57, 59, 63
  leader, 55–61
  members (ship), 53–55, 59
  psychology, x, 45, 48, 53–61
Group Psychology, 55–61, 64
Guam, 97, 112
Guantanamo Bay, 17, 74, 76–77, 79, 90–91, 145, 153, 178
Gulf War, 97
Guatemala, 98

habeas corpus, 87,123, 135
Habermas, Jurgen, 157–160, 173, 179
Hagee, Reverend, xii
Haliburton, 166
Haiti, 97
Hamas, 10, 100
Hamdi vs Rumsfield, 135
Hamdi, Yaser Esam, 134
Hardt, Michael, 94–95, 112, 146, 177
Harvey, David, 95, 112–113
hate speech/legislation, 169
herd instinct, 57, 61
Hobbes, 12, 18, 69, 87
Howard, John, 3, 20, 48
Homeland Security, 6–7, 9, 21, 103, 146, 148
human dignity, 121, 124, 127
human rights, viii, ix, 2, 7–8, 13, 28, 70, 76, 78–79, 90, 92, 100, 104, 106, 110–111, 121, 143, 152–155, 161
  and counterterrorism, 143

human rights (*cont.*)
  discourse, 153
  and freedoms, ix
  groups, 152
  international, 151–156
  universal, 153, 155–157
  Universal Declaration of, 152
humanitarian intervention, 85–86, 94, 109–110, 154–5
Huntington, Samuel P., 83
Hussein, Saddam, 66, 104, 152

Ignatieff, Michael, xi, 17, 23, 77, 88–89, 101, 107–108, 110, 114–143, 149, 154–155, 160, 178
illegal enemy combatants, 74, 116
IMF, 94–95
Immigration, 3, 4, 11, 22, 92, 148
international courts, 156
intelligence
  services, 145
  sharing, 91
International Court of Justice, 153
International Criminal Court, 151, 153
international law, 152, 176
Iran, 98, 109, 111, 154
Iranian Revolutionary Guard, 111
Iraq (is), x, 7, 29, 44, 59, 65–66, 74, 78, 80, 97–100, 105, 108–109, 111, 113, 117, 130, 147, 152, 156, 179
  dead, 132
  embargo, 50
  invasion of, 6, 9, 24, 54, 91, 103, 130–132, 159, 166
  occupation of, 165–166
  oil fields, 9
  post-Iraq, 75
  U.S. policy, 24
  war on (in), 11, 19, 54, 69, 75, 133
  weapons programs, x
Islam, 25
Islamic
  extremists, 14, 75
  fundamentalist, 92
  militant, 81, 84
  radicalism, 22
  terrorists/ism, 109, 140

Israel(i), ix, xii, 32–34, 42, 48, 104, 111
  government, 32
  occupation of Palestine, 108
  pro-Israel, 32
  self-hatred, 32–34
Israeli-Palestinian conflict, 32–34, 44

Johnson, Chalmers, 87–88, 115, 150
judicial
  oversight, 145
  review, 77, 134–135
just war, viii, 42, 53, 132

Kagan, Robert, 100
Kant, Immanuel/Kantian, 43, 142, 156, 158
Kaplan, Amy, 88, 90–91, 112, 114, 150, 177
Karimov, Islam, 114
Kelley, David, 49
Kierkegaard(ian), 46, 65
Kipling, Rudyard, 107, 110
Klein, Naomi, 9–10, 20, 22, 105, 114
Kosovo, 97–98, 107
Krauthammer, Charles, 101
Kuwait, 113
Kyoto protocols, 151

Lafer, Gordon, 9, 22, 66
laissez-faire, 8
Lane, Christopher, 26, 41
Latin America, 80, 97, 167
Lebanon, 97
Le Bon, Gustav, 44, 49–51, 55–56, 66
Leeden, Michael, 100
Lefort, Claude, 18–19, 23
legal
  constraints, 69, 72
  order, 71–72, 78
  rights, 155
  safeguards, 17
  structure, 156–157
Lehrer's News Hour, 132
lesser of two evils, 116–142
Levy, Bernard-Henri, 109
liberal (ism)
  balancing act, 140
  capitalism, 93, 154

commitments, 119
conceptions, 116
doctrine, 139
freedom, 93
humanism, 85
humanitarianism, xi, 111
ideal, 138
individualism, 154
institutions, 83, 101, 122, 134, 137–138, 144
legal-order, 72
markets, 3
post-liberal, 9–10, 15, 7
response to terror, 139–141
societies, 8, 77, 147
states, 86
theory, 18
wars, 105
liberal democracy/tic, 116–117, 139–141, 145, 147, 166–172, 175
exception, 75–78
paradigm, 17, 146
politics, 86, 165
practice, 117–118, 148
principles, 3, 17, 82, 143, 167
regimes, 76
systems, 144
tradition, 139
libertarian, 15, 22
lies, lying, ix, x, 2, 29, 32, 34, 41, 68, 82
accounting for, 53–61
explanations for, 49–61
in war on terror, 43–67
politicians, x, 49–61
responsibility for, 49–61
Locke, John, 141

Machiavellian(s) (ism), viii, 46–48, 65, 68
Magna Carta, 87
Manichean, 36, 40, 48, 61, 82, 147
McCain, John, xii, 111
McCellan, Scott, x, xiii
mendacity, 43–64
metaethics, 142
Middle East, 9–10, 22, 84–85, 94, 97, 100, 105,111
Mill, C. Wright, 99

Mill, J.S., xiii
militarism/tic, xi, 102–103, 111, 143, 166, 168
military
adventurism, 97, 166
aggression, 156
bases, 103
campaigns, 133
dictatorship, 98
draft, 29
institutions, 95
intervention, 101
spending, 99, 112, 151
supremacy, 96
tribunals, 4, 77, 148
moral
conscience, 60
deliberation, 137–138
hazard (argument from), 128
imagination, 132
judgment, 43
philosophers, viii, 27
truth, 137
value, 136
MOSOP, 178
Mossadegh, Mohammed, 98
Mouffe, Chantal, 167, 179
Mugabe, Robert, 152
multiculturalism, 13
Muslim, 7–8, 13, 20–3, 29, 66, 126
mutual respect, 137–138

narcissism, narcissistic, x, 35–38, 40, 55, 57, 60, 159
constructions, 31–32, 40
identification, 36
libido, 59
satisfaction, 37
'NASCAR dads', 169
NATO, 98
national
identity, 63, 157
interest, 29, 46, 69, 172
security, 3, 11, 65, 69, 146, 172
Negri, Antonio, 94–95, 112
Neocleous, Mark, 150, 177
neoconservative (ism), ix, xi, 10, 19, 22, 44, 54, 69, 99, 101, 105, 112, 168

neoliberal (ism), ix, xii, 3, 6, 8–10, 20, 22, 62, 92–93, 95, 98–99, 105, 147–148, 163–172
neo-imperialism, 84–85
Netherlands, 153
Nicaragua, 97
Nietzsche, Friedrich, 38, 153, 178
Nigerian government, 178
'noble lie', 69
non-combatant immunity, viii
normative ethical theory, 27
normative judgments, 33
Northern Alliance, 134
North Vietnamese, 97
NSA wiretaps, 4, 77
nuclear
 non-proliferation, 96
 weapons, 96

Obama, Barack, xii, 111, 179
object-relations, 37
oil, 97
'Other', 24, 157, 166, 175
Owens, P., 44–45, 64

Pakistan, 111
Palestine, 10, 100, 104, 154
Palestinians, xii, 33, 42, 80
 anti-Palestinian prejudice, 34
Panama, 97
paranoia, 5, 14
Pataki, Tamas, 35–38, 42
Patriot Act, 4, 46, 72, 88, 145
patriotism, 14, 63, 103
 constitutional, 158
Pearle, Richard, 99
Pentagon, 103, 110
Pentagon Papers, 49–51
permanent state of emergency, 76
Persian Gulf, 113
Philippines, 97, 112
Plato, 39
PNAC, 100
Poland, 43
police, 1, 4, 7, 22, 78, 145
 states, xi, 2, 4 , 21, 145
Politics, 57
politics
 anti-security, xii, 149, 172

collective, 154
contemporary, 161–162, 164
cosmopolitan, 157
democratic, xi, 11, 43
democratic transformation of, xii, 144, 177
egalitarian, 163, 172
global, 95
group, 62–63
imperialist, xi, xi, 112
liberal-democratic, 2, 68, 171
and media, 162
moral condition of, xiii
of fear, 12
of security, ix, 11, 144
of terror, 53
philosophical response to, viii
'politics most unusual', viii, xii, 172
populist, 62
post-9/11, x, xi, 69, 171
secular, 86
U.S., 13, 103, 111, 166
political
 absolutism, 82
 apathy, 62, 167
 authority, 70, 81–83
 campaigns, 162
 community, 161, 169
 conflict, 174
 conservatism, 82, 171
 constituencies, 53, 161
 culture, 148, 158, 162, 168
 decision making, 136
 deliberation, 137
 dissent, 62
 elites, 69, 163, 170–171
 equality/inequality, 149, 168, 172
 ethics, 118–120, 130, 133, 136, 138–139, 160
 freedom, 165
 fundamentalism, 13–14, 18
 ideology, 163
 identification, 157
 inequality, 162
 judgment, 116
 leaders, 48, 68–69
 legitimation, 157
 life, xi, 2, 68, 175
 participation, 148, 157, 167–168

pluralism, 63–64, 173–4
reforms, 145
representation, 151
space, 167, 176
status quo, 48
theology, 83, 147
theory, viii
violence, 24–42, 159–160
POW conventions, 90
PNAC, 100
pre-emptive
    killings, 125, 127–128
    strikes, xi, 100–101,112
    war, 119, 131
prejudice(s), ix–x, 8, 19, 24–42, 44,
    52–53, 61, 116, 136–137, 140,
    144, 148, 151, 157, 159–160,
    167–169, 172–173
    religion/ious, 34, 166, 176
preventative war, 131–133, 136, 143
prevention of terrorism bill, 72
progressive populism, 170
propaganda, x, 32
    security, 63
protection
    constitutional and legal, xi
Psychologie des foules, 44
psychic defense, 28, 30, 169
psychic humiliation, 153
psychoanalysis, 168
psychoanalytic, x, 6, 25–29, 35, 40, 52
Puerto Rico, 112
    public opinion, 2
public safety, 12, 122–123, 126, 130

race, xii
racial profiling, 13, 126, 169
racially discriminatory policies, 28–29
racism, x, xii, 24–42, 52, 92, 110, 144,
    157, 159–160
    causal accounts, 28
    cognitive and affective, 26, 52
    prejudices and violence, 25–42
    state, 169
    symptoms and cures, 30
Rawls, John, 40, 42, 139, 142
Reagan, Ronald, 97
realpolitik, 100, 154
regime change, 101, 111

religion/religious, 24–42, 58, 69,
    81–83, 86
    affiliations, 63
    authority, 81–82, 147
    beliefs, 69
    character of, 37
    commitments, 175
    communities, 54
    conflict, 58, 174
    conservatives, 82
    extremism, xii
    faith, 165–166, 174
    fundamentalism, 19, 59, 68–69, 81,
        86, 144, 159, 166
    inspired terrorism, 81
    justification, 48
    minorities, 78
    moralizing, 68
    obscurantism, 82
    pluralism, 36, 39
    and prejudice, 24–42
    and/in politics, 39, 68, 82, 86
    religiose, 35–40
    Right, 13–14, 54, 147
respect for difference, 174, 180
respect for persons, 2
retreat to process, 133–139
return of the repressed, 82, 168
Rich, Frank, 54, 65–66
Rights, 8, 13, 17–18, 117, 119,
    121, 138, 146–152, 155,
    167–168
risk-management, 5, 166
Robertson, Pat, 59, 102, 114
rogue states, 91, 166
Roosevelt, F.D.R., 88
Rorty, Richard, 171, 179
Roy, Arundhati, 150
rule of law, 70, 146, 150, 153, 156,
    168, 175
Rumsfeld, Donald, 20, 75, 79, 86–87,
    108, 113, 178
Russia, 105

San'a, 125
Saudi Arabia, 10,100, 104, 111,
    113–114, 134, 154
Saudi monarchy, 49
Scanlon, T.M., 142

Schmitt, Carl, 64, 70–73, 76–78, 81, 83, 85–87, 89, 91
secret rendition, 28, 46, 69–70, 123
sectarian conflict, 49
secular principles of justice, 40
secular reason
  principle of, 36, 38, 180
secularism, 13, 83, 99, 147
securitization, 8, 13, 15, 20, 34, 53, 78, 145, 149, 160, 168
security
  agencies, 7
  agenda, xi
  and anti-security, xi, 149, 172
  apparatus, 8, 19, 72
  concept of, 149
  discourse, 3, 5, 18
  halting security paradigm, 144–150
  illusion of, 15, 83, 143
  insecurity, ix, 6, 48, 68, 103, 143
  laws, 140
  and liberty, 16–18, 133–134
  logic of, 19, 162
  measures, 4, 12, 143–144, 147–148, 168
  national, 165, 171
  obsession with, 13, 144
  outsourcing, 9
  paradigm, ix, xi, 2, 4–6, 144–145, 148–149
  policy, 154
  politics of, ix–x, 1–23, 68, 144
  post-liberal, 8
  and rights, 140
  and risk, 5
  state, 2, 5, 7, 150
  threats, 63
separation of
  church and state, 38–39, 147
  powers, 146
Serbian war criminals, 153
Sharia law, 109
Shaw, Devin Zane, 75, 88
Shumpeter, Joseph, 167
Social psychology, 57
Somalia, 97

Sovereignty, viii, x–xi, 2, 26, 68–91, 94, 102, 119, 153–154, 157, 160, 172
  law and violence, 70
  popular, 168, 175
Soviet, 93, 110
Spain, 98
Spanish-American War, 97, 111
'state of exception', viii–ix, xi, 2, 34, 64, 68–89, 73–78, 83, 90, 122, 144, 160, 176
Steinmetz, George, 98
stereotyping, 61, 85
Strauss, Leo, 69
Straussian, 99
Straw, Jack, 21
suicide bomber, i
Supreme Court (U.S.), 134, 142, 146, 148
  decisions, 77
  justices, 135
supreme emergency, 119
surveillance, 2, 4–7, 9, 13, 22, 76–78, 91, 146–147
  electronic and biometric, 2

Tabuga, Maj. Gen. A.M., 141
Taliban, 104, 109
terrorism/terror/ist
  age of, 52
  antidote to, 9–10, 156
  attacks, 73, 84
  campaign, 132
  counterterrorism, 6–7, 11, 72, 77, 92, 117–118, 130
  defining, viii, 11
  emergency, 70, 72–73
  enemy, 8, 19, 85
  fears about, viii, 3, 5, 12
  global war on, 91
  groups, 63
  international, xi, 120, 139
  Islamic, 66, 68, 85
  legislation, 88, 145–146
  moral challenge of, viii
  moral justification, viii
  Muslim, 166
  Organization, 111, 156

responses to, ix, 122–124, 130, 143
risk of, 13, 150
security from, 14
state, non-state, 25, 79–81, 169, 176
suspects, 3–4, 6, 72, 74, 104, 125, 148
threats, 5–7, 13, 15, 46, 73–74, 112, 132, 140
theocracy, 83
theology and politics, 81–83
Thomas, Clarence, 135
ticking bomb situation, 123
Tobin Tax, 178
Tocqueville, 12–13, 22
tolerance/intolerance, 8, 36, 39–41, 43, 168
torture, ix, 2, 15, 17, 28, 32, 46, 53, 58, 61, 64, 68–70, 75–76, 78–79, 104, 108, 119, 121, 123–124, 126, 129–130, 148, 152, 177–178
  absolute ban on, 128, 129
  legal justification for, ix
  moral permissibility of, viii
  psychological, 129–130, 141
  U.S. sanctioned, 44
'torture memo', 75
'torture warrant', 129
Trotskyists, 100
Turkey, 109

unconscious phantasy, 35
unilateral/multilateral, 98, 131, 136
United Arab Emirates, 113
United Nations (UN), 66, 88, 99, 151, 156, 170
UK, ix, 4, 6, 11, 44, 14, 20–23, 48–49, 74–75, 77, 80, 87, 92, 104, 113, 145, 152–154
UN Security Council, 151
US
  army, 100
  citizens, 4, 17, 31–33, 72, 77, 148
  Constitution, 38
  court system, 90, 116
  domestic policy, xii, 10
  elections, 162

empire, 90, 94–5, 99, 102–4, 106–12, 178
exceptionalism, 176
executive, 135
foreign policy, xi–xii, 10, 69, 140, 150–151, 161
hegemony, 98, 151, 162
imperialism, 83, 90, 92, 95, 97, 99, 101–103, 106–112, 144, 150–151, 154–155, 158, 161–162, 168, 173
impunity, 76
innocence, 31
interests, 14, 91, 10
law, 74
self-image, 31, 159
sovereignty, 90, 94
unilateralism, 156, 159
utilitarian justification, 47
Uzbekistan, 104, 114

Vietnam War, 50, 111
violence
  discursive, 160
  extremist, 18
  institutionalized, 37
  internal and external, 161–162
  modes of, 144
  and politics, 24–42
  political character of, x
  psychological underpinning, 25
  religion, 58
  sovereignty, 68–89
  sources of, 160
  state and non-state, 79–81

Waldron, Jeremy, 17, 23
Walzer, Michael, 119, 141–142
war crimes, 153
  tribunals, 153
war on terror, xi–xii, 1–3, 7–13, 17–18, 20, 31–32, 41–44, 63, 69, 72–77, 82–86, 92–94, 97–98, 103–104, 111, 116–117, 120, 122, 125, 135, 141, 144, 152, 160, 162, 168, 176–177
  ameliorative responses to, 160
  critical response to, 144

war on terror (*cont.*)
  moral calamities of, 172
  moral failure of, 116–118
waterboarding, 75–76, 129
Waxman, Henry A., 65
ways forward, xii, 143–180
weapons inspectors, 132
Weimar, 70
Western nations, viii-ix
  capitalism, 93–94
  culture, 116
  democracy, ix. 13–14, 43, 64, 78, 106, 146, 162
  governments, 74, 152–154
  hegemony, 94
  powers, 84, 155
  societies, xi, 8, 90,148, 162–163
  values, 92
'The White Man's Burden', 107, 110

Wilsonianism, 85
wiretapping, 17, 65, 72, 148, 177
Wittgenstein, Ludwig, 61
WMD, 9, 24, 44, 49, 65, 75, 88, 97, 130, 132, 152, 166
Wolfowitz, Paul, 99
World Court, 151
World Trade Centre, 110
Wright, Jerimiah, xii
WTO, 94

xenophobia, 8, 92

Yemen, 125
Young, Iris Marion, 156, 178
Young-Bruehl, Elisabeth, 25, 28–29, 41

Zimbabwe, 152
Žižek, Slavoj, 169–170, 179